Shattered Innocence

Shattered Innocence: A Practical Guide for Counseling Women Survivors of Childhood Sexual Abuse

Neil Weiner, Ph.D.
Private Practice
Mesa, Arizona

Sharon E. Robinson Kurpius, Ph.D.
Arizona State University
Tempe, Arizona

Taylor & Francis
Publishers since 1798

USA	Publishing Office:	Taylor & Francis 1101 Vermont Ave., N.W., Suite 200 Washington, DC 20005 Tel: (202) 289-2174 Fax: (202) 289-3665
	Distribution Center:	Taylor & Francis 1900 Frost Road, Suite 101 Bristol, PA 19007-1598 Tel: (215) 785-5800 Fax: (215) 785-5515
UK		Taylor & Francis, Ltd. 4 John Street London WC1N 2ET Tel: 071 405 2237 Fax: 071 831 2035

SHATTERED INNOCENCE: A Practical Guide for Counseling Women Survivors of Childhood Sexual Abuse

1 2 3 4 5 6 7 8 9 0 BRBR 0 9 8 7 6 5

This book was set in Times Roman by Brushwood Graphics, Inc. The editors were Holly Seltzer and Lisa Speckhardt. Prepress Supervisor was Miriam Gonzalez. Cover design by Michelle Fleitz. Cover illustration by Angela F. Anderson. Printing and binding by Braun-Brumfield, Inc.

A CIP catalog record for this book is available from the British Library.

∞ The paper in this publication meets the requirements of the ANSI Standard Z39.48-1984 (Permanence of Paper)

Library of Congress Cataloging-in-Publication Data
Weiner, Neil.
    Shattered innocence: a practical guide for counseling women survivors of childhood sexual abuse/Neil Weiner, Sharon E. Robinson Kurpius.
    p. cm.

    1. Adult child sexual abuse victims—Counseling of. 2. Abused women—Counseling of. I. Kurpius, Sharon E. Robinson. II. Title.
HV6570.W45 1995   95-13954
362.7'64'082—dc20   CIP

ISBN 1-56032-347-7 (case)
ISBN 1-56032-348-5 (paper)

"Those hurts and pains that we experience in childhood don't just magically evaporate as we grow older. They rumble around in us, and when we have reached a level of strength, maturity, insight, and awareness to handle them, they come up to be worked through. This is one of the ways our inner being is loving to us. It gives us every opportunity to heal the hurts we need to heal, and it gives us that opportunity when we are strong enough to handle it."

(anonymous author)

Contents

Preface

We spent many mornings sharing cream cheese and bagels while debating how best to write this book. Initially, the book was conceptualized as a self-help book for women who had been sexually abused as children. However, as our ideas evolved and became focused, it became evident that the information and approaches we wanted to share would be most useful to mental health professionals working with victims of childhood trauma, particularly child sexual abuse. Therefore, this book has been designed as a guide or handbook for mental health professionals who want to know more about working with female clients who were sexually abused as children.

Much of the information presented in this book can also be useful to clients who are in their own recovery process. The ideas shared can serve to let them know that they are not alone, that childhood sexual abuse is devastatingly prevalent, and that women everywhere are struggling with the effects of having been abused. Although the examples and discussions may be most relevant for females, male clients can also benefit from reading this book. Many of the issues and problems evolving from having been abused are similar for men and women.

This book presents background essential to understanding child abuse, gives a four-stage theoretical model for intervention, and offers suggestions for using a variety of techniques designed to facilitate therapeutic progress. For each of the four stages of recovery, case examples are discussed. In addition, information is given that can help the therapist accurately diagnose the occurrence of childhood sexual abuse, conceptualize the effects of family, stage of development, and spirituality on the victim, and evaluate the client's progress toward recovery. Ego splitting is differentiated from multiple personality disorder. Strategies for reintegrating split ego parts are related, and case examples are given. Finally, components of what we believe are essential for a healthy life are described and ideas for continued growth are presented.

This book would not have been written if it were not for the many women who shared their stories and worked through the pain of recovery. It is not an easy journey, and one must be courageous to face the hurt and betrayal of childhood sexual abuse. Hopefully, our ideas for facilitating this recovery process will help therapists be more effective with clients who want to stop being victims or even just survivors of sexual abuse. Hopefully, clients will recover from the effects of the abuse and move on to living rich and fulfilling lives.

Acknowledgments

First we acknowledge Frank Noble for his thoughtful suggestions regarding the content of this book. Although Dr. Noble died before this book was completed, his ideas have made this a richer work.

We also thank various colleagues who read sections of this book and provided us with useful ideas. These individuals include Patricia Kerstner, Augustine Baron, and Barbara Kerr. In addition, we thank both Connie Cowan for her suggestion regarding the use of "shattered innocence" in our title and Richard Kinnier for challenging our ideas and being our devil's advocate. Also, we would like to thank our children, Ricia and Jared Weiner, and Erin "Emmy" Robinson, for their youthful perspectives and willingness to give us feedback (positive and negative) on our ideas.

The inspiration for the chapter entitled "The Journey Within: Meeting It" came from Stephen King's novel *IT*. When we contacted him about this chapter, he graciously agreed to read it. His words of support and encouragement were greatly appreciated.

Most of all we acknowledge the women whose stories appear in this book for their courage in sharing their journeys to recovery. Many of them read drafts of the chapters and provided insights gained from having struggled with their own It and moving on to health.

Chapter 1

Children: Sugar and Spice, Everything Isn't So Nice

A double-propeller plane soars quietly above a typical suburban town. The camera mounted on the right wing records houses nestled in small clumps of evergreens, oaks, and carefully manicured lawns. Near the center of the town, majestic churches and synagogues wait to swallow up parishioners for religious events and ceremonies. Gleaming schools disgorge students who have soaked up their daily dose of mathematics, English, and social studies and now run gaily into the sunshine. The wide angle lens of the camera focuses on one of the two-story homes near the outskirts of this community. A white picket fence surrounds this Tudor-style house framed in bright red roses and yellow daisies.

As the camera pans the house and its lawn, it fails to capture the 7-year-old girl huddled on the backyard swing, her arms clutching her legs tightly against her chest. Nobody sees her. She is invisible. Her motionlessness reminds one of a doe frozen in the headlights of an oncoming car. Like the doe, she is suspended in time. She is lifeless, blankly staring into space as she attempts to comfort herself by hugging herself tightly. Her unhappy face seems barely attached to her body as a single tear runs gently down her cheek.

Suddenly, a remarkable metamorphosis occurs. The little girl shakes her head, sheds her invisibility, and returns to the reality of the world around her. With a sudden jerk, she leaps off the swing and skips toward the kitchen door. Her movements catch the attention of the plane's camera, which now focuses on a smiling, skipping child entering her home for dinner.

The next day this little girl can be observed at school struggling with her spelling lesson and twisting her hair as she tries to memorize the word "Wednesday." On Sunday, she can be seen squirming in her choir seat waiting for the pastor to finish the sermon so she can sing the hymn the children's choir has been practicing all month. She looks like a healthy, happy child, but deep inside she hides a dark secret.

This innocent child is a victim of sexual abuse. To the casual observer, the reality of her abuse is invisible. Indeed, in our society, she and other children who are sexually abused are all invisible. No matter their race, religious affiliation, or where they live—a scenic suburban home, a pastoral rural farm, or an inner-city housing project—they are invisible because we ignore their plight.

Who is this little girl we just described? She could easily have lived next door to you, been a playmate at the park, or sat next to you at school. She could be almost anyone you pass on the streets. It is even possible that this little girl is the person you see in the mirror every morning or the client sitting across from you in your office.

Is this child and others like her who have been sexually abused a rarity in our society? The answer is a resounding NO! Many, many children are victims of sexual abuse.

Recent statistics indicate that as many as one in every three girls and one in every five boys will be sexually abused before they reach the age of 18 (Cooney, 1988). Almost always, they are abused by someone in their family or a family friend. These are frightening statistics and testify to how common sexual abuse is in our society (Finkelhor, Hotaling, Lewis, & Smith, 1990; Ratican, 1992).

What exactly is sexual abuse? Sexual abuse occurs when a child has sexual contact with any adult or older child (National Center on Child Abuse and Neglect, 1990). This contact may happen when an adult uses trickery, coercion, or threats or misuses the natural curiosity of children to involve a child in sexual behavior. Sexual abuse of children can occur through physical contact such as fondling their bodies sexually, kissing them in an inappropriate manner, or forcing the child to engage in sexual acts (oral sex, anal sex, masturbation, or vaginal intercourse). Sexual abuse also includes giving children unnecessary medical treatment, such as enemas or washing them in a sexually provocative manner, as well as showing them adult or child pornography, telling them explicit sexual stories, and involving them in voyeurism where they watch the adult behave sexually or the adult watches them behave sexually. More subtle forms of sexual abuse occur when adults tell children inappropriate sexual jokes or make remarks about a child's body.

How many children have been hurt according to this definition? According to D. E. H. Russell (1986) in a landmark study of 930 San Francisco women, 38% of the respondents reported that they had been abused by the time they were 18 years old. According to this study, 89% of the abuse occurred at the hands of family members or close family friends. Other studies have shown that 11% of sexual abuse victims are younger than 5 years old and another 60% are between 5 and 13 years old.

If sexual abuse is so prevalent among children, why don't children tell anyone what is happening and why do they commonly forget that it ever took place? The best explanation is that it is too horrible for these children to live with consciously so they forget that it ever happened or distort what happened. Like our invisible little girl, they hide a dark secret deep inside.

Counselors and psychologists call this process dissociation. Children often dissociate in order to repress the memory of the sexual contact. We all have the ability to dissociate so we can continue to cope with our lives after a traumatic experience. These experiences can range from being in an automobile accident to being sexually abused as a child.

Although not about sexual abuse, many stories written for young children are full of trauma, malevolence, and evil directed at children. These stories also depict how children creatively cope with what is happening to them.

CHILDREN'S STORIES

To better understand children's reactions to their worlds and their responses to traumatic events, it is helpful to read children's literature. Three well-known stories have been chosen to illustrate how trauma can affect children. The story of *Alice's Adventures in Wonderland* (Carroll, 1865/1968) depicts one's ability to fall into unconsciousness and how a child, Alice, handles the confusion and lack of stability that is part of the unconscious world. The adventures of *Peter Pan* (Barrie, 1911) are filled with elements of the unconscious fighting abandonment and adult tyranny. In *The Wonderful Wizard of Oz* (Baum, 1900), Dorothy's journey is an excellent example of how the unconscious can protect children and help them to fight back.

Alice's distortion of reality is the core of *Alice's Adventures in Wonderland* (Carroll, 1865/1968). This tale chronicles Alice's journey as she descends with the white rabbit into the hole of her unconscious. Here the world is one of confusion that can turn quickly from a friendly tea party to mayhem, from a sleepy dormouse to the Queen of Hearts shouting, "off with her head!" Never too certain of her safety, Alice experiences a variety of reality distortions in Wonderland.

Both time and space become distorted or unreal. For example, the white rabbit constantly flashing his watch and saying, "Oh dear! Oh dear! I shall be too late!" emphasizes for the reader the ongoing time distortion in the story. Time distortion is an essential part of one's childhood experience. It is not unusual for children traveling with parents to ask, "Are we almost there? Are we there yet?" Telling these impatient children that you will be there in an hour is meaningless to them since their concept of time differs from that of adults.

Alice can also shrink to be ten inches tall or grow to be taller than the trees—a distortion of the reality of the space we occupy in relation to other objects. Other distortions in the story include visual hallucinations, such as the vanishing Cheshire Cat. Alice's ability to dissociate is related by the story's author: ". . . And once she remembered trying to box her own ears for having cheated herself in a game of croquet she was playing against herself for this curious child was very fond of pretending to be two people." (Carroll, 1865/1968, p. 19). Like most children, Alice has no difficulty being two of herself, and there are few external concrete anchors to hold her in what we adults would call reality. The distortions depicted in *Alice's Adventures in Wonderland* are vivid reminders of how scary this world can be for children, and that children have an amazing ability to change their perceptions of reality in order to cope with what is happening to them.

Another popular children's story, *Peter Pan*, can be interpreted as explaining how children protect themselves from abandonment and trauma. The stage play and the movie, *Hook*, each depicted Peter and the lost boys as having the time of their lives in their adventures against Captain Hook. The abandonment and trauma issues originally presented by J. M. Barrie are minimized.

In the original version, however, Peter Pan has vague, unhappy memories of being deserted by his mother, "Long ago . . . I thought . . . that my mother would always keep the window open for me; so I stayed away for moons and moons and moons, and then flew back; but the window was barred, for mother had forgotten all about me, and there was another little boy sleeping in my bed" (Barrie, 1911, p. 152). But, as the leader of the lost boys, Peter searches desperately for a kind, compassionate mother for them. Wendy, a young adolescent girl, is chosen to fly to Neverland to fulfill this role. When they meet her, the lost boys are so happy that "[they] all went on their knees, and holding out their arms cried, 'O Wendy lady, be our mother' . . . [Then Peter told her] 'what we need is just a nice motherly person.'" (p. 97).

Like Peter and the lost boys, Wendy, John, and Michael also have experienced not being wanted. When Wendy was born her practical father viewed her birth and her eventual childhood illnesses as expenses he could not afford; therefore, he considered giving her away. "For a week or two after Wendy came it was doubtful whether they would be able to keep her, as she was another mouth to feed." (Barrie, 1911, p. 3). The same financial concerns arose with the births of John and Michael, "but both were kept" (p. 4). Fortunately for Wendy and her brothers, they were deeply loved by their mother, who was willing to take the financial risk of keeping them. As very young children, all of the children in *Peter Pan* experience feelings of being unwanted.

In the tale, Wendy and Peter act as parents for the lost boys; however, their parenting is challenged by the lurking evil symbolized by Captain Hook and the pirates. The adults in this world are sinister, and the children must hide underground to be safe and protected. The lost boys' only defense lies in the magical ability of Peter Pan to fly and fight fearlessly for them.

The story of Peter Pan, the child who never wanted to grow up, illustrates the defenses available to children when the adults in their worlds are menacing, rejecting, or frightening. Children can literally or figuratively hide, creating some magical fantasy character to protect them, or fly away in their minds to escape the adults. The children in *Peter Pan* live in a make-believe world in order to cope with the reality of being unwanted.

The third story, *The Wonderful Wizard of Oz* by L. Frank Baum, conveys another aspect of childhood trauma, the qualities needed by children to face overwhelming odds. This book parallels *Peter Pan* in the description of the child's significant parental figures. Dorothy's Aunty Em and Uncle Henry are described in severe and dour terms: "The sun and wind . . . had taken the sparkle from her eyes and left them a sober gray; they had taken the red from her cheeks and lips, and they were gray also. She was thin and gaunt, and never smiled, now. . . . Uncle Henry never laughed. He worked hard from morning till night and did not know what joy was. He was gray also, from his long beard to his rough boots, and he looked stern and solemn, and rarely spoke." (p. 2) The bleakness of the parental figures extends to the panorama facing Dorothy when she leaves the house, which itself is portrayed as dull and gray, like everything else that led to the horizon. Dorothy escapes this grayness and sullenness when she is vaulted by a whirling cyclone to Oz, a land of marvelous beauty that sparkles with sunshine and bright colors.

The land of Oz is inhabited by witches (good and bad), Munchkins, wizards, and an assortment of monsters. In order to leave Oz and return home, Dorothy has to make a dangerous journey, during which she enlists the services of a lion who needs courage, a tin woodsman who wants a heart, and a scarecrow who wants a brain. This journey can be viewed as a metaphor for Dorothy recovering three basic components of herself—courage, love, and rational thinking. Each of these aspects can be injured in a child trying to cope with a traumatic life event such as being sexually abused.

First, children who are traumatized have extensive fear symptoms and lack the courage to face them. For example, in *Hope Under Siege: Terror and Family Support in Chile*, Ritterman (1981) refers to the epidemic fear that rages in environments ruled by tyrants. "Fear—accumulated from past atrocities, even without specific memories coming to mind—can explode in people at any time, paralyzing them, deterring them from seeking justice, acting as free men and women (p. 228)." Children who are sexually abused are tyrannized by the abuser and live in fear of further abuse. In such a daily world, the word "courage" has no meaning to these children and may only become meaningful when as adults they gather all of their courage to confront what happened to them.

The second result of trauma is the severing of heart connections, losing the trust necessary to love or to accept being loved. The sexually traumatized child often learns that she is to put everyone's needs before her own. In time, she learns that she has no legitimate needs (Gelinas, 1983). Relationships are characterized by a lack of trust. Love and caring are obliterated by recurrent patterns of abuse. Although she desperately wants to be loved, the sexually abused child learns not to become vulnerable by trusting her heart to others.

The third major aftermath of sexual trauma is irrational thinking or thought distortions. They may take the form of recurrent images, obsessive ideas, hallucinations, nightmares, or a short circuiting of the abstract thinking process. For example, one client who was recovering from childhood sexual abuse remarked in a therapy session that she takes all statements literally and was confused by any abstract references. To avoid the confusion caused by abstraction, she limited her employment to data entry on computers, where everything is black and white. In addition, she shied away from all relationships that were not sexually-based, because these were the only relationships in which she concretely understood what was expected of her.

In our children's stories, Peter, Alice, and Dorothy experience thought distortions. The story of Dorothy, however, is the most descriptive of the loss and recovery of courage, love, and thoughts anchored in reality. Through her adventures in Oz, Dorothy recovers these three components of herself. She faces her fear of the wicked witch and learns courage. She places her friends' needs above her own and learns the true meaning of love. And she realizes that the Wizard is a fraud who cannot rescue her from her distress and unhappiness and that she must rely on her own thinking and problem-solving. The magic slippers, which she had with her all the time, symbolize that the power to return home (to heal herself) was already hers. Others could not return her home or repair the damage caused by trauma. The resources were always within her. She had only to rediscover them.

The transformation of Dorothy as she returns home to Kansas is mirrored in the abrupt changes in her uncle and aunt. Losing Dorothy shocked them into recognizing the depth of their love for her. Aunty Em greets Dorothy affectionately, "'My darling child!' she cried, folding the little girl in her arms and covering her face with kisses" (p. 205).

Sometimes, only when we lose something do we realize how much it means to us. When children are sexually abused, they lose part of themselves and forget how valuable that part is and how much love it needs. Like Dorothy, victims of childhood sexual abuse must find within themselves the power to return home, to become whole again, to heal. It is well worth the effort and pain of searching within ourselves for the power to return that part home.

Tales such as these, especially *Peter Pan* and *The Wonderful Wizard of Oz*, tell how children can escape from reality in order to cope with trauma. In these children's stories, trauma is depicted as confusion brought about by an assault on the child's conscious functioning and sense of worth. Escape from this assault can occur by flying to a far-off magical land or by being carried by the wind and rapidly falling out of space. Each child is transported to a land that does not exist in reality, but once the child has been transported in such a manner, the laws of conscious functioning no longer apply—the initial trauma no longer exists in the child's mind.

A discussion of children's stories would not be complete without mentioning the most wonderful story about the power of love to make things (or people) real. *The Velveteen Rabbit or How Toys Become Real* (Williams, 1922/1983) tells a tale about the process of becoming real—the process of experiencing the type of love necessary to return safely from trauma.

> "What is REAL?" asked the Rabbit one day, when they were lying side by side near the nursery fender, before Nana came to tidy the room. "Does it mean having things that buzz inside you and a stick-out handle?"
>
> "Real isn't how you are made," said the Skin Horse. "It's a thing that happens to you. When a child loves you for a long, long time, not just to play with, but REALLY loves you, then you become Real."
>
> "Does it hurt?" asked the Rabbit.
>
> "Sometimes," said the Skin Horse, for he was always truthful. "When you are Real you don't mind being hurt."
>
> "Does it happen all at once, like being wound up," he asked, "or bit by bit?"
>
> "It doesn't happen all at once," said the Skin Horse. "You become. It takes a long time. That's why it doesn't often happen to people who break easily or have sharp edges, or who have to be carefully kept. Generally, by the time you are Real, most of your hair has been loved off, and your eyes drop out and you get loose in the joints and very shabby. But these things don't matter at all, because once you are Real you can't be ugly, except to people who don't understand." (pp. 14–16)

The story goes on to relate how the Velveteen Rabbit became a live rabbit. The little boy's love for him serves as a catalyst for the rabbit's evolution.

These children's stories, *Alice's Adventures in Wonderland*, *Peter Pan*, *The Wonderful Wizard of Oz*, and *The Velveteen Rabbit*, have a common link to the traumatic abuse of children. In each one, a child is in a state of confusion or is devalued by adults and is motivated by the search for love and caring. By being devalued, children become things or objects that can be used for whatever purpose the adults want.

MYTHS AND BEING DEVALUED

Joseph Campbell (1988) in *The Power of Myth* relates the potential for destruction inherent in being devalued. In the process of devaluing, a person becomes an "it," an object for use. Campbell tells the Native American Blackfoot tribe's origin legend about their buffalo dance. In this myth, an ancient Blackfoot tribe attempts to drive a buffalo herd over a cliff so that the tribe can get meat for the winter. However, each time the herd approaches the cliff, it veers off. One day, a young girl from the tribe sees the buffalo on the cliff and promises to marry one of them if the herd flings itself over the cliff. To her astonishment, part of the herd crashes down the side of the cliff, and the old shaman buffalo carries her off to be his bride.

The girl's father discovers she is missing and, tracking the old buffalo with the help of a magical magpie, he finds the rest of the herd. Hiding in a buffalo wallow, the father asks the magpie to find his daughter and then sets up an ambush. The old shaman buffalo discovers the treachery and sends the herd to trample the father. The girl suffers such anguish over the death of her father that the compassionate husband-to-be (the old shaman buffalo) promises her that if she can bring her father back to life he will let her leave.

Singing a revivifying song, the daughter awakens her father. At this solemn moment, the buffaloes make an agreement with the girl. They will teach her the buffalo dance and when their families are killed, if the tribe does the buffalo dance and sings her song then the herd will come back to life.

This story of the sacred union between humans and animals is contrasted with the wholesale slaughter of the buffalo by frontiersmen as depicted in George Calin's paintings of the old West. These frontiersmen sharpshooters took the skin of the buffalo and left the carcasses to rot. As Campbell (1988) points out, the frontiersmen turned the buffalo from a thou to an it.

An "it" easily loses worth and can be treated as an object—or depersonified. In contrast, the "thou" denotes value and honoring of the other's humanness (Buber, 1970). Too often, children become an "it" in their homes and their humanness is devalued. This devaluing, the shift from a "thou" to an "it," is the same attitude that can lead to the sexual and physical devastation of children.

SUMMARY

If you were silently nodding your head as you were reading the preceding paragraphs, you are not alone. Many innocent victims of childhood sexual abuse are becoming visible. They are stepping out from behind the illusion of the purity of white picket fences and cozy suburban homes. They are clambering up from basement tenements in the inner cities and emerging from the rural farmhouses. They are the rich and famous, the poor and unknown, the secretary and the executive, the cleaning woman and the university professor. All are seeking to understand themselves better, searching for an identity, and wanting to take the shame and guilt away from having been a victim of childhood sexual abuse.

One of the celebrities who recently spoke out about the effects of being sexually abused is Marilyn Van Derbur Atler, the 1958 Miss America. Atler (1991a, 1991b) recalls the fateful evening when she addressed an adult survivor group for the first time. "Tonight I break my silence. That means shining a bright light into the blackness where my night child has been hidden for so many, many years. It means speaking the unspeakable word—the ugliest six-letter word in the English language—incest." (1991b, p. 78) Born into an affluent, influential family, she recounted how she experienced a long series of mental and physical reactions to being sexually abused by her mother and then by many others as she grew up and how she was finally hospitalized for paralysis. Like the little girl at the beginning of this chapter who was sitting on the swing and who seemed to be invisible and frozen in place, Atler escaped the trauma of sexual abuse by becoming paralyzed. She concluded her remarks by hoping that "the child may be mute today, but someday the child will speak her name and your name. The child will speak every single name! And we will take away the children's secrets, we will take away the rapist's power" (p. 151). Most of all, we will give back to the adult victim her dignity and her courage to be who she is without shame and guilt.

Others among the rich and famous who have added their names to this list of survivors of childhood sexual abuse include La Toya Jackson, Roseanne, and Oprah Winfrey. Their stories are ones that paint a picture of glamour and fame on the outside and a private hell on the inside. Roseanne, for example, states that while she was growing up, she mutilated her body by cutting herself, abused drugs and alcohol, ran away from home, and hitchhiked five times across the United States. She was not only running away from her home, she was running away from herself and her own sense of worthlessness—her victimization.

Many of the stories of those still searching for an identity are just as moving. They involve repressed memories, flashbacks, substance and food abuse, and suicidal ideation, to mention a few of the symptoms. These untold millions are in all stages of discovery and recovery from being sexually abused as children.

Hopefully, our double-prop plane circling the Tudor house with the white picket fence can land in a new environment—one that is populated by caring, supportive families and friends. One in which self-help groups provide a forum to make the unspoken, spoken. One where ministers and therapists help guide victims to non-victim status. And most of all, an environment where trust and caring replace the childhood scars created by betrayal and abuse.

Chapter 2

Child Abuse Across Time and Cultures

The feudal lord wrenched the baby from the clutches of its shrieking mother. Holding the baby's leg, with one supreme heave, he whirled the infant around and sent it soaring in an arc above the village. The baby's mother screamed in panic as he tore her dress from her body, threw her to the ground, and brutally raped her. After completing the act, he harshly informed her distraught father that it was the duty of every married serf to have sex with him on her wedding night. He had just come to collect an overdue payment.

This story, related by Ken Follett (1990) in the historical novel, *Pillars of the Earth*, accurately depicts the cruel treatment of peasants who were the property of feudal lords. Treated as objects, the women and children in particular were used for the lord's pleasure without concern for their safety or welfare. As part of his right as lord, he could brutalize them in any way he saw fit, and no one interfered. The peers of the lord did not think he was acting beyond his rights or that such behaviors were cruel or unjust. After all, he owned these peasants, and they were his to do with as he pleased.

Although modern society has evolved and has become more civilized in what is considered acceptable treatment of others, abuse of children is still shockingly commonplace, women continue to be sexually brutalized (one in seven women will be raped sometime in her lifetime), and child sexual abuse continues to be a major problem, with between 35% and 45% of women being sexually abused before they reach the age of 18 (Roland, 1993; Russell, 1986). In light of the continuing frequency of these acts of violence, it appears as if we have not come very far from the days of the feudal lord.

It is difficult not to ask, Why do these things still happen? Why does a civilized society let this violence continue? While we cannot provide a simple answer to these questions, perhaps if we understand the treatment of children (and women) across time and cultures, we might gain some perspective on why this type of violence is still a prevalent problem in what we think of as one of the world's most advanced societies—the United States of America.

AN HISTORICAL PERSPECTIVE

Throughout history, children have been considered the legal property of their parents, particularly their father. According to the doctrine of patriae potestas, the father was invested with absolute control over the lives of his children, and, therefore, could treat them in any manner he deemed appropriate. Regardless of the cruelty of treatment, there was little or no interference from others.

It may surprise you to know that the *Bible* reports many stories of the harsh treatment and sacrifices of children. In fact, in over 2,000 references to children in the Old Testament, there are no empathic statements about the needs of children. Most passages describe child sacrifices, stonings, beatings, and obedience to all the wishes of their parents and other adults. For example, Abraham offered to kill his son if that was God's wish. Herod slayed innocent children to ensure that he would remain king, and baby Moses survived the Pharaoh's order to kill all male children by being put in a basket and set upon the river. Children belonged to those in power, and those in power could do as they wished with these children.

It seems as if the Golden Rule for parents with respect to their children was not, "Do unto others as you would have them do unto you." Instead, it was "He that spareth the rod hateth his son, but he that loveth him correcteth him betimes" (*Proverbs* 13:24). More recently, this has become the adage, "Spare the rod and spoil the child" and has been used as a justification for all forms of punishment or discipline in families, for corporal punishment in schools, and for ritualized beatings by religious cults (Cooney, 1987). These acts (sanctioned by some religions) would now be labeled physical child abuse.

History has also recorded periods when sexual contact between adults and children was not only acceptable but was an established part of "civilized" society. Sexual contact between children and adults in ancient Rome and Greece was common, with boys being particularly victimized in boy brothels. These brothels were accepted as part of the established society and were frequented by Rome's leading male citizens—senators, teachers, and other patricians. Recently, two bestselling books, *Marius* and *The Grass Crown*, which chronicled the historical events leading up to Julius Caesar's rule of Rome, related the sexual preferences of one of the leading characters for young boys. While this was not an advocated lifestyle, he was not viewed as aberrant because of it. He was expected to be discreet in his behavior and still have the traditional family unit for appearance's sake. In both novels, no one seemed to be concerned about the welfare of the young boys who were the source of his sexual pleasures. It was the outer appearance of dignity and decorum that was of utmost importance—not who was hurt. The same conscious "looking the other way" also occurred when the victim of the abuse was a wife. Although the physical and sexual abuse of wives was not infrequent during Roman times, as long as the male carried out his public duties and still supported his family, what he did in the privacy of his home was his own affair and certainly was not mentioned or criticized by others.

Physical and sexual abuse of children was not just common in Biblical times or in ancient history. In the Middle Ages, many peasant mothers practiced infanticide in order to survive life's hardships themselves. Since infants were considered to be less than human and were the property of the parents, a mother might dispose of her own newborn in order to get a position as a wet nurse among the wealthier families. It was unseemly for young mothers of the upper classes to breast-feed their own babies; therefore, it was a common and expected practice to hire a wet nurse to take care of this baser need of the newborn. No one asked the wet nurse about her own baby, nor did anyone care as long as she had sufficient milk for the infant she was hired to suckle.

For a young woman who happened to have a baby out of wedlock, her plight was even more devastating. If the Church found out that she was an unwed mother, she would be excommunicated and forced to live as an outcast from society. If she disposed of her infant and this was discovered by the Church or the legal authorities, she would be either decapitated or put into a sack and thrown into a river (Chase, 1975). There was no understanding or forgiveness for her. The crime was not so much that she destroyed her baby but that she had the baby without having a husband. In any case, if the mother was poor, if there was famine or war, or if she just felt overwhelmed by the demands of staying alive, there were few alternatives. And, since children were valued so little, no one closely questioned the disappearance of a newborn.

The practice of disposing of one's baby in order to become a wet nurse or just to survive continued well into the nineteenth century. In Paris, at least a quarter of all births were to single mothers, and half of the children born to these women were abandoned or allowed to die. According to Jules Simon, a prominent French politician in the late 1800s, over 180,000 infants perished each year in France during this time period.

In many societies, particularly agrarian and primitive cultures, female children were considered a curse and were killed at birth. They were viewed as burdens since they could not work in the fields or help support the family. They were just another mouth to feed, and, therefore, they were unwanted and disposable.

Just as the Church in ancient times had not interfered with the brutalization of children, during the Renaissance Martin Luther supported the killing of any deformed newborn (Cooney, 1988). Luther, the founder of the Lutheran religion, believed that a child's deformity was caused by the devil, which meant that the child had to be destroyed. It was also during this period in history that children were buried alive in the foundations of new buildings in order to be a blessing on the building and to ensure its longevity.

Historically, it has not been unusual for the Church, for society, or for parents to mutilate a child in order to make the child more valued. For example, boys were castrated in order to allow them to continue singing in high voices in church choirs, to serve as guards for queens, or to be eunuchs for a master's harem. Parents living in poverty have purposefully crippled or mutilated their children so that they can be more pathetic and successful beggars. Sadly, this practice still exists in many parts of the world today.

In 1993, ABC aired a feature on female circumcision (*Day One: Female Circumcision*). The host of the program, Forrest Sawyer, pointed out that between 85 and 100 million women and girls alive today have been subjected to female genital mutilation ranging from removal of the clitoris only to total removal of the vulva and clitoris. This procedure is not done in a hospital or by any medical personnel. Typically, it is a female village elder who performs the ritual on young, unsuspecting girls who are brought by their mothers for the circumcision (Levin, 1980). No medication is given, and hemorrhaging and infection are common. Not only would a woman be a social outcast if she was not circumcised, but it is also taboo to seek medical attention after the painful clitorectomy. It was noted that this procedure increases the woman's chance of having stillbirths, becoming sterile, and contracting AIDS and other sexually transmitted diseases. What, then, is the purpose of this tradition?

The purpose of the mutilation is to desensitize females so that they will not enjoy sex and become promiscuous, and to increase their husband's sexual pleasure (Slack, 1988). Not only are the genitalia mutilated, but afterward, the woman's vagina is sewn almost shut to the point that some women cannot even pass their menstrual blood. The husband forces entry after marriage and is assured that his bride is a virgin. Many woman are resewn after the birth of a child to ensure further pleasure for their husband.

From early childhood through adulthood, their sexuality is associated with pain. As one Gambian woman said on the ABC program, "Pain is part of womanhood. We women are here to suffer." Sadly, this is what most of them still believe, although leading women in 25 different countries are trying to fight this tradition in African culture. Many Americans would be surprised to learn that many women in the U.S. have also been circumcised as children.

In an effort to prevent such atrocities, the United Nations Convention on Rights of the Child passed a resolution "to protect children from all forms of physical or mental violence, injury, or abuse. It urges effective and appropriate measures to abolish traditional practices that are prejudicial to the health of children" (ABC Special, 1993). In 1993, a congresswoman introduced a bill into the United States House of Representatives that would make female genital mutilation a crime. The House has yet to act on this bill and the United States has still not ratified the U.N. Convention's resolution. Perhaps those responsible for endorsing both the resolution and the bill should be reminded that the victims of this abuse are not adults making informed decisions, but small children who cannot protect themselves.

History is replete with adults inflicting harm on children in the name of good. For example, the general belief during the Middle Ages that infants were sinful and on the verge of turning into evil creations or into the devil himself could be viewed as a widespread example of adults projecting their own unconscious hostilities onto children. Certainly the behavior of adults toward children, especially infants, has been designed to severely control them. In many societies, babies were restrained by corsets, stays, backboards, puppet strings, or swaddles. Many were tied to chairs to prevent them from crawling on the floor "like animals."

After infancy, children were controlled through the use of monster and ghost stories or by being exposed to some horrifying scene. For example, the frescoes from the Roman era depict masked adults terrifying children, and even today, it is not uncommon for parents to tell children about the monster or boogie man who will get them if they do not do as they are told. During the French revolution, children were taken to hangings and guillotines and then whipped when they got home so they would remember what they saw.

Prior to the 1900s, there was little truly kind or sympathetic adult treatment of children. One of the first books to acknowledge the feelings of children was *The Tattler,* which described how an infant must feel about being born into the European Victorian society. DeMause (1988) pointed out that it was one of the very few books on children that showed any empathy at all. "I have not found a description with this degree of empathy in any century prior to the eighteenth" (p. 16). During this era, extremely repressive child-rearing practices were in vogue and children were severely punished according to religious sanctions. They were viewed as small adults and expected to behave with that level of maturity. Children were allowed little or no "childhood," and if they failed to behave appropriately, their parents might flog them. Girls were often forced to wear chastity belts, and boys frequently underwent painful circumcisions and occasionally had toothed rings attached to their penises to prevent masturbation. Not surprisingly, it was during this time that the patriae potesta doctrine, which said children are owned by their father, was established.

CHILDREN AS POSSESSIONS

In early colonial America, children were also viewed as chattel of their parents. The Elizabethan Poor Laws allowed destitute English children to be exported to America to work as apprentices, where they were treated as little more than slaves. The state government of Massachusetts in 1628 passed the Stubborn Child Act, which allowed children to be put to death for not obeying their parents.

It was not until 1871 that abuse of children gained national attention when the Society for the Prevention of Cruelty to Animals intervened to stop the repeated physical abuse of Mary Ellen Wilson by her foster mother. As a result of the publicity from this case, the Society for Prevention of Cruelty to Children was founded in 1874, and laws were eventually passed that required law and court officials to prevent the abuse of children. Rarely were birth parents classified as abusers, however, as the Society for Prevention of Cruelty to Children did not want to intervene in the "natural" balance of power between parents and children and, therefore, ignored the abuse of children.

In 1924, the Fifth Assembly of the League of Nations established the doctrine of parens patriae, which said the state and courts had the power and duty to protect minors. It was not until 1938, however, that the Fair Labor Standards Act was passed. This Act impacted children's rights with respect to employment by prohibiting interstate commerce to businesses not adhering to child labor guidelines.

In spite of these advances and prohibitions regarding child labor and schooling, children were and continue to be the victims of violence in the family. In 1962, Kempe, Silverman, Steele, Droegemueller and Silver caught the public's attention with their explosive article entitled, "The Battered Child Syndrome." With this article, the American public was shocked into awareness of the prevalence of the abuse of children. Only then did all 50 states pass legislation prohibiting the abuse of children.

In spite of the tremendous strides that have been made in protecting children from abuse and violence, surprisingly, we still often inadvertently teach small children that violence against them is an accepted part of life. For example, nursery rhymes, fairy tales, and children's songs depict violence against children. The old woman who lived in the shoe got so frustrated with her children that she "whipped them all soundly and sent them to bed." The cradle in Rock-a-Bye Baby fell out of the tree, tumbling the poor baby with it. Hansel and Gretel fully expected to be baked and devoured by the old witch, and Little Red Riding Hood narrowly escaped being eaten by the Big Bad Wolf. Snow White's stepmother tried to kill her because Snow White was the more beautiful of the two. Cinderella is treated as a kitchen servant and emotionally abused by her wicked step-mother. From an early age, children learn that they can be hurt by adults and that in some ways, this is acceptable, particularly if the adult is their parent or parent-substitute.

For ages, many adults have failed to believe that incest was harmful to children. In many countries that have royalty as the governing system, marriages between parents and children, cousins, and siblings were viewed as a way to preserve not only the royal bloodline but as a way to keep the wealth and power in the family. For example, only recently did a member of the Japanese royal family marry someone outside the family. It was only at the close of the nineteenth century that incest was no longer viewed as an acceptable practice among Mormons in the United States (Cooney, 1987). Prior to this time, incest was justified as a way to keep Mormon girls from marrying outside their faith.

The notion that a child is less than a person still persists. Although child prostitution and pornography are illegal and officially condemned in the United States, they are unofficially tolerated, even though they are not condoned (Kempe & Kempe, 1984). It has been estimated that, in America, one in three to four girls and one in five to six boys will be sexually molested before they reach the age of 18. The figures for being physically abused are even higher.

In 1992 alone, the National Committee for Prevention of Child Abuse (NCPCA, 1993) reported that nationally there were 2,936,000 cases of reported child abuse, of which 17% were for sexual abuse. This shockingly high number is probably just the tip of the iceberg since it does not include those cases that were never brought to the attention of authorities. According to recent government statistics, since 1985 there has been an average 6% increase in reported child abuse each year. Only 6% of this abuse occurred in out-of-home settings such as day care and foster care facilities. That means that 94% of the abuse occurred in home-related settings. The NCPCA also reported that the parental relationship accounts for 75% of the relation of the perpetrators to victims. These data would suggest that violence toward children (physical, sexual, and emotional abuse and neglect) has not decreased as society has become more civilized. Instead of improving, the situation seems to be getting worse.

SUMMARY

The reports of child abuse "continue to climb at a steady rate, apparently fueled by increasing economic stress and substance abuse as well as greater public awareness of and willingness to report maltreatment" (National Committee for Prevention of Child Abuse, 1993, p. 20). It is evident that children are still the helpless victims of adult violence, with the number of reported cases of child abuse increasing yearly. At the beginning of this chapter, we described the feudal lord raping his peasant serf and killing her baby. Have we really come very far from this scenario? When national statistics indicate that one in three to four girls and one in five to six boys are sexually molested and that one in seven women will be raped during their lifetime, the answer, sadly, must be no.

Chapter 3

Labels Are Not Always Accurate: Identifying Sexual Abuse

Whether treatment of women and children is dictated by religious or by secular powers, across the ages men have controlled the interpretation of what are acceptable behaviors toward women and children. If the history of women who have sought therapy is examined, it is evident that the patriarchal political climate even shaped what has been viewed as the causes of women's mental health problems.

THE MENTAL HEALTH VIEW OF SEXUAL ABUSE

In an excellent work called *Trauma and Recovery*, Judith Lewis Herman (1992) catalogs the "forgotten history" of psychological trauma. It is forgotten because the implications of trauma are too horrendous for society to accept; therefore, its existence is denied and assigned to oblivion. The cause for this denial may be that the witnesses have to take sides when the trauma is caused by humans; we cannot remain neutral. We have to choose between the victim and the perpetrator.

Since power usually resides with the perpetrator, it is easiest to take the perpetrator's side and not interfere with the interaction between the victim and perpetrator. In contrast, the victim demands that the witness understand her pain and take some action to relieve it or at least to remember it. One powerful weapon used by perpetrators is silence and secrecy, and the witness and victim collude with the perpetrator when they remain silent. If the victim breaks the silence and reveals the secret of the traumatic acts, the perpetrator attacks the credibility of the victim by marshalling an impressive array of arguments such as, "It never happened," "The victim lies," "The victim exaggerates," "The victim brought it upon herself," and, "In any case, it is time to forget the past and move on" (Herman, 1992, p. 8). The victim and her story become devalued as the perpetrator redefines reality to fit his needs. If this redefined reality fits the sociopolitical climate of society, it is accepted as real.

There have been a few brief periods in history when men have been interested in women's reality. One of the most significant of these, from a mental health perspective, was during the late 1800s when the mental disorder of hysteria became a major focus of investigation. Jean-Martin Charcot, a French neurologist, cataloged the symptoms of hysteria after doing in-depth observations of women diagnosed as hysterics. His major conclusion was that the symptoms were psychological in nature.

Building on Charcot's work, Sigmund Freud and Pierre Janet sought to discover the cause of hysteria. In order to do this, they talked at length with women experiencing hysteria. This was the first time that men of science had actually "listened" to women. Like Charcot, Freud and Janet each arrived at the conclusion that hysteria was psychological, and further noted that it resulted from psychological trauma. "Unbearable emotional reactions to traumatic events produced an altered state of consciousness, which in turn induced the hysterical symptoms" (Herman, 1992, p. 12). Janet called this process dissociation, a term that is prevalent in the psychological literature today.

Brever and Freud reported that hysteria could be found among the "people of clearest intellect, strongest will, greatest character, and highest critical power" (quoted in Herman, 1992, p. 12). Experiencing hysterical symptoms was not a sign of weakness but rather was a way for the mind to cope with the memories of traumatic events.

As he continued his investigations, Freud (1905/1953) heard women tell him about sexual assault, abuse, and incest. As he listened and followed "the thread of memory," he uncovered major traumatic events occurring during childhood. After extensively studying 18 women, Freud (1896/1962) wrote an article entitled *The Aetiology of Hysteria* in which he stated, "I therefore put forward the thesis that at the bottom of every case of hysteria there are *one or more occurrences of premature sexual experience*, occurrences which belong to the earliest years of childhood, but which can be reproduced through the work of psychoanalysis in spite of intervening decades." This was the first time anyone had documented that childhood sexual abuse results in psychological trauma for its victims.

Sadly, Freud's message was not accepted either by his professional colleagues or by the French and Viennese society of the late 1880s. Within a year of publishing his findings, Freud had recanted his opinion. Apparently, he could not accept the implications of his hypothesis—since hysteria was so common among women and if their stories were true, then the "perverted acts against children" were endemic not only among the proletariat of Paris but among the respectable families of Vienna. This was just too incredible. By turning his back on his own theory, Freud identified with the perpetrators and joined the conspiracy of silence and secrecy.

Freud (1920) then proposed a major theory of human development that totally denied women's reality and reinforced women's inferiority. While sexuality remained a major focus, the context in which it occurred was reframed by Freud as one of fantasy and desire, dissociated from the reality of experience. Later Freud wrote, "I was at last obliged to recognize that these scenes of seduction had never taken place, and that they were only fantasies which my patients had made up" (Herman, 1992, p. 14). Thus ended the first age of listening to women's tales of sexual trauma.

The patriarchal society was not ready to believe that childhood sexual abuse existed. While men of science like Charcot and Freud saw themselves as benevolent rescuers, uplifting women from their degraded condition, they never for a moment envisioned a condition of social equality between women and men. Women were to be the objects of study and humane care, not subjects in their own right (Herman, 1992, p. 16). By the close of the nineteenth century, men had heard more than they wanted about women's lives and turned once again to the safety of the father-protector role. Society was not ready to face the challenge required by believing the depths of sexual oppression of women and children.

Indeed, it has been and continues to be difficult to acknowledge that widespread sexual abuse of children occurs in our so-called enlightened, modern society. Yet, women who have been sexually abused as children are turning up in record numbers in mental health agencies, counseling offices, and hospital waiting rooms (Browne & Finkelhor, 1986; Vanderbilt, 1992). The following case is a composite of many such women seen in therapy and is a typical example of a woman who was sexually abused as a child.

DIAGNOSIS OF CHILDHOOD SEXUAL ABUSE—THE CASE OF LINDA

Since graduating from a small Midwestern college, Linda, a 33-year-old woman, has taught high school English. She comes from a large family but has not seen them for the past 6 years. When asked about this during her initial counseling interview, Linda responded that she just has been too busy; however, she does talk to her mother a couple of times a year on the telephone.

Linda entered counseling in distress about a physically and emotionally abusive relationship with a man. This relationship was the latest in a series of failed relationships, all of which were abusive. Linda has been in relationship counseling twice before and individual counseling once. Her previous counselor diagnosed her as having major depression.

When questioned about other problems, Linda reported that she was at times suicidal, drank more than she should, had an intense fear of being touched, had "female problems," felt emotionally numb, suffered from frequent nightmares, and was about 30 pounds overweight. When asked if anyone had ever touched her inappropriately, Linda started sobbing and nodded yes. Gentle probing revealed that from the ages of 8 to 12, both her brother and uncle fondled her and forced her to have oral sex with them. She feels dirty and ashamed about what happened and believes that somehow it must have been her fault—that she is a bad person who deserves to be with men who hurt her and who prove to her that she is worthless.

This composite of several cases portrays one of the numerous ways that a diagnosis of sexual abuse is encountered. In the case of Linda, the initial information about the childhood sexual trauma was recalled in the first session. However, it is often the case that no conscious memory exists of this abuse, and only the many presenting problems are discussed in the first counseling sessions. Awareness of being abused may not surface until much later in the therapeutic process.

When memories of being touched, fondled, being forced to touch someone else sexually, or even of having sex as a child start to surface, the question frequently asked is—even if conscious memories do exist, can they be trusted? Was I really abused? These questions are also being increasingly echoed by friends and family members of those who report being sexually abused as children.

DID IT OR DIDN'T IT HAPPEN?

The battle lines are being drawn between those who believe that childhood sexual abuse is widespread and has a significant, harmful impact on the adult survivors (Bass & Davis, 1988; Bruhn, 1990; Farmer, 1989), and those who refuse to believe the prevalence of the problem. On one side are counselors, therapists, psychologists, and their clients who are facing the devastation resulting from this abuse. On the other side are accused parents and others who claim that memory is suspect and that these "victims" have been unduly influenced by well-meaning but overzealous groups and mental health professionals (False Memory Syndrome Foundation, 1991, 1992b, 1993; Gardner, 1992; Loftus, 1993).

Representing those who believe that such abuse exists and has existed for ages, Ellen Bass and Laura Davis (1988) have written a landmark self-help book, *The Courage to Heal*, for women who have been sexually abused as children.

Relying on numerous studies that place the incidence of childhood sexual abuse of women under the age of 18 at 33%, these authors have attempted to support women who suspect or know that they were abused. They tell their readers, "If you are unable to remember any specific instances . . . but still have a feeling that something abusive happened to you, it probably did (p. 21). To say 'I was abused' you don't need the kind of recall that would stand up in a court of law" (p. 22).

Countering this stand are others who doubt either the validity and incidence of these claims of childhood sexual abuse or the reliability of memory. They feel that many well-intentioned therapists, counselors, and support groups suggest to vulnerable clients that their symptoms match those of people who have been sexually abused. This suggestion results in a fantasized scenario of the abuse. Also, they claim that since memory does not function like a video camera, it is subject to what is known as the "false memory syndrome."

In fact, more than 2,400 families presently belong to a foundation that calls itself the False Memory Syndrome Foundation (FMSF). Founded in 1992, the Foundation consists primarily of accused family members and a professional advisory board of psychiatrists and psychologists who are alarmed by the increasing accusations and confrontations that are splitting or destroying families. In their pamphlet (FMS Foundation, 1992a), they attack aspects of the recovery movement. "*Courage to Heal* has been referred to as the Bible of the Incest-Memory Recovery Movement. We feel this book is a political statement that preaches anger and revenge" (p. 17). Also, on the subject of memory and the ability of the brain to repress traumatic information, the FMS Foundation (1992a) states, "Psychiatrists advising Foundation members seem to be unanimous in the belief that memories of such atrocities cannot be repressed. Horrible incidents of childhood are remembered, as the children of concentration camps remember vividly the experiences suffered by them" (p. 2).

Is it possible that the same controversy that erupted a century ago with the discoveries of Charcot, Janet, and Freud again threatens to engulf the mental health and lay communities? These early mental health professionals all realized that past traumatic experiences can dominate the present functioning of people. For example, Janet recognized that unassimilated fixed ideas caused by trauma seriously impair the assimilation of subsequent experiences. He felt that traumatized patients' emotional development stopped at these key points of trauma. Freud accepted this view initially and thought that the hysterical presentations of his clients were due to childhood sexual seduction. However, Freud recanted this view and for numerous reasons developed his theory of the role of fantasy in mental health problems. His patients' stories of sexual abuse were consigned to an elaborate system of developmental fantasies.

The controversy over the prevalence of childhood sexual abuse and the accuracy of repressed memories is becoming more dichotomized. The debate is being taken up by scholars supporting each side of the argument. Regardless of who is right and who is wrong, we should not lose sight of the women who are suffering and need help from qualified, caring therapists. These women may come to therapy being keenly aware that they have been sexually abused or, like so many, being aware that something is drastically wrong with their lives but not being able to identify what exactly it is. Too often these women are misdiagnosed as having a more "acceptable" mental health problem.

Typical Misdiagnoses

Many victims of childhood sexual abuse have been misdiagnosed or diagnosed based on one aspect of their complex symptomatology. Some of the major diagnostic labels applied to adult survivors of sexual abuse include major depression, anxiety, borderline, phobic, sexual dysfunction, histrionic, paranoid, and posttraumatic stress disorders. These diagnoses are accompanied by the reporting of intense feelings of guilt and shame, poor self-esteem, somatic complaints, learning difficulties, marital difficulties, drug and alcohol abuse, and severe perceptual disturbances (Briere & Runtz, 1988; Cunningham, Pearce, & Pearce, 1988; Finkelhor, Araji, Baron, Browne, Peters, & Wyatt, 1986). With this wide array of presenting complaints, many therapists feel overwhelmed and do not know how to proceed to help these women effectively.

Although the consequences of sexual abuse are very diverse, most therapists are in agreement that if it is not diagnosed and treated, many other interventions are doomed to failure (Ellenson, 1986; Gelinas, 1983). In fact, Blake-White and Kline state in their 1985 article on incest that when problems are brought to the surface, the patient may appear worse. In reality, untreated sexual abuse can relegate a person to a lifetime of depression and anxiety (Blume, 1990; Courtois, 1988).

While it is generally agreed that these women often need therapeutic intervention in order to come to peace with having been abused, what are some of the factors or events that cause them to suspect that abuse has occurred?

Keying Awareness

For many survivors of sexual abuse, key events or developmental milestones will trigger delayed aftereffects of the trauma. These intrusive aftereffects or symptoms can range from frightening flashbacks or body memories to debilitating panic attacks or even psychosis. The victim may feel acute anxiety or depression, or even experience a pervasive numbness. The responses of these women may range from a shattering of the normal routine of their lives to seeking intensive crisis intervention, including hospitalization. Women who have prior knowledge of being sexually abused often agonize over how to deal with these aftereffects, while women with no previous conscious memories are often confused, frightened, and tormented by their experiences.

Events that trigger these reactions fall into three categories. The first category involves life transitions that normally are seen either as life-enhancing, enjoyable, developmental milestones or as negative, hurtful losses. The second category involves events that trigger memories of the abuse experience because of the events' similarities to the abuse or the symbolic representation of the sexual abuse. The third category includes either a family member breaking the silence or memories being stimulated by media reporting of sexual abuse.

Life transitions. These special milestones of most people's lives can cause difficulties for the abuse victim. Whereas for most people life transitions can be overwhelmingly happy, memorable, or can cause appropriate grief, such as when a death occurs in the family, the feelings of an abuse victim can be triggered unmercifully by these transitions.

1. *Marriage or intimate relationships*—The closeness required in intimate relationships is very difficult for victims of sexual abuse. Their trust in others has been shattered at an early age and the demands of intimacy can cause panic and crisis for them. Also, the sexual demands of intimacy can precipitate emotionally painful recall of sexual abuse or other intrusive symptomatology, such as physically re-experiencing the pain of attempted penetration.

2. *Birth of a child*—Giving birth to an infant or even experiencing the birth of a family member's or friend's baby may serve as a catalyst to regress to the victim's own childhood. It may also cause an emotional crisis if the victim fears that she has the potential to abuse or neglect the baby.

3. *Age of a child*—As children of the survivor of childhood sexual abuse reach the age that the survivor was when the abuse began, painful memories are often stimulated, causing physical, emotional or psychological reactions.

4. *Graduation from college or promotions on the job*—Most survivors have been brainwashed to believe that they are bad, inadequate, dirty, and so on. Achievement or rewards can trigger feelings of not really deserving the accolades. Survivors often feel that they are impostors and do not deserve recognition for their achievements. Therefore, when they com-

plete milestone tasks such as graduating from college, getting an advanced degree, or receiving promotions at work, they experience cognitive dissonance. Their perceptions of themselves are at variance with the honors they are receiving, and as a result, memories may begin to surface.

5. *Death of the perpetrator*—It is often the case that when the perpetrator dies, painful memories surface for the first time. With the actual physical removal of the abuser from this world, victims frequently experience a newfound safety. The perpetrator can no longer carry out threats to kill the victim or other family members. Children believe these threats, and this belief becomes deeply embedded in their psyche. Many perpetrators threaten to kill or actually do kill the child's pet to frighten the victim into silence.

6. *Divorce*—The tragedy of divorce can be a potent reminder of abandonment issues. Also, if children are involved in the bitter struggles to win allegiances, this can replicate family of origin issues, particularly in cases of incest where the mother has abdicated her wifely role and intentionally denies that a daughter is being sexually abused by the father.

7. *Severe Illness and Medical Procedures*—Life-threatening experiences such as having a heart attack or being diagnosed with cancer are potent reminders that many victims of sexual abuse have always wanted in some ways to die rather than to live with the crushing implications of the abuse. For example, a client almost died of cancer and during a mastectomy began having flashbacks of being sexually abused by her uncle and a family friend. The removal of her breast seemed to trigger the memory of the loss of her sexual innocence as a child.

Events analogous to or symbolic of the abuse. These can include:

8. *Sexual assault or rape*—These events can occur either inside or outside of an intimate relationship. The use of force during sex or feelings of being in a powerless position can ignite powerful memories of prior victimization. Often women experience sleep disturbances and intrusive physical and emotional symptoms during their waking hours.

9. *Sexually transmitted diseases*—These diseases can be reminders of the feeling of being dirty that often results from childhood sexual abuse. Frequently victims believe that having a sexually transmitted disease is a deserved punishment for being sexually abused, for the acts of the perpetrator. Survivors often feel responsible for what happened to them even though they were only children.

10. *Failures in therapy*—Many survivors have been in various individual and group therapies without benefiting from the therapy. Sometimes after another perceived failure, repressed memories begin to surface as the victim feels a sense of hopelessness of ever getting better.

11. *Returning home for visits during college or after marriage*—The discrepancy between other environments and the home environment can trigger extreme reactions as the survivor experiences the differences between functional and dysfunctional interpersonal systems. This awareness can occur either when contemplating the visit or during the actual visit.

12. *Sensory reminders/sensual exposure*—The smell of the cologne of the perpetrator, a boss who is similar to the abuser, or even music that was playing during the sexual assault can cause flashbacks or body memories of the experience. The severity of these symptoms will typically frighten the survivor, although they alert her that there is something wrong.

13. *Voids in memory*—Many survivors have significant gaps in their childhood memory. It is not uncommon to hear reports that "I cannot remember anything before the age of 13." Sometimes the stimulus of looking at childhood pictures or meeting an old classmate can release a torrent of memories of the abuse.

14. *Pelvic exams or physicals*—Any physical examination of the genital region and breasts, or an exam that is performed while the patient is nude, can be devastating for the survivor. Being touched in these areas is associated with abuse both remembered and forgotten.

15. *Anniversary of the abuse or holidays when abuse occurred*—These time markers serve as time bombs for stored feelings or thoughts. They can unexpectedly trigger memories or emotional and physical responses associated with being abused as a child.

Disclosures. These can include:

16. *Family members*—If siblings, cousins, nephews, or one's own children disclose being sexually abused, the charge can facilitate the reoccurrence of memory in the survivor. These revelations are extremely distressing as the survivor tries to deny that something so awful actually happened to her and to the other person.

17. *Media*—The recent extensive media attention given to childhood sexual abuse survivors by talk shows, popular magazines, and newspapers can trigger a flood of reactions in survivors. Especially difficult for these individuals is the sensational reporting or the trivializing of such a hurtful event.

18. *Survivor impulses or sexual abuse perpetration*—The realization of sexual fantasies, thinking about hurting children sexually, or actually participating in sexual abuse can cause a reliving of one's own abuse. This form of retrieval can be extremely traumatic for all involved.

Presenting Problem of Clients

With any diagnosis of sexual abuse, clients can usually be categorized into one of three groups. One group consists of women who seek out treatment specifically for the remembered sexual abuse. Another group seeks treatment for issues other than sexual abuse but is aware of being sexually abused. The last group is unaware of having repressed memories because of denial or dissociation (Faria & Belohlavek, 1984) and comes to therapy for a variety of other presenting problems. Within each of these three groups, the accuracy of diagnosis is juxtaposed with the accuracy of memory.

The smallest category of clients ask for help with sexual abuse and have conscious memories of what happened to them as children (Faria & Belohlavek, 1984). Sometimes they have been carrying around this secret for years. In other cases, the memories were triggered by experiences associated with some part of the abuse. Examples of such experiences include the death of the perpetrator, flashbacks during sexual activities, a son or daughter reaching the same age as when the abuse occurred, a boss or coworkers re-enacting the components of the abusive relationship with the victim, moving away from the childhood home, or even the smell of alcohol or aftershave lotion used by the perpetrator.

For women who are aware that they have been abused as well as for women whose abuse history is masked or withheld, there is almost always the presence of perceptual disturbances along with certain thought disturbances (Ellenson, 1986). Also, there are extreme personality disturbances like those discussed in the general diagnosis section above. These may include asocial, avoidant, submissive or passive-aggressive personality characteristics. In addition, acute clinical symptoms such as depression, anxiety, and somatic complaints may be present (Wheeler & Walton, 1987).

If sexual abuse is not acknowledged and treated, the patient's life will often be controlled by past patterns and symptoms. Some victims will not tell the therapist even if asked about possible sexual abuse. These women tend to believe that if they do not say aloud what happened to them, it did not really exist. This is the ostrich approach to coping with the betrayal of sexual abuse; it is not productive in that symptoms do not go away and the hurt continues to fester. Many victims, however, feel a relief to finally have permission to vent (Gelinas, 1983).

The therapist's inquiries need to be respectful when patients are asked if they have ever had sexual contact with family members or others against their will. An experienced therapist understands that even if there are memories, many parts of the experience and other incidences may be dissociated or denied. Dissociation occurs when a person is faced with a situation that arouses extreme anxiety, grief, or despair, and she represses the memories and the accompanying painful affect. Denial occurs when a component of reality is not acknowledged so as to dismiss it from conscious awareness. This banishment helps to maintain an intrapsychic homeostasis. With sexual abuse, particularly incest, it is not uncommon that "most victims of sex abuse have very few memories of the actual incest" (Blake-White & Kline, 1985, p. 396).

Whether women who do not actually remember their sexual abuse were really abused has become the focus of national controversy. In order to diagnose sexual abuse among women with no conscious memory, a therapist has to understand the rudiments of memory functioning. In an article published by the New York Times Company, Goleman (1992) reported that Dr. Kihlstrom of the University of Arizona indicated that memory is highly susceptible to reinvention. Loftus, a specialist in eyewitness testimony, further iterates that in her experiments she demonstrated that suggested memories can be induced. For example, in her preliminary study (Loftus & Coan, in press), relatives of subjects told them that at age 5 they had been lost on a family shopping outing. Accepting this explanation as true, the subjects gave further embellishments about this made-up experience.

Memory is also subject to grafting of details onto an unrelated incident. Furthermore, the process of condensation can occur. "For example, a detail belonging to one event can be combined in memory with similar occurrences as one incident" (Olio, 1989, p. 95). With all of this perplexity in the retrieval of memory, how can one proceed to diagnose sexual abuse and to investigate its occurrence?

The key may be in realizing that if a person has been sexually abused, it usually occurred with someone that they loved and who betrayed them. The entire experience is painful, frightening, confusing, and often life-threatening. When memories are retrieved through hypnosis, visualization, or other methods, these memories are paired with an overwhelming fear of what happened and the consequences of breaking the barrier of silence. Even though memories are not always accurate, Terr (1990) states that "corroborating evidence and repeated behaviors or dreams that reflect traumatic events serve as checks on spontaneous recall" (p. 333). As a result of their outpatient therapy groups for incest survivors, Herman and Schatzow (1987) found a compelling link between memories of sexual abuse and corroborating information. Of the 53 women who participated in these therapy groups, 33 (64%) did not have full recall of these events and 14 (28%) had severe memory deficits. Despite the lack of vivid recall, 39 (74%) of these women obtained confirmation that the abuse did happen from other reliable sources, such as family members, close friends, and neighbors. Surprisingly, 6 (11%) of the women did not even attempt to gain confirmation. Perhaps the fear of really knowing (playing ostrich) was more powerful than the desire to know and to begin the journey to recovery.

SUMMARY

We feel that a respectful, careful diagnosis is possible with victims of sexual abuse whether or not they have memories. If a therapist pays attention to the constellation of presenting symptoms and listens carefully to the client's reports, possible sexual abuse can be cautiously explored and, if uncovered, hopefully healed. When memories are not available, techniques exist that are not suggestive and do not implant memories, but allow the client to discover what is in her own inner world as her unconscious is ready to reveal it to her.

Therapists and clients must keep in mind that the journey is not one of police work. We cannot be detectives seeking to prove conclusively what the mind and body are presenting. Memories are subject to distortion, condensation, grafting, symbolization, fantasy, displacement and a host of other mental mechanisms. In the final analysis of the complex problem of sexual abuse, the mandate for the therapist and client is not to ensure that the client's historical truth is recovered. Rather, the mandate is to ensure that the meaning of what is discovered is processed so that the client is not bound by the past but faces the present and future unfettered. Hopefully, this will be done with minimal contamination from the therapist.

We now have the opportunity to act on what Freud and other pioneers initially discovered about sexual abuse of children and its impact on the adult survivor. However, we must recognize that we are still struggling with the same questions and controversies that they did a century ago. It is hoped that we do not turn our backs on this distressed population and, like Freud, assign them once more to a disbelieving therapeutic community and society.

Chapter 4

The Journey Within: Meeting *IT*

At some point in her life, in order to recover from being sexually abused, every survivor has to confront the trauma of being betrayed by a trusted adult. This journey within is painful, and the path that must be taken is lined with sharp rocks and dangerous cliffs. Although this difficult journey is unique for each survivor, there are also amazing similarities.

Stephen King, the well-known writer of horror novels, seems to have a fundamental grasp of this perilous journey. In his bestseller, *IT*, King (1987) weaves an effective but frightening metaphor for the re-experiencing of the childhood trauma and the healing process. Pearls of wisdom for those struggling to recover are hidden within the pages of this horrifying but still enlightening novel. Although the children portrayed in *IT* are primarily boys, the process of re-encountering the trauma in order to eventually let go of it is the same regardless of one's gender.

The setting for *IT* is Derry, a small town in rural Maine. Downtown Derry is located along a stream, with the rest of the town scattered along the valley and hills that provide a picturesque backdrop for the tale. The canal running through town and a wild patch of nearby land called the Barrens provide those hideaways that children typically treasure for forts, secret meetings, and times hidden from adults. This seemingly quiet, idyllic American scene, complete with Easter Egg hunts, Old Cape houses, and Canal Day festivals, hides a secret evil that preys on the children of Derry and that is often manifested in the callousness, apathy, and cruelty of the adult citizens.

Scattered across the country, six adults who were childhood friends receive unexpected phone calls from the one friend, Mike Hanlon, who hasn't left Derry. Mike, now the town's head librarian, summons each of them to return to their hometown to confront the evil that has reappeared after 27 years of silence to feed on Derry's children. Like so many childhood friends, as adults these six have lost touch with each other. Unlike most children, however, they have almost totally forgotten about Derry and their lives as children—until they receive the nighttime phone call. As children, these seven, known as the Loser's Club, had made a sacred pact that if the "evil" (It) ever returned to Derry, they would come home to fight it again. Those who had left Derry had repressed the horrifying events of their childhoods and even their promise to return. Like a forgotten voice beckoning them from the past, the unwanted phone call triggers their remembering process. The shock of hearing Mike's voice jolts each to begin remembering pieces of what had happened to them as children—the events that resulted in their blood-pact, their promise to reunite to fight the "evil" living beneath Derry.

The six who left Derry are all very successful in their careers and, according to 1985 standards, would be considered rich. In spite of this financial wealth, all of them are childless. Each person—Stan, Richie, Ben, Eddie, Beverly, and Bill—seems to be missing an important ingredient of him- or herself and isn't truly at peace with what life has given him or her. As Mike tells them, "Things are out of order with your own lives, too, you know. None of you left Derry untouched . . . without It's mark on you." (p. 487).

Stan Uris, who as an 11-year-old child had cut the palms of each friend's hand to make the blood-promise, is the most successful young accountant in Georgia and perhaps all of the Southeast. Outwardly, Stan seems to be a well-off, happily married man, except his wife just can't become pregnant. There are no medical complications. Stan explains to his wife, "Sometimes I think I know why. Sometimes I have a dream, a bad dream, and I wake up and I think, 'I know now. I know what's wrong.' Not just you not catching pregnant—everything. Everything that's wrong with my life." (p. 51). After receiving the fateful call to return to Derry, Stan quietly goes upstairs and commits suicide in his bathtub. As he is dying, he uses his own life blood to scrawl "It" on the bathtub tile. Facing his childhood trauma was not an option for Stan. Death was easier and more acceptable.

Richie "Records" Tozier is L.A.'s most successful disc jockey. The popularity of the many different characters' voices he has created has shot him up to the top of his profession. After talking to Mike, Richie realizes, "Now he had to go back to being himself, and that was hard—it got harder to do that every year. It was easier to be brave when you were someone else" (p. 61). Even as a child, Richie found it easier to be someone else. Known as Trashmouth, he was always wise-cracking and seemed to have no control over what he would say next. Needless to say, this trait constantly got him into trouble, particularly with the three school bullies. It was as if his quick mouth was his compensation for being small and wearing thick glasses.

The third member of the group, Ben Hanscom, is found in Nebraska. Referred to by *Time* magazine as "perhaps the most promising young architect in America" (p. 67), Ben lives his life alone. No matter where he is in the world, however, he returns to a friendly bar in a small town outside of Omaha every Saturday night for a quiet chat with Ricky Lee, the bartender, and for a few beers. Although he is not aware of it, this may be Ben's attempt to put order and roots in his life. After talking to Mike, Ben drives his Cadillac to his Saturday-night stop, fills a stein with Wild Turkey whiskey, and drains it. Ben tells Ricky Lee that he got a phone call from an old friend whom he had forgotten, but what really scared him was realizing that not only had he forgotten Mike, he had forgotten everything about being a kid. "I mean I'd forgotten all about it. . . . Did you ever hear, Ricky Lee, of having an amnesia so complete you didn't even know you had amnesia" (p. 76). When Ben gets ready to leave the bar, he tells Ricky Lee, "I'm scared almost insane by whatever else I may remember before tonight's over, but how scared I am doesn't matter, because it's going to come anyway" (p. 78). Ricky Lee sees in Ben "the face of a man who has died deep in sin and now stands hard by hell's smoking side door" (p. 77).

The fourth childhood friend, Eddie Kaspbrak, is now the owner of a profitable New York limousine service. Suffering from numerous psychosomatic complaints, he has a medicine chest that looks like a well-stocked pharmacy. Eddie, who grew up with an overwhelming, suffocating mother, is now married to the same type of woman. "Eddie did not need a shrink to tell him that he had, in a sense, married his mother" (p. 85). When his nighttime call comes, Eddie knows he has no choice but to "get moving and keep moving or stand in one place long enough to start thinking about what all of this meant and simply die of fright" (p. 80). He knows that he has to return home to Derry—"the place where, once you're in there, they don't ever want to let you out" (p. 83), ". . . the place where when you go there, you have to finally face the thing in the dark" (p. 88). For Eddie, returning to Derry is like being a "man standing at the mouth of an old mine shaft that is full of cave-ins waiting to happen, standing there and saying goodbye to the daylight" (p. 95).

Beverly, the only female in the group, has become a successful Chicago dress designer. She is dominated by a physically and emotionally abusive husband, Tom, who beats her and thinks of her in such endearing terms as "whore, slut and cunt." When her call comes, her husband catches her packing for the journey back to Derry. Irate that she is smoking a cigarette, which he has strictly forbidden, and that she is daring to think of taking a trip without his permission, he takes his leather strap and starts hitting her. While striking her across the breasts with the strap, he tells her, "Got to give you a whuppin. . . . Sorry about that, babe" (p. 110). Almost unconsciously, she fights back for the first time, bloody-ing him with his own weapon. Their bedroom is demolished as the violence esca-lates, and Beverly flees for her life. Tom yells at her as she runs barefoot out of their house, "I'LL KILL YOU, YOU BITCH! YOU FUCKING BITCH!" (p. 116).

Mike's last phone call is to Bill Denbrough, an author of bestselling horror novels, who is on movie location in London, England. As a child, Bill was the unofficial leader of this group of misfits known as the Loser's Club. After he talks to Mike, 20-year-old memories flood back into Bill's consciousness. "Memories were suddenly trying to crowd in. It was as if a black sac in his mind were bulging, threatening to spew noxious (dreams) images up from his subconscious and into the mental field of vision commanded by his rational waking mind—and if that happened all at once, it would drive him mad." (p. 127) Awakening from a form of suspended animation, Bill senses memories "waiting to be born. They're like clouds filled with rain. Only this rain would be very dirty. The plants that grew after a rain like that would be monsters" (p. 134).

For the first time in many years, Bill also remembers the gruesome murder of his 6-year-old brother, Georgie. As Bill prepares to leave for Derry, he begins to stutter as he had as a child, and the childhood scars on his palms made during the blood-promise have reappeared. He tells his wife, Audra, that he has no choice but to go back to Derry. "Unless you're willing to take the pipe or eat the gun or take a long walk off a short dock, you can't say no to some things. You can't refuse to pick up your option because there is no option. You can't stop it from happening any more than you could stand at home plate with a bat in your hand and let a fastball hit you. I have to go. That promise . . . it's in my mind like a fuh-fishhook" (p. 135).

The one who never left Derry, Mike Hanlon, is the only African-American in this group. As the self-designated watchman of the memories, Mike's job is to wait for the evil to return and to summon his childhood friends whose careers he has followed and phone numbers he has faithfully collected. While tracing Derry's history from 1740 to 1985, he discovered that every 25 to 27 years, an evil envelops the town and numerous children disappear or are found half-eaten and mutilated. Yet, this pattern has never received national attention. A "curtain of quiet" cloaks these recurring events.

When the cycle of murders begins again and becomes too numerous and horri-ble to explain rationally, Mike hears the voice of the Turtle telling him to call the others home. (In the Hindu religion, the turtle is the second incarnation of the god Vishnu who succors the pious and destroys evildoers.) Mike realizes that he has no choice but to make these calls when It uses the blood of a small boy It killed to write "COME HOME COME HOME COME HOME" on the concrete retaining wall close to the little boy's half-eaten body.

By some twist of fate, Mike and his six childhood playmates were selected to stop the evil that preys on Derry. As a child, Bill remembers thinking, "We're being drawn into something. Being picked and chosen. None of this is accidental." (p. 347). This chosen circle of seven had made a blood-pact to come home to Derry to fight It again, if they did not defeat It as children. When the murders begin again in 1985, Mike has the responsibility of telling the others that the fight against It is not over. As children, they had not destroyed It.

Each of the adults who left Derry has repressed the horror of the events of the summer of 1958. Despite successful careers and some marriages, no children have been born to remind them of the terror of being children, the terror they barely survived. Their adult lives seem somehow empty and hopeless, and each hides an unknown fear that threatens to engulf him or her. It seems as if they have all been biding time until they are required to return to the scene of their original trauma and to confront It as a group.

What is this trauma or evil that destroys children? For the group returning to Derry, It took many forms. A clown with a white painted face and a leering red vampire smile, carrying balloons that floated into the wind, killed Bill's brother, Georgie. For everyone else, the evil took the form of their most terrifying thoughts—Richie saw a snarling werewolf; Eddie was presented with a decaying leper who wanted to give him a blow job; Ben barely escaped the grasping hands of a mummy; Mike was attacked by a giant, ghastly bird; Stan was almost trapped by dead children; Bill saw Pennywise the clown with Georgie's face; and Beverly heard voices in the bathroom drain and was splattered with blood belched from the sink. No adult saw what each of these children saw. The horror was reserved especially for children. Perhaps for that reason, only those with childlike beliefs in the power of magic and in the power of good can triumph over It.

Journeying back to their childhood home rekindles the memories of the friendships and love among the members of the Loser's Club, as well as memories of the encounters with It and the school bullies. What these seven people initially had in common as children was being terrorized by Henry Bowers, Belch Huggins, and Victor Criss. Their fear of Henry and his gang was the common threat that first bound them together.

The members of the Loser's Club had a vast array of the problems that cause children to be shunned or ignored by their classmates, problems that made them different. Bill, known to his friends as Big Bill, struggled to overcome a severe problem with stuttering. Ben dealt with all the cruelty especially directed at children who are fat. Ben was so large that Richie nicknamed him "Haystack Calhoun." Bev Marsh was the rough girl from the other side of the tracks who didn't dress or talk with the sophistication of girls from the "right" families. Richie Tozier was a wisecracking kid with "Bucky Beaver" teeth and coke bottle glasses. Not only did Eddie Kaspbrak have an over-protective mother who rushed him to the emergency room if he fell and skinned his knee, he had to have his aspirator constantly in hand to fight asthma attacks. Fastidious Stan Uris was Jewish in a town where this made him an oddity and others uncomfortable, and Mike was an outcast because he was Black.

These castoffs were haunted by various manifestations of the clown and by the bullies led by the insanely cruel Henry Bowers. Like a pendulum swinging between dread of the terrors of Henry and It and the innocence of childhood, these seven bonded as a single entity to protect themselves against Henry and his gang. Henry heaped his hatred on each of these children, with each act becoming more violent and cruel. He carved an "H" in the fat of Ben's stomach, and on the fateful day when the seven melded as a group, he was chasing Mike with the intent of putting a firecracker in the front of his pants. Fleeing for his life through the Barrens, Mike stumbled on the six others. As if sensing a confrontation when Mike burst upon them, they were lined up like soldiers with their hands and pockets full of rocks as ammunition. In their standing together against Henry and company, these seven began to sense their full power and love for each other. Speaking for all of them, Bill yelled at Henry, "We're through t-t-taking your shit, B-B-Bower. Get ow-ow-out" (p. 662). When all seven unleashed a torrent of well-aimed stones, the bullies turned tail and ran. All the torment and pent-up anger of being Henry's victims seemed to be released with this cathartic fusillade.

More important, however, was the feeling that the circle was now complete for the fight against It. "Bill looked from Mike to Richie, Richie met his eyes. And Bill seemed almost to hear the click—some final part fitting neatly into a machine of unknown intent. He felt ice chips scatter up his back. *We're all together now*, he thought, and the idea was so strong, so *right*, that for a moment he thought he might have spoken it aloud; he could see it in Richie's eyes, in Ben's, in Eddie's, in Beverly's, in Stan's. *We're all together now*, he thought again. *Oh God help us. Now it really starts. Please God, help us*" (pp. 666-667). Then, as is typical of children, the fight and this thought were forgotten, and they started playing with their firecrackers.

The Loser's Club didn't reckon with Henry's hatred and need for retaliation. Knife drawn, Henry along with his gang chased the group into the sewer system of Derry. Once in the sewers, Big Bill and the others remembered that It came out of the sewers. Winding their way through the stench and raw sewage of this underground world, they finally came face to face with It. This time It, who was female, had taken the form of a huge black spider feeding in an enormous web deep in the bowels of Derry.

The battle began. Bill and the spider lock minds in what King labeled the Ritual of Chud, and It tried to throw Bill out into the macroverse. Flung mentally through space, out of the blue and into the black nothingness of the deadlights, Bill passed the Turtle, who told him there is only Chud and that he must help himself. As he was being hurtled through space, Bill also understood that there was also Another, the Final One who created all. With this childlike understanding, Bill mentally shouted that he believed in Santa Claus, the Tooth Fairy, the good of policemen, that mothers and fathers love their children, that courage is possible. "OH SHIT, I BELIEVE IN ALL OF THOSE THINGS!" (p. 1013). Crying out in pain, the Spider let go of Bill and retreated. The terrified children thought they had mortally wounded It and It had crept off to die. Only Stan and Bill had their doubts that It was dying.

When the children tried to find their way back to the surface, however, they found that Eddie, who had always seemed to have a compass in his head, didn't know the way. Showing her love for them, Beverly reunited them in the sex act, in the essential human link between this world and the infinite. They recaptured their childhood innocence in that act of unselfish love, and Eddie safely directed them to the surface. Once there, Stan cut their palms and they joined in a blood pact, promising to return if they had not killed It.

When the children return to Derry as adults, they have to recapture their childhood belief in magic and reenter the sewers to battle the Spider again. This time the circle is reduced to only five warriors. Stan is dead, and Mike is fighting for his life after Henry, who escaped from the insane asylum, tried to carve him into pieces. In this second journey, Bill again becomes locked in a deadly mental battle with It. Spraying the Spider with his aspirator, Eddie weakens her and she loosens her grip on Bill. Richie mentally charges the Spider and, as he too is whipped into the blackness toward the deadlights, he shouts "Pull us back! Pull us back or I'll kill you! I . . . I'll Voice you to death!" (p. 1021). The Spider screeches in pain and tries to shake them off, to leave them on the Outside. Realizing that It has a death grip on Bill and Richie, Eddie sacrifices himself as he triggers the aspirator into the Spider's eye and down her throat. As Bill and Richie are mentally thrown back into their bodies, screaming in agony, the Spider flees. She lays her eggs as she retreats. Ben, Bill, and Richie charge after her. Discovering the eggs, Ben stamps the potential for life, for perpetuating the horror of It, out of each egg. Augmented by the force of that Other—the force of love and unforgotten childhood magic—Bill and Richie physically combat the Spider. It is only destroyed when Bill reaches deep within It's heart in a fantastic surrealistic journey to the nexus of It's power. Bill rips that heart apart and the horror ends.

Above ground, Derry is also being literally torn apart as the earth belches and swallows whole sections of the town. When Richie, Bev, Ben, and Bill emerge from the sewer pipes, over half of downtown Derry, the feeding pen for It, has been destroyed.

King's portrayal of the journey back to Derry, back to what happened to them as children, is an emotional and potentially psychologically shattering experience for these adult children. Only five are able to make this journey. For them, it is a journey of healing. Rational, logical, fastidiously orderly Stan chose to die rather than confront again the illogic and "dirtiness" of fighting It. Mike, who had remained in Derry, had no need to reconfront It since he had never lost his memories. As for the others, however, the facing and killing of It frees them from these memories and within the week they each are beginning to forget, not only the horror of the past few days, but each other and why they had been together in Derry. Their minds are free, and they each can now really go on with living.

As he weaves this tale, King vividly depicts the three major themes that trauma victims eventually have to experience or confront in order to recover. These three themes are the effects of repression, adults' conspiracy of silence, and the defeat of evil through love and childhood magic.

REPRESSION OF MEMORIES

In the beginning of the book, six of the friends cannot remember the traumatic events that shaped their childhood and clouded their adult development. They have repressed these memories. When Ben Hansom gets his call, he explains to the bartender, "I had a call from an old friend tonight. . . . I'd forgotten all about him. . . . After all, I was just a kid when I knew him, and kids forget things, don't they? Sure they do. You bet your fur. What scared me was getting about halfway over here and realizing that it wasn't just Mike I'd forgotten about—I'd forgotten everything about being a kid . . ." (p. 80).

Most survivors of sexual abuse also either forget what was done to them or repress the information. In their self-help book, *Courage to Heal*, Bass and Davis (1988) state that children begin to forget the trauma of sexual abuse even as it is happening. In fact, just like the adult characters in *IT* who returned to the sewers of Derry to fight the evil, most sexual abuse survivors have to sludge through the mud and garbage of abuse that has been stored in the depths of their unconscious—garbage that has been securely hidden from any awareness.

CONSPIRACY OF SILENCE

A second major theme concerns the conspiracy of silence or what King has called the "cloak of quiet" of adults. The adults in Derry either don't recognize the evil that has swallowed their town or punish the children who break the silence. After Bill's brother, Georgie, dies, Bill's parents never talk about the tragedy and don't even share their grieving with each other. In fact, Bill feels the warmth sucked out of his household, leaving only a "cold place on the couch between his mother and father" (p. 316). His brother's room is left exactly as it had been before the murder, as if Georgie was only out playing and would return any second. The process of living has stopped in this household, and no one talks about it.

When Mike Hanlon discovers that the horror and murders occur every 25 to 27 years, he is stymied by the suppression. While interviewing the 90-year-old former head librarian, Mike is told that the cycle was known by some residents but to let it go and to stop asking questions. "A lot of the old-timers do, although that is one thing they won't talk about, even if you load them up with booze" (p. 156). Those old-timers who are aware of the cycle just want to forget whatever has happened.

Mike also tries to confront the chief of police about the mysterious murders, but he is met by stony silence. The chief talks about runaways and accidents. Frustrated, Mike asks the chief if a 3½-year-old could have run away before he was murdered. "Rademacher fixed me with a sour glance and told me it sure had been nice talking with me, but if there was nothing else, he was busy. I left" (p. 159).

Beverly Marsh as a child lived with her physically abusive father and a mother who worked as a waitress most of the time. In her first encounter with It, Beverly is washing her hands when blood gushes from the wash basin and splatters the towels, the mirror, the wallpaper, the floor. Bev screams hysterically and runs for the living room where her father is watching television. Unable to tell him what has frightened her, she is only able to say "the sink . . . in the sink . . . the . . . the" (p. 378). But her father doesn't see the blood. Her hysteria is just another excuse for a beating, another occasion where his "worrying" about her justifies his hitting her hard enough to leave purple bruises. The bruises are noticed by other adults and her friends, but no one ever says anything out loud. It is a family matter, and it is best to say nothing.

Silence is also the legacy of sexual abuse. Many adults don't want to consider the extent of the problem, or they blame the victims for enticing the abuse. In most families in which sexual abuse occurs, there is a code of silence. Children are told, "This is our secret," or are coerced into silence by threats of physical harm to themselves or other members of their family.

Even today, the False Memory Syndrome Foundation is trying to tell the public that either the victims or their therapists are making up these tales of sexual abuse. This assertion should sound familiar from the information presented on the history of abuse in Chapter 2. Even though Freud was initially convinced that a large majority of his well-off, female Victorian clients had suffered from inappropriate and premature sexual contact, he repudiated his own theory when it became obvious that neither his professional colleagues nor the existing Viennese society would accept the reality of his conclusions. He changed his position to one that contributed to the conspiracy of silence.

LOVE AND MAGIC

The third theme of the novel, love and magic, involves overcoming evil by re-experiencing love and childhood innocence. The reparation of hurt and damaged children only occurs when they experience genuine love and caring and recapture the magical qualities of their childhood innocence.

In *IT*, there are two evils, both deadly. The most haunting evil, known to the children as It or Pennywise the Clown, is also the more lethal. Taking the form of each child's worst fears, It is palpably real and feeds on whatever human life it touches.

The second evil is man's inhumanity as manifested in the actions of many Derry townspeople and in the hatred and cruelty of Henry Bowers and his gang. King likens these bullies to the forest creatures Dorothy must avoid in the *Wizard of Oz*. As Dorothy crept through the dark forest, she chanted, "Lions and Tigers and Bears, oh my! Lions and Tigers and Bears, oh my!" In similar fashion, the children in *IT* think, "Bowers and Huggins and Criss, oh my! Bowers and Huggins and Criss, oh my!" (p. 456). While the danger emanating from these three bullies is ever-present, the children initially can frequently avoid Henry and his friends by constantly being alert.

In addition to these three bullies, the evil in *IT* also works through other humans. For example, King's novel begins with three teenage toughs brutally beating Adrien Mellon, a homosexual, and throwing him off a bridge into the Derry Canal, 23 feet below. Pennywise only gets Mellon because of these teenagers' hatred of someone who is different. Beverly Rogan's violently jealous husband follows her to Derry and under the influence of It meets his death. Years earlier, a group that called itself the White Legion of Decency set fire to a night-club for Blacks, and everyone trapped inside burned to death. The men of Derry once slaughtered a bank robber and his gang when they drove into town. When the gun fight was over, no one admitted to having taken part in the ambush. "In

Derry, They let things happen, they always do, and things quiet down, things go on, It . . . It . . . sleeps . . . or hibernates like a bear . . . and then it starts again, and they know . . . people know . . . they know it has to be so It can be" (p. 931). It and Derry have become one, and in the end, both have to be destroyed. Perhaps King is telling us that people who use others for their own needs or who hurt others are fertile ground for evil and sow the seeds of their own eventual destruction.

Even parents participate in hurting their children. Beverly Marsh's father beats her while at the same time telling her it's for her own good and he is doing it because he loves her. Eddie's mother has the pharmacist put a harmless water solution in his aspirator. This encouragement of Eddie's psychosomatic illness keeps him from becoming independent and leaving her. Ben's mother is only happy when she is stuffing food in him and won't admit that he is obese and rejected by the other children. After Georgie died, Bill's parents seem to have forgotten that he is alive and needs their love.

Evil not only lurks in such dark, forbidding places as sewers, cellars of houses, and mine shafts, it also has a strong foothold in these families. To combat this evil (It), forces of good must be summoned—the innocent love shared by children, their belief in magic, the wisdom of the Turtle, and the power of Final Other.

In order to begin this battle, each adult has to remember his or her childhood. Mike's telephone call is the catalyst. Not only must they remember, they have to re-experience the hurt. When Bill remembers, he starts to stutter. Eddie breaks the same arm that he broke in childhood. Beverly received beatings from her father, and now is brutalized by her husband. As each adult returns to Derry, the same form of It that threatened them as children attacks them as adults. They experience body memories (Richie's pain in his eye, Eddie's throbbing arm, the reappearing of the scars on their palms) and flashbacks.

Sexual abuse survivors also often experience body memories and flashbacks. Body memories are physically re-experiencing the abuse somewhere in the body. Flashbacks are the re-experiencing of the sensations of the abuse in the present time frame.

The importance of love in the recovery process is aptly portrayed by King in the love shared by the children. By standing together in the rock fight against Henry and his gang, the seven children unite, forming a loving, innocent whole. After the first encounter with the Spider, this wholeness is threatened. Beverly realizes that she has the power to bring them back together by making love to each of the six boys. It is an act of love that unifies them again.

Many abused children feel unloved and unlovable, particularly if the abuser was a family member. These victims of incest often think, "If my dad (mom, grandfather, uncle, or other relative) treats me as if I'm no good, worthless, then how could anybody else love me?" Being abused confirms that they are no good, not lovable. The journey back to health often requires accepting the caring and love of others and feeling that this love and caring is deserved.

Another important part of recovery is recapturing one's childhood belief in good and trust in the world. This innocence and reaching out for the magic of life is crucial. When Bill fights the Spider, he thinks, "Chud, this Chud, stand, be brave, be true, stand for your brother, your friends; believe, believe in all the things you have believed in . . ." (p. 1057). This childhood belief in the goodness of life is the force that defeats the darkness.

Big Bill called his bike Silver. Flying heedlessly down the streets yelling, "HI-YO SILVER AWAYYYY!" Bill could become the Lone Ranger, John Wayne, Bo Diddley, "anybody he wanted to be and nobody who cried and got scared and wanted their muh-muh-mother" (p. 221). Silver was Bill's magical escape from the hurt and coldness in his home. When the children decided to kill It, they molded silver slugs for their slingshot. As children, they believed in the power of silver to destroy evil.

When Bill's wife becomes catatonic from the terror of seeing It, Bill breaks the evil spell by riding her recklessly on his bike, Silver, shouting "HI YO SILVER AWAYYYYY!" (p. 221). He uses the bit of childhood magic left from defeating It to restore Audra to her sanity, but to do this, he had to have a child-like belief in the power of magic to heal. This magic was formed from the love the adults had for each other and the love Bill had for Audra. The message is to trust and believe, don't give up hope.

For sexual abuse survivors, there is usually no belief in God or in any good in the world. Trust in themselves or in others is minimal or totally missing. Their world constricts in affect and experience as they turn inward. It is as if they are saying, "Why venture out? You'll only get hurt." To heal from the abuse and to get on with their lives, they have to be taken back to that pristine childhood state where anything is possible if you can only imagine it. They need to relearn how to believe in the good and the joy that life can offer.

RESOLUTION OF TRAUMA—THE CASE OF ANN

In the following section, we will introduce Ann, an adult survivor of incest. Using the metaphor for abuse and recovery presented in *IT*, we will trace Ann's abuse and emergence into health and relate this to the events the children experienced in *IT*. First, however, we want to present a brief history of Ann.

A 38-year-old woman, Ann is divorced and the mother of a teenage daughter. She is a victim of sexual abuse perpetrated initially by her father, but which later included her mother and her mother's boyfriend. Her father first sexually abused her when she was only 4 years old and continued until she was 12. Her mother's sexual abuse continued well into Ann's adulthood.

Prior to starting therapy with one of the authors, Ann had over 10 years of counseling with eight different therapists. These therapists most frequently diagnosed her as being manic-depressive, and she was hospitalized several times. She was told that she had a chemical imbalance, that she never would be well, and that the drug Lithium would be "her best friend for the rest of her life."

Ann has also had several physical health problems, including numerous staph infections, an ectopic pregnancy, and a hysterectomy. She also has a history of cutting herself around the vagina. Her most prevalent health concern was numerous infections in her left breast. Although treated with antibiotics and surgery, these infections were never totally cured.

With this background in mind, let's explore the case of Ann. Since she was involved in therapy with one author, the term "I" will be used to refer to the author/therapist and "we" will be used when discussing Ann and the author/therapist.

The Betrayal of Trust: The Clown

The evil in *IT* is represented by Pennywise the Clown, who enraptures children with floating balloons and with his painted-on smile. He entices children with his promise of caring and fun, with his tricks and games, with his safe image of Ronald McDonald- and Clarabelle-type clowns. Most of all, he entices them with promises of an adult who is in tune with a child's need for the circus, for the smell of roasting peanuts wafting in the air, for animals doing tricks, and for everything that makes children happy and secure. This clown, Pennywise, pulls the cruelest of hoaxes. Through his promises, he beckons children to their death.

For Ann, the Clown is represented by her parents. When we first started therapy, Ann thought of her mother as a loving person who would sacrifice anything for her; however, she had few childhood memories. She looked forward to her mother's visits but admitted that she was not close to her father, who she considered to be a cruel and selfish man. Ann could not explain why she wanted to move far away from where her mother lived, and she experienced a fear reaction when asked whether she wanted to live near her. She claimed to be close to her mother but then literally reacted with fear at any mention that she might relocate closer to her home. There was a push-pull quality to her relationship with her family.

For many sexual abuse victims like Ann, their relationship with their perpetrator seems paradoxical. Why do abused girls and women stay so emotionally dependent on their abusers? Why do they seek out other relationships similar to the one they had with the abuser?

The answer to these questions probably lies in the status that parents and other family members give children and in the special nature of abuse when children are so young. For example, infants will attach to a figure during the first 9 months of life. The cries of the infant are signals for nurturance, safety, and social stimulation, and the infant bonds with the figure who meets these needs. This attachment process is called imprinting. Bessel A. van der Kolk (1987) believes that an infant seeks increased attachment in the face of any external danger, even threats emanating from the attachment object itself. When the attachment object withdraws safety and nurturance and becomes abusive, paradoxically, the attachment is in many ways strengthened.

Many children who have been sexually abused incorporate an inner sense of badness. Participation in forbidden sexual activity and any pleasure derived from it convinces the child of his or her badness. Also, the adults many times scapegoat the child in order to relieve their own guilt. Accusing the child of instigating the sexual contact or even calling her a whore or a slut is common. Like Pennywise, adults who sexually abuse children are betraying the trust of these children by violating their innocence and belief in the goodness and caring of adults.

Symptoms of Childhood Abuse

All of the seven adults in Stephen King's novel lead relatively empty adult lives. The overt symptoms of this emptiness range from Bev's abusive husband to Eddie's extensive psychosomatic symptoms. The covert manifestations are embedded in the hopelessness and fear that lurks underneath the surface in spite of their outward riches and successes.

Ann, too, experienced futility in her life. When she began therapy she wrote: "This is real typical—so much energy I put out and nothing accomplished—kind of like the wind-up doll that's been overwound and keeps bumping its head against the wall! I know that this obsessive-compulsive stuff is a major problem for me—I have identified it, but I can't stop it."

In addition to this sense of hopelessness, she entered an abusive marriage. Her alcoholic husband periodically degraded her, both in private and in front of her daughter, and dominated her life. In spite of leaving him, her present life was still meaningless. "I have contemplated ending my life over many hours—how can I do it with as little hurt as possible to those I love so much. Also, I am nothing—a major disappointment to those who have dared to love me."

Feelings of meaninglessness and hopelessness are often experienced by sexual abuse victims. The erosion of their basic personality patterns because of early trauma leads to a bewildering array of symptoms. Sexual abuse victims have been described as dependent, self-defeating, hysterical, hypochondriac, and alienated. Depending on the particular symptom array at the time of diagnosis, victims are labeled borderline, narcissistic, depressive, obsessive-compulsive, manic-depressive, schizoid, panic disorder, chemical dependency, sexual disorder, and others.

Even with all these reactions to abuse, most victims lack one of the fundamental indicators of mental health—intimate relationships with others and themselves. They believe that others have to be defended against because they will engulf you or abandon you, and the real self must be defended against because victims feel that at the deepest levels they are bad.

Awakening the Memories: The Call

In *IT*, Mike Hanlon is the keeper of the memories for the childhood friends. Having researched and cataloged the evil, he calls the others home. When the call comes, it triggers bits and pieces of haunting, unwanted memories for each adult. These memories are like dead bodies being spit to the surface of awareness.

Ann also got a call from her unconscious. As the memories emerged, Ann began to experience reactions similar to those of the characters in *IT*. In another letter, Ann tells how she started to remember her father's sexual abuse. "I am staring at my mom's perfume bottle on the dresser and thinking how I feel. I could squeeze that heavy glass bottle until it shatters. I'm not breathing—just barely—I just want him to go to sleep! THERE IS SCREAMING GOING ON IN MY HEAD. I have to be quiet. Oh God this is not a dream. This really happened, didn't it." As a child, Ann had stared at her mother's perfume bottle on the dresser in order to dissociate from what was happening to her.

Memories can return in a variety of ways. Some are seen in intense visual images. Others are body memories, such as physical sensations in the mouth, vaginal area, or along the thighs. Sometimes the memories come back as voices in pain. Whatever the form of the memory, many are triggered by associated experiences. For example, the Old Spice that a therapist was wearing in a counseling session triggered one client to relive her uncle brutally raping her. The smell of his Old Spice cologne was overwhelming to her when he pressed his face against hers during the rape. The scent of the cologne stimulated a total recall of what he had done to her.

Revisiting the Abuse

When the childhood friends come home to Derry, they are confronted by the silence of the town, which is still ignoring the underlying evil feeding off it. They are also attacked by people from their past (Henry) and by people from their present (Bev's husband). No one sees what they see or helps them.

Ann, too, was attacked when she began to revisit her abuse. As she started to remember what happened, her husband escalated his drinking as well as his emotional and physical abuse of her. Ann wrote, "I want my husband. I want to lean on him, but he is pushing me farther and farther away." Eventually she divorced him as she realized that she had recreated the relationship with her father in the present.

Ann also had to confront her relationships with her mother and father as her memories began to flood in. Ann wrote about telling a friend about her father sexually abusing her. "I never looked her in the face as I told her that I had done something that was so horrible that I had been forced to forget it when I was a kid. As I finished my wine, I hardened my heart. I told her that I went to bed with my dad, not once, but many times. I'm not trying to defend myself, but I was so confused. My dad told me I needed to help him hold our family together. He needed me! I felt that I had to protect my mom. She wasn't able to love him (as he put it) and he would get so angry with her. I didn't give her all the details. I just told her that I only wanted my dad to love me. This was the only way. And it was sickening, gross and I hated it, but my daddy needed me. At those times I felt like he loved me. I had not looked at her since I'd started talking. At that point I looked up at her and saw tears running down her face. I just saw red. I yelled at her, Dammit . . . Don't be sad for me. I am trash. I hate that little girl." Like so many sexual abuse victims, Ann turned her anger against herself instead of the person who betrayed her.

Soon after revealing to her friend that her father had abused her, Ann brought her mother to a counseling session. After calmly listening to Ann tell about the sexual abuse, Ann's mother demanded to know if anyone else in the family knew. Only when Ann shook her head, no, did her mother comfort her. Immediately after the session, Ann's mother strongly encouraged her to get medication, to stop counseling, and to stop seeing a best friend who was supportive of Ann getting therapy. This mom, whom Ann had attempted to protect all her life, busily set up roadblocks to any new information emerging, information involving the mother's encouragement of the sexual abuse and her participation in it.

Later, Ann wrote, "My mom always loved me. That's what I believed until Monday. When I left your office I think I was kind of in shock. I sort of felt as if someone had just told me that she died. I guess, in a way the relationship I had had with her for all these years did die on Monday. I guess I really had love and need confused. She definitely needed me and I think that I was so desperate for her to love me that I interpreted that need to be love. I took care of her. I protected her. I hurt for her. I tried to be someone she could be proud of. I comforted her. I nursed her. I took up for her, always thinking that some day I'm gonna do good enough and this void, this empty hole in my heart is going to be filled. Yep, some day I'm gonna do something right and I'm gonna be loved. If you sacrifice enough, you might be loved. That meeting with my mom today crushed that." Ann's mother was not there for Ann. As Big Bill experienced with his parents, for Ann there was only emptiness and cold where warmth and caring should have been.

The journey of discovering and confronting childhood sexual abuse is heart-breaking, painful, and lonely. When sexual abuse occurs, the abuser will usually deny it. No one in our society wants the stigma and possible legal consequences attached to this revelation. Also, many times abusers have rationalized their behaviors so as not to be sensitive to the hurt they are causing. Such rationalizations might include statements such as: she (the child) liked it, I was only teaching her about sex, she was provocative, or I was drunk and didn't know what I was doing.

Elliana Gil (1983) cautions incest victims against trusting that their families will respond positively to their confronting the abuse. "Some abusive parents will deny the event completely, and turn on you once again, implying that you are sick, crazy, or disturbed to make such an accusation. Your fantasy of getting a long-deserved apology or some effort at compensation or comfort may be quickly dispelled" (Gil, 1990, p. 77). Even friends and spouses might tell victims that it happened in the past and they need to forget it and just get over it. A religious argument might be used to support this advice. Such an argument might be that God wants them to forgive the abuser and stop feeling sorry for themselves. Statements and advice like this are often very hurtful to the childhood sexual abuse survivor since they negate the importance and devastation of what happened.

The Road to Health

In order to fight the evil, the members of Loser's Club not only re-experience past behaviors, they also have to rediscover their childhood trust and innocence. Bill starts stuttering again. Eddie breaks his arm. Bev again makes love to Bill. Each must physically and emotionally return to their child being. Upon returning to Derry, Bill muses, "How much of us never left the drains and the sewers where It lived . . . and where It fed? Is that why we forgot? Because part of each of us never had any future, never grew, never left Derry? Is that why?" (p. 488). With the recapturing of the hurtful as well as happy experiences of their childhood, something magical happens. The adults now have the capacity to fight the evil using childhood tools—desire and belief.

With the occurrence of her breast infection, Ann's childhood is recreated. As a child she had a staph infection that her mother told her came from all the dirty things she did. That staph infection seemed to be resistant to the antibiotics, as was her breast infection as an adult.

As Ann struggled with her memories, she regressed to other childlike behaviors. At various times, she forgot how to take care of her bills, do housework, and make meals. Often feeling younger than her teenage daughter, she clutched teddy bears and other stuffed animals for security. She also repeatedly called me for reassurance when she was feeling insecure or alone.

The magic of childhood does eventually return. She became involved with a church youth group and learned for the first time how to let go in childlike play. She enjoyed water balloon fights, went boating and swimming on the Colorado River, and became involved in zany skits. She had fun.

Ann rediscovered her inner child, Annie, but didn't know how to relate to her. "Because I never really ever experienced any nurturing, I have no idea how to nurture Annie. Nurturing, boundaries, specialness, all of these are alien to me. That is why I am feeling so unstable. I really don't know what to do with this child inside me." One goal of therapy was to help Ann integrate the childhood ego state, Annie, into her adult personality.

Therapists who work with sexual abuse victims are well aware of their different ego states. Abused children often become arrested in the ego development stage at which the abuse occurred. The earlier the abuse, the more damage is done to the child's ego development. Developmental theorists have postulated that the psychological disorders labeled borderline personality, narcissistic personality, and schizoid personality have their roots in neglect or trauma occurring before the person is 3 years old.

Herman (1992) compares the road to recovery for sexual abuse victims to immigrating to a new country. "They must build a new life within a radically different culture from the one they have left behind" (p. 197). They have to recreate their lives. In a therapeutic relationship with a skilled mental health professional, these victims begin the process of recovery by recapturing hope. Hope is a future with goals and intimate relationships.

Emerging into the Light: The Phoenix

The final battle in Derry takes place in the lair of the Spider. As Richie and Bill kill the Spider, Bill realizes that it is their remembered childhood and love for each other that allows them to strike the actual blows. As It dies, the walls of the canal crumble and downtown Derry collapses into the sewer. Without It, Derry no longer has a reason to exist.

Having confronted their greatest fear, Richie, Bev, Bill, and Ben begin to change, to heal. The scars on their hands disappear, and Bill's stuttering diminishes. Even their memories start to fade, but this time it is a process that sets them free to live more meaningful lives. As the tale ends, Bill thinks, "Not all boats which sail away into darkness never find the sun again, or the hand of another child: if life teaches anything at all, it teaches that there are so many happy endings that the man who believes there is no God needs his rationality called into serious question" (p. 1135).

Like the children who confronted It, Ann must confront her personal evil—the awful truth that she did not have loving, protective parents. Through the long, arduous process of therapy, Ann decided that she "has no parents." As she withdrew from her mother, gifts started to flood Ann's mailbox. Profuse statements of love appeared in letters from her mother, and this love was emphasized in telephone conversations. Her mother pleaded with Ann to move back to her hometown, but, like the children in *IT*, Ann stood true and was brave. She didn't keep the gifts, and the counseling office became a museum filled with coffee mugs, plaques with witty sayings, clothes, and other assorted bribes from Ann's mother. In a final act of independence, Ann told her mother that she wouldn't take care of her mother's needs any longer. She began to claim her freedom.

Behavioral changes started to happen. Ann left a relationship with a man who was abusive. She became more protective of her daughter, who had two different boyfriends, both of whom had abusive tendencies. Her daughter got an almost straight "A" report card. Ann met new, caring friends. Now, she no longer takes lithium, and her breast infection has healed. Other changes are still occurring in Ann's life, some slowly and some quickly. As she is recreating her life, she struggles with recapturing the trust of childhood. Still, regardless of the difficulties in her recovery, Ann is firmly committed to creating a healthy life for herself.

In order to have this healthy life, Ann must learn to let go of the role of victim. While appropriate self-boundaries need to be established, she must allow herself to feel all of the emotions that were formerly denied. Opportunities to achieve, to use her special talents, must be grasped. In spite of the risk of being hurt, intimate relationships must be experienced. And finally, as one former client stated, "the abuse becomes boring now . . . I have many more things that consume my energy." When getting on with life is more inviting than continuing to identify as a victim, childhood sexual abuse survivors can integrate the abuse into their lives and move beyond the terror of their personal It. It will no longer have dominion over them.

Chapter 5

The Family: Fertile Ground for Childhood Sexual Abuse

As more clients are becoming aware of being sexually abused as children, therapists are beginning to understand that the family system provides a fertile ground for sexual abuse to occur and that the family maintains the secrecy of the abuse. In addition, it is increasingly being recognized that the child's developmental stage at the time of the abuse impacts her reactions and recovery process. Therefore, an understanding of theories of ego identity and of the psychosexual, cognitive, and moral development of children can provide a useful framework for appropriately conceptualizing and intervening with adult women who were sexually abused as children.

THE FAMILY

Contrary to popular opinion, for the most part, children are not being hurt by random others or by strangers who hang around school yards. Most frequently, the assault originates with those closest to them—their fathers, mothers, grandparents, older siblings, aunts and uncles, baby-sitters, neighbors, family friends, and other extended family members. Occasionally, strangers do sexually assault children, but usually it is a member of the child's family who betrays the child's trust.

Recently, Calof and Leloo (1993) eloquently spoke about the extent to which society has deluded itself regarding family involvement.

> A few years ago, I believe in the Year of the Child, an abundance of materials regarding child abuse was produced and distributed by various service and civic organizations. Not a bad idea. Unfortunately, the primary theme of these materials was, If you are being abused, tell your parents. Well, the problem with this, of course, is that, statistically speaking, it is your parents who are abusing you. Sure,

51

there are strangers in trenchcoats at the school yard fence, but the incidence of child abuse outside the family pales in comparison to the child abuse and torture that is meted out in families. Imagine the child who was being abused by his parents reading such material. Surely, his conclusion would have been he wasn't being abused, or he was somehow different and deserved it, or some other equally damaging conclusion. Thankfully, the message has metamorphosed to Tell SOMEONE, but the denial still persists. We don't want to think we as a culture are engaging in self deception when we pride ourselves as pro-family (Calof & Leloo, pp. 37-38).

If so much physical and sexual abuse exists within certain families, it would be helpful to explore the attributes of these families, the common behavior patterns within these families, and the characteristics of adults who perpetrate sexual abuse. In addition, mental health professionals need to understand the different profiles of male and female perpetrators in order to work effectively with the adult children who were abused.

Family Attributes

In most cases, families that engage in childhood sexual abuse appear to be no different from most other families. In fact, Swanson and Biaggio (1985) point out that "the external appearance of the family may be unremarkable and even normal, but upon closer examination, the pathological internal mechanisms of the family become apparent" (p. 669). The description of families in which sexual abuse occurs, therefore, must take into account major, hidden dysfunctions, such as alcohol and drug addictions, intergenerational sexual abuse, and the influence of physical or social isolation. Any or all of these family characteristics can allow child abuse to happen. Alexander (1991) noted that there is a circular and reciprocal relationship about sexual abuse that occurs within a family context. Once it occurs, it can become self-perpetuating.

Alcohol and drugs seem to significantly impact the occurrence of sexual abuse. There is evidence to suggest that with incestuous fathers, almost 50% have an addiction problem (Meiselman, 1978). When an individual is under the influence of alcohol and drugs, there is lowered inhibition against engaging in typically prohibited behaviors, and boundaries between right and wrong become blurred. One such prohibited behavior is incest. Many clients in therapy relate stories of their sexual abuse in which the perpetrator was either drinking or taking drugs. For example, one survivor reported that when she was 8 years old her father used to take her to his favorite bar and have her wait in the car. Periodically, he and his friends would come out and drink with her. During these visits, she remembered being sexually pawed and molested by both her father and his friends. Another survivor recounted that as a 4-year-old child she would mix drinks for her parents' parties with the guests exclaiming about how "cute" her bartending was. After the guests had gone home, her father would slip into her room and sexually abuse her. Involving children in situations where drugs and alcohol are being used makes children especially vulnerable to being sexually abused.

Besides addictions, individuals who have grown up in families in which members have been sexually abused seem to be especially susceptible to continuing the legacy of sexual abuse. Kaufman and Ziegler (1987) reported that the intergenerational transmission of sexual abuse is approximately 30%. In a study of 118 incestuous fathers, Finkelhor and Williams (1992) found that 70% of these fathers said that they had themselves been victims of childhood sexual abuse. These shockingly high figures have also been substantiated for males who are preoccupied with sex. Carnes (1991) reported that 81% of the male sex addicts he studied were victims of childhood sexual abuse. It should be remembered that while these statistics also indicate that not everyone who has been sexually abused as a child becomes a perpetrator, a highly sexualized family atmosphere surrounding a child is much more likely to precipitate perpetration.

This is aptly demonstrated by a story related by a female client who was happily married but wanted to work on ridding herself of compulsive sexual fantasies. In these fantasies, she saw herself having sex with young adolescent girls. During the course of her therapy she found out that her aunt had molested her from the ages of 10 to 13. The molestations transpired while she was spending her summer vacations in another state with her aunt. Later, the client haltingly admitted that she had repeated the same sexual acts on her two younger sisters when she returned home at the end of the summer.

A third factor that is characteristic of families in which sexual abuse takes place is isolation, both geographic and social (Wurtele & Miller, 1992). For some families, frequent moves serve to hide family secrets such as physical or sexual abuse. For other families, frequent moves because of economic conditions or because of occupations such as the military or sales positions contribute to family destabilization. Due to limited longevity in any one location, these families never become socially integrated into their communities, and this isolation may permit the adults to fulfill their sexual and emotional needs through their children. Social and physical isolation not only preserves the hidden nature of sexual abuse, it typically inhibits the child from experiencing, through close friendships, any healthy family interactions. Consequently, childhood sexual abuse victims believe that sexual contact with adults is their fault. Somehow they caused it, and they are dirty, unworthy, and unlovable. When a child lives in a family that has isolated itself, there is no one available to counter these cognitive distortions.

The impact of frequently moving was depicted by one survivor who related that her family moved about every 2 years. There was never any notice about the moves; her father would just announce that they needed to get their things together for the movers by that weekend. She learned that she could never count on security or safety in her outer life or in her inner family life since her father was molesting her. Making friends seemed out of the question and any continuity in her schoolwork was unraveled by her family's frequent relocations.

Family Behavior Patterns

Families in which sexual abuse occurs are dysfunctional in many ways. In such families, there typically is poor communication, poor conflict resolution, and triangulation, with the child given adult roles that satisfy parental needs (Alexander & Friedrich, 1991; Kirschner, Kirschner, & Rappaport, 1993). When combined, these three dysfunctional patterns contribute to the breakdown of any possible healthy family functioning.

Poor communication covers a variety of verbal and nonverbal behaviors. If a married couple does not confide in one another, they each feel isolated and lonely. Unlike couples in healthy relationships, couples with poor communication do not share their dreams, hopes for the future, fears and doubts, or any other truly personal aspects of their lives. These couples are unable to really connect or touch each other in a deeply personal manner and, as a result, they feel cut off from most forms of adult nurturance (Lang, Langevin, Van Santen, Billingsley, & Wright, 1990). In addition, since these couples fail to respond to nonverbal cues, individual feelings are not recognized, much less discussed. Poor verbal and nonverbal communication negatively affects the psychological and spiritual closeness of a couple. As these deteriorate, the sexual relationship, which is also a form of interpersonal communication, will deteriorate.

When problems or conflicts do surface, couples with poor patterns of communication do not know how to argue fairly or how to discuss their differences. Therefore, conflict resolution does not occur or is marked by distrustfulness by both partners (Lang et al. 1990). In couples where problems are not resolved, there seems to be a stockpiling of grievances and "mountains are made out of molehills." Instead of working through their differences, these couples often behave toward each other in passive-aggressive or outright aggressive ways. Since these couples do not communicate with each other in an honest, open fashion, they are unable to resolve their differences in a way that is beneficial to the relationship.

Typically, a notable power imbalance exists in the couple's relationship, with one partner coercing the other to defer to his or her view (Wurtele & Miller, 1992). The spouse in the one-down position is afraid to speak up or confront the spouse in the power position. In this kind of family atmosphere, the child is taught that he or she is helpless and that needs are only fulfilled for the strongest. Also, in this type of family, the dominant spouse may add physical domination to his or her mental and emotional domination. When conflicts arise, children soon learn to keep quiet or risk being hit or beaten. One sexual abuse survivor related knowing that if she disagreed with her parents she would be slapped so "why bother?!" When there is poor communication and conflict resolution, there is distrust and little closeness between the marital couple. At this point, the boundaries between the adults and children get blurred, and children become inappropriately involved in the lives of the parents.

Perhaps the most harmful consequence of growing up in families where sexual abuse happens is the triangulation of the child into parental roles. Triangulation is the inappropriate use of a child to carry out tasks normally performed by the adult spouses or to act as a go-between for the parents. As noted earlier, these couples lack satisfying emotional relationships both within and outside the marital relationship. Although most report that this problem started well before marriage (Lang et al., 1990), the marital relationship and the children in the family are detrimentally affected by the couple's poor emotional interaction. When these couples do have emotional outbursts, they may share their feelings with the children instead of their spouse, they may utilize the children as confidants, or they may have the children act as messengers for material that they do not want to tell the spouse directly themselves. One survivor reported being utilized as a spy to watch her father after he got off work and to trail him on her bike to a neighbor's house. At the house she was expected to peek in the window to check on him. By forming this alliance with her daughter, the mother forced the daughter into an adult role in a triangulated relationship—the daughter, the mother, and the father. The child became an integral member of the adult's marital relationship by having to take on the inappropriate behavior of spying on her own father.

Parentification takes place when a child is expected to take over the roles of the adults. This can occur because the parents abdicate their responsibilities, are absent, or are intoxicated. Some examples include taking primary responsibility for raising younger siblings, taking care of all the household tasks, and taking care of the emotional and sexual needs of the parents. As would be expected, the child who must assume these adult responsibilities rarely gets her needs met and learns to deny or repress her own needs.

Characteristics of Sexual Abuse Perpetrators

In families where there is poor or little honest communication, where the adults do not know how to resolve differences, and where the children are triangulated into adult roles, the probability of abuse occurring is greatly enhanced, especially when one or more of the adults in the home have characteristics typical of sexual abuse perpetrators.

Sexual abuse most frequently occurs in the immediate or extended family, which includes close family friends. According to Russell (1986), 89% of sexually abused children are abused by relatives or family acquaintances. Who are these friends and relatives who become perpetrators? What characteristics are common among them?

The best information available has been derived from descriptive studies of incestuous fathers and female sex offenders. Characteristics of both of these groups will be discussed. Perhaps the reader can then extrapolate their behavioral and personality patterns to other sexual offenders.

A study of incestuous fathers delineated five distinct types of fathers who sexually abuse their children (Finkelhor & Williams, 1992). Regardless of which category these men fell into, however, almost two-thirds of them confessed that they had been sexually attracted to their daughters for years before the actual abuse commenced.

The first type, the Sexually Preoccupied, comprised 26% of the group of fathers. They indicated a clear, conscious sexual interest in their daughters, usually from birth. Their relationship with their daughters was always contaminated by their sexual attraction to them.

A second type, labeled Adolescent Regressives, seemed to be arrested in the developmental stage of early adolescence. When their daughters reached puberty, their own early adolescence sexuality became activated and they satisfied their adolescent sexual drives through their daughters. Comprising about one third of incestuous fathers, these men had become fixated at the adolescent stage of sexual development and had failed to reach mature adult sexuality.

About 20% of the sample were clustered into a category labeled Instrumental Self-Gratifiers. These men had tremendous self-recriminations for their incest. During the incest, they reported that they attempted to fantasize about their wives or pretended their daughters were adults. Somehow, while it did not remove the guilt they felt, they were able to rationalize their behaviors.

Ten percent of the sample fit into the fourth type, the Emotionally Dependent. These fathers are characterized as lonely, dependent men who sought an exclusive, marital prototype relationship with their daughters. Instead of working on the marital relationship, they directed their marital affections and needs to their daughters.

The last type, Angry Retaliators, also consisted of 10% of the fathers. These embittered men acted out their frustrations with their lives directly on their close relationships. These men justified physically or sexually abusing their daughters by blaming their wives for neglecting them, their daughters for looking too much like their wives, or whatever reason they could think of for their behaviors. Like most fathers across all of the groups, these men blamed others for their acts.

In contrast, women who sexually abused children took more responsibility for their acts than did the group of incestuous fathers. Studying 110 female sex offenders, psychologist Ruth Mathews (cited by Vanderbilt, 1992) was able to identify four classifications of female sex offenders.

The first she labeled the Teacher-Lover category, in which an older woman initiates a younger boy or adolescent into sex. This relationship is often socially sanctioned, and a number of movies have glamorized it. In stories of the old West, a boy was not a man until he had visited a brothel and been sexually initiated by a prostitute. For example, in *Lonesome Dove*, a well-known made-for-television western, the boy Knute enters the brothel a boy and exits a man. Other movies depicting this type of relationship include *Summer of '42* and *The Graduate*. The reality, however, is that this kind of abusive relationship can be just as damaging as others that are sexually abusive.

The second cluster of female sexual perpetrators was called the Experimenter-Exploiter. Typically women who fit this category were girls who came from overly rigid and moralistic families and who explored their sexuality while babysitting younger children. Having little knowledge about sex, as teenagers these women seemed to be drawn by the mystery and forbiddenness of the topic. The Predisposed, the third group, were themselves physically abused as children and now sexually molest their younger siblings and their own children. They are caught in the cyclical perpetuation of sexual abuse.

The fourth classification was comprised of the women who were coerced by males. Most of these women were themselves abused as children and remain vulnerable to male threats or inducements to join into sexually abusing children.

Both groups of male and female abusers contribute to the perpetuation of sexual abuse that has rippled through some families for generations. Even though their motivations seem to be diverse, their brutal, unloving acts leave emotionally and psychologically crippled children in their wake.

Summary of Family Involvement

Sadly, the majority of sexual abuse can be described as a family affair. It frequently exists in the midst of alcohol and drug addiction, intergenerational sexual abuse, and the isolation of family members. In these families poor communication, poor conflict resolution, and the triangulation of children seem to be the rule rather than the exception. Even though most sex offenders can be categorized into relatively distinct groups, their motivations seem to be diverse. Regardless of motivation or type of offender, the consequences of their sexual abuse of children are overwhelmingly harmful and pervasive.

The depth of hurt and damage is often influenced by the child's age and level of development. Therefore, we want to present a brief overview of theories of child development to help the reader better understand the vulnerabilities of children.

AN OVERVIEW OF CHILD DEVELOPMENT

As children grow from infants to young adults, they pass through many stages of development. This development can be conceptualized from many perspectives. Those chosen to be briefly reviewed are considered to be those most relevant to understanding the impact on the child of being sexually abused. Specifically, Erikson's theory of life span and ego identity development, Freud's theory of psychosexual development, Piaget's theory of cognitive development, and Kohlberg's conceptualization of moral development will be reviewed.

Ego Identity Development: Erikson

An ego psychologist, Eric Erikson (1963, 1968) conceptualized identity or human development as occurring over the entire life span. His theory delineates eight stages of development divided according to life tasks that must be mastered. In each of the eight stages, life tasks focus on psychosocial factors that have significance in a person's ego development. These eight stages are: (a) trust versus mistrust, (b) autonomy versus shame, (c) initiative versus guilt, (d) industry versus inferiority, (e) identity versus role diffusion, (f) intimacy versus isolation, (g) generativity versus stagnation, and, (h) integrity versus isolation.

The first stage, general trust or basic mistrust, lasts roughly the first year or so of a person's life. When in this stage, children are more helpless than at any other time in their lives and need the love, protection, and nurturance of others to survive. If these needs are met, children learn to trust those around them. If these needs go unmet, the child will learn to mistrust his or her world and will feel insecure in the world.

The second stage, autonomy versus shame and doubt, begins when the toddler is about 2 years old and lasts until he or she is approximately 4 years old. During this stage, the child learns to master bodily functions and starts doing simple self-care tasks. For Erikson, the crucial developmental task of this stage is developing the psychosocial ability to make a choice for oneself. The child who is supported by his or her parents begins to learn the basic experience of the autonomy of free choice. If the child's social environment encourages him or her to begin to make decisions while protecting him or her from unnecessary shame and failure, the child is reinforced for initial attempts at self-determination. The seeds of autonomy are sown. When a child is punished for trying to be autonomous, self-doubt and shame result. Children do not think that the punisher is wrong, but believe that they must be inadequate or inept because they were punished. As adults, these children try to hide themselves from the scrutiny of others lest they be judged as inadequate. Those children who do not successfully begin to achieve autonomy suffer from self-doubt and its resulting shame.

During stage three, lasting from approximately age 3 through age 5, the child moves into a period when he or she struggles with learning initiative and responsibility in social interactions, particularly those with parents. An unsuccessful outcome of these interactions results in guilt. According to Erikson, the child is "on the make" during this time. Boys and girls enjoy aggressive behavior that is directed toward capturing and owning the opposite-sex parent, which, of course, must end in failure. Not succeeding causes the child to again identify with the same-sex parent. By identifying with this parent, the child is preparing for eventually becoming a parent. As this occurs, the basis for adult initiative and responsibility are learned. If the failure is exaggerated by unnecessarily severe punishment, the child will experience guilt, which leads to feelings of unworthiness as an adult. Women who were sexually abused during this stage may develop troubled sexual patterns such as promiscuity, dressing and acting seductively, hiding their sexuality, having a sexual dysfunction, or even trying to be nonsexual. In addition, these women may have difficulties successfully parenting their own children.

For Erikson, the next stage of development occurs when children are between 6 and 12 years old and are in elementary and middle school. During this time, the child is learning traits that lead to industry or inferiority. As the child begins to establish contacts outside the home, peers and adults such as teachers have an important role. Successful relationships with these others allow the child to become productive and to win recognition through what he or she has created. The danger of not succeeding is that the child will learn that his or her "tools and skills" needed for interacting with the external world are not adequate, resulting in feelings of inferiority.

The last stage relevant for children is the identity versus role diffusion stage. Covering the junior high and high school years, ages 12 through 18, this period is characterized by children becoming more autonomous and beginning the transition from being children to young adults. This may be a time when parents are confused and even threatened by the changes happening in their children as they start to "grow up." Peers play a dominant role during this time period as children struggle to find out who they are as individuals separate from their parents and family. This is a very difficult time and is fraught with anxiety. Sometimes children overly identify with heroes of the day or with their crowd in order to feel safe and as if they are "fitting in." Not succeeding in establishing an individual identity results in role diffusion for the young adult.

When a child is consistently sexually abused, she may become arrested at the stage of psychosocial development she was in when the abuse occurred. For example, a female client whose abuse was documented by her older sister as occurring when the client was between the ages of a few months and 4 years lived a very isolated life. She had no significant relationships, worked over 70 hours each week, did not use makeup or even bother to comb her hair and brush her teeth, and did not buy furniture for her home. If one were to conceptualize how her psychosocial stage of development was arrested by her being sexually abused, it is evident that she had not learned to trust others and avoided intimate human interactions (stage one, trust vs. mistrust), that she had not developed appropriate self-care skills (stage two, autonomy vs. shame), and that her personal presentation manifested her feelings of unworthiness and guilt (stage three, initiation vs. guilt).

Psychosexual Development: Freud

Freud (1920) postulated five stages of psychosexual development, and individuals can become stuck or "fixated" at any one stage regardless of the ages associated with that stage. The first stage, the oral stage, lasts from birth through the first year of life. For the infant, all gratification is experienced through the mouth. Everything from food to toys to hands and feet is put in the mouth. Feeding becomes a major area of conflict as the infant is involved in receiving (oral accepting) and taking (oral aggression). Since infants are so helpless, they must depend on others to provide food and drink and to meet oral needs. If an infant experiences difficulty in this area, personality traits evident as an adult might include impatience, pessimism, envy, and aggressiveness. Psychologists might refer to an adult who exhibits an excessiveness of these traits as orally fixated.

The second stage, the anal stage, occurs during the second to third year of life. The primary activities are giving and withholding. The child learns retention and expulsion control over his or her bowels during toilet training. If the child over-controls, adult personality traits associated with "anal retentive" behavior include stinginess, obstinacy, and compulsive orderliness. At the opposite extreme are traits associated with anal expulsive behavior—cruelty, destruction, acquiescence, dirtiness, and messiness.

The phallic stage (ages 3 through 5) has the genitals as the focus of attention and heterosexual relationships as the core activities. During this time, the child vies with the same-sex parent for the attention of the opposite-sex parent (known as the Oedipal complex). Children are curious about their own and others' bodies. Personality traits developed during this time include ability to relate to others, assertiveness, self-respect, gregariousness, and chastity. Unsuccessful passage of this stage may result in self-hate, timidity, isolation, promiscuity, and avoidance of heterosexuality.

From ages 6 to 12, the child enters a period of latency in which the sexual instinct is dormant and the child's attention is focused on learning other life skills. The child gets pleasure from learning, builds interpersonal skills, and is active in peer group relationships. During this time, social learning and conscience development occur.

The last psychosexual stage of development is the genital period beginning during puberty and lasting until death. The adolescent becomes involved in heterosexual contacts and begins to become a productive member of society. The person reaching this stage of psychosexual development is fully able to love and to work.

If we again look at the female client described above who had such poor self-care skills, it is easy to see how her psychosexual development was fixated between birth and the age of 4. She was considerably overweight and used food as a way to nurture herself (oral stage). For her profession, she had chosen to be a bank auditor. This job required minute attention to detail and allowed her an acceptable outlet for her compulsive orderliness and need for detail (anal stage). Finally, she avoided all sexual contact and was basically asexual (phallic stage). She was partially arrested in the first three stages of psychosexual development, and a skilled therapist would need to reparent her through each of these stages.

Cognitive Development: Piaget

Jean Piaget is probably one of the most influential writers on children's thinking and reasoning processes. Based on years of observing children's behaviors, he believed that by interacting with people and objects, children developed their knowledge of the world and their role in it (Wadworth, 1971). He hypothesized that there are four stages of cognitive development— sensorimotor, preoperational, concrete operational, and formal operational (Steward & Koch, 1983). According to Piaget, these stages are sequential and a child must successfully pass through one in order to progress to the next.

The first stage, sensorimotor development, occurs during the first 2 years of life. Children explore their world through their senses as the children develop their motor skills. The primary developmental task is coordination as they learn to crawl, walk, and begin to speak.

During preoperational development, language development and being able to manipulate objects to get what one wants are the primary developmental tasks. The child learns symbolic and intuitive thought and begins to be aware of quantity and the similarities and differences between objects. Symbolic thought allows the child to create images that can represent something else. Imaginary play facilitates this development. As the child develops intuitive thought, he or she can begin to take the perspective of another in a very simple fashion.

The third stage, concrete operational thinking, lasts during most of the elementary school years. Children acquire the ability to understand principles and apply these principles to concrete objects such as doing addition and subtraction. They also gain an ability to classify objects into categories (for example, circles, squares, and triangles) as they begin to mentally organize objects. For the child, everything is still somewhat black and white and thinking is anchored in reality.

The final stage, formal operations, begins as the child thinks more abstractly. Adolescents think in terms of what would be "ideal." Relationships between things such as events or statements can be made as thinking becomes more deductive in character. Adolescents begin to reflect on their world and think about ideas, and as they become older, their thoughts become more systematic and rational. Not all adults successfully attain formal operational thinking, particularly if there is severe trauma in their past.

As we again look at the female client described earlier, it is evident from her behaviors that she has not progressed to the formal operational thinking of adults. For example, she lacks coordination. She trips over things, her gestures are jerky, and her bodily movement lacks fluidity (sensorimotor stage). Although she sees similarities and differences in objects, she has a poorly developed imagination and lacks creativity (preoperational stage). The majority of her thinking is very concrete, and she has even chosen a profession where this type of thinking is essential for success (concrete operational stage). Abstract thinking is difficult for her, and she even has to struggle to understand simple jokes, to project into the future, and to empathize with others.

Moral Development: Kohlberg

Building on the initial ideas of Jean Piaget, Kohlberg (1976) presented a six-stage model of moral development with three global levels of reasoning. The first level, preconventional reasoning, applies to children under 9 years of age. During this time, children learn to receive rewards and avoid punishment. This is accomplished by believing in the power of right of authority figures such as parents, grandparents, and teachers. Children also learn that behaving in certain ways can be justified, making the behavior acceptable. During this level of moral reasoning, children are basically selfish and concerned with getting their own needs met.

Following the rules set up and enforced by society is the core of the second level of moral reasoning, conventional morality. It is important to children to meet the expectations of family and significant others, usually through conformity. This level of development lasts from early adolescence to adulthood. A slight shift is made from needing to be seen as a good person by others to wanting to do what is socially and legally correct for the benefit of society.

The last level of moral development is postconventional reasoning. As mature adults, individuals act according to their own personal sense of right and wrong. They consider issues from multiple perspectives and behave in ways that reinforce their personal reasoning about morality. Factors such as a sense of justice, equality, and respect for others influence judgments and behaviors. According to Kohlberg, this stage evolves over one's adult life span.

If we again look at our female client, we see that she constantly believes that she is going to be punished for whatever she does, even though she strives to make her work perfect. Stuck at the preconventional reasoning stage of moral development, she is petrified of any authority figure. During the first few counseling sessions, she insisted that the door to the counseling office remain open. For this client, one of the primary initial goals of therapy was to establish trust so that she would not be so fearful of being in a room alone with the therapist and so that she could begin to talk about her fears of being judged and punished. Helping this client move through the stages of moral development is a slow, laborious process that may not be accomplished during the actual process of therapy.

Summary of Development Issues

By understanding how a child develops in these many dimensions, one can better understand how to work with the adult woman who was sexually abused as a child. Questions about her age at the time of the abuse will help the mental health professional better understand her emotional, psychosexual, cognitive and moral functioning at that age. In turn, this information will give the mental health professional greater latitude in interventions appropriate for the needs of the little girl who was hurt and betrayed.

Chapter 6

Ego Splitting—How Children Survive

In this chapter, four case studies that depict the process of mentally protecting one's self from early childhood sexual abuse will be presented. These cases illustrate why traditional talk therapy can be a slow, ineffective remedy for women who were sexually abused and why it is important to treat the abuse itself as well as the attitudes and cognitions that have resulted from the abuse.

As an introduction to the case presentations, we first describe the splitting phenomenon that frequently accompanies severe trauma and the childhood thinking that can be arrested in time even as the survivor ages. The discussion will focus primarily on the splitting phenomenon with most details of the cases not presented.

Ego splitting is a normal reaction to trauma. For example, people who have been in a car accident will describe how action seemed to slow down and how they watched what was happening as if they were above the car. This is simply a way for the mind to handle the impending trauma through the process of dissociation.

All Around the Town, a bestseller by Mary Higgins Clark (1992), aptly describes how children dissociate when they are being abused. "After a while she found ways to slip away from them, in her mind. Sometimes she just floated on the ceiling and watched what was happening to the little girl with the long blond hair. Sometimes she felt sorry for the little girl. Other times she made fun of her" (p. 7). Later in the story, we find out that the little girl, Laurie, dissociates into four states. Unlike the person who develops schizophrenia, she is able to access each of these states to help her recover from the effects of being sexually molested for 2 years. As Laurie progresses in therapy, she begins to have more control over which ego state emerges. In contrast, schizophrenia is a mental illness that can be controlled by medication but never cured.

EGO SPLITTING

It is important for therapists to recognize that during physical or sexual trauma, children will usually mentally dissociate. Dissociation is a concrete process and, depending on the severity of the trauma, can occur in many ways. Braun (1988) proposed the BASK (Behavior, Affect, Sensation, Knowledge) model of dissociation. According to Braun, either during the experience or afterward, behavior, affect, sensation or knowledge is split from the person. If the trauma is frequent or severe enough, the split will be long-term and will last until intervention occurs. This splitting process is the generative dynamic behind much of the extensive symptomatology presented by sexual abuse clients and, thus, renders ordinary talk therapy ineffective with these adult survivors of sexual abuse.

An example of what occurs for the child being abused might help to illustrate the concrete nature of splitting. A 38-year-old client was able to remember and abreact her sexual molestation by her father. The abuse first occurred when she was 8 years old and continued until she was 11 (many perpetrators will stop when puberty approaches because of fears of pregnancy). Her father would come into her bedroom in the middle of the night and perform cunnilingus on her or have intercourse with her while she was in a deep sleep. After the first couple of times this happened, she would try to stay awake or sleep very lightly. As an adult she developed a sleep disorder that had resisted a variety of treatments, including that offered by a sleep disorder clinic.

During the sexual abuse, she had dissociated into five ego states that had dispersed into various areas of her bedroom. One of the ego states was located under the bed and took all the fear with her. We later discovered that this ego state was the source of the overwhelming fear reactions that the woman had experienced throughout her life. Until we treated the sexual abuse, the fear responses appeared to be random and not linked to anything in her present life. In the process of therapy, we learned that her fear response was being triggered by anything that resembled the atmosphere and events surrounding the sexual abuse—heavy breathing sounds, the scent of her father's cologne, a feeling of being out of control, or the sound of the tick-tock of her bedroom clock. In a sketch of this ego state, the client drew a little girl huddled in a fetal position, clutching her knees while hiding under the bed.

The second dissociated ego part had taken the pain sensation of the experience with her. She was seen facing a wall, with her back turned toward everyone. The pain was mostly physical and included the tearing in her vagina, the weight of her father lying on her so that she had difficulty breathing, and the pain associated with him holding her arms down. The resulting symptoms in her present life from this dissociation included a numb feeling in her body during all sexual activity and many gynecological difficulties.

Hovering over her childhood bed, the third ego part took the affective components of despair and sadness with her. She saw what was happening and felt the hopelessness of being betrayed as the sense of childhood safety and security were demolished. The client experienced this betrayal in her present life as periodic depressions that were relieved by drug therapy but were never cured.

The fourth ego part was in the doorway of her bedroom looking out. A younger ego state, this little girl did not see what happened nor did she have any knowledge of the abuse. She kept her connection to her father because he had not done anything and he was still her loving parent. As an adult woman, she still did not recognize her father's alcoholism or the inappropriateness of many of his comments and behaviors. Out of all the children in the family, she was the only one who still defended him and rescued him from financial and emotional distress.

Hiding in a stuffed animal, the last ego state contained the anger. She was angry at the betrayal of trust and angry at her father's lack of genuine caring and love. As a child, she was never allowed to express anger and, as most children do, she thought that whatever had happened to her was because she was bad. As an adult, she still did not express any anger and suffered from a host of physical problems including asthma and arthritis.

Like this woman, many sexual abuse survivors can identify the parts of them that dissociated during the trauma. If the abuse is chronic or violent, the adult victim will continue to operate with certain cognitive, psychological, and emotional handicaps. For the client in the previous example, each ego part had to be identified and brought back into consciousness, that is, reintegrated with the adult person.

With this overview of typically dissociated ego parts, let us introduce you to Maria. Her experiences and the charting of her ego parts represent the complexity of the splitting response that is often necessary for a child to psychologically survive physical and sexual abuse.

MARIA—FINALLY UNDERSTANDING HER PAIN

Maria is a 36-year-old woman who has not been married and who currently lives alone. She grew up living with her parents, maternal grandparents, and a brother who is 15 months older than she is. Her grandfather was the only one identified by Maria as providing any nurturing, and his death when she was 30 years old was especially traumatic for her.

Maria has vague memories of her abuse starting very early in her life. The abuse included her mother becoming so furious when Maria would cry that she would choke Maria and throw her against the wall. Maria has many clear memories of her parents screaming at each other and her mother constantly telling her how awful her father was and that she needed Maria's protection. It was not unusual for her mother to talk about killing him. In addition, Maria has many feelings associated with being sexually abused by her father, by a family friend, and by her grandmother.

Maria remembers her childhood as being scary and remembers feeling alone most of the time. At the age of 12, she often felt suicidal and knew that her "brain didn't work right." She began her therapeutic journey when she was 20 years old and over a 16-year period has seen nine therapists. Her clinical diagnoses have included bipolar disorder, schizophrenia, borderline personality, and acute depression. Psychiatrists have prescribed many medications for these disorders, and Maria has frequently attempted to self-medicate with cocaine, marijuana, Librium, alcohol, and various prescription painkillers.

Her physical condition has been striking in that she has numerous physical problems and reports that for most of her life she has not felt well. When she began therapy with one of the authors, Maria did not mention her physical discomfort, and it was only after 6 months of therapy that she mentioned physical problems. These problems have included numerous precancerous moles, a ruptured appendix, collapse of the canal between her bladder and kidney, fibroid cysts, and a fibroid tumor that caused her to have a hysterectomy. Recently, she needed another operation to remove adhesions resulting from previous surgeries. Although Maria has above average intelligence, at age 6 she was diagnosed as learning disabled and has consistently had difficulty with verbal communication.

When Maria first presented herself for therapy, she had almost no affect and reported feeling numb most of the time. In spite of having a secure job as a technical writer, she reported that her life fluctuated between feeling suicidal and depressed with intermittent periods of anxiety. Her relationships were distant and often ended in misunderstandings that left her feeling unloved. She indicated that if she had the courage to end her life she would have done so a long time ago, and she was hopeful that an auto accident or some other accident would grant her wish to be dead. Although Maria had been through therapy that focused on her many different diagnoses, she felt that none had worked for her, which added to her feelings of hopelessness.

Maria started to make progress only when she was able to identify the splitting process that occurred during her childhood and realized that many of her adult symptoms were related to childhood traumas. It was as if she had become frozen in time when she experienced the traumas, and her present adult life was constantly being filtered through her past child ego states.

Maria was able to identify 25 ego states. Using her technical skills, she organized them by charting them. While organizing these "subparts" (client's term), she understood for the first time that the moods that had consumed her her whole life matched many of these subparts. Additionally, soon after she finished her chart, her suicidal thoughts began to lessen and for the first time she felt hope that her life could change for the better.

At different times in her life, Maria has operated from all 25 subparts. The many diagnoses and physical ailments seem to correspond to various periods in her life during which one of the subparts was most dominant. For example, when Maria first went to therapy she was in what she called the "dead" state. She had a flat affect, reported being seriously depressed, and was barely able to function at work. After a short amount of work on her depression, she reverted to the "scared" state. In this subpart, she cried all of the time and stated that she was scared to go to work or to drive to a class she was taking. Much later in the therapy, she accessed the "anger" and "hate" states. In these subparts, most often she would become angry at herself, but occasionally she would experience anger at others, including her therapist. Later, the anger and hate shifted to her parents and grandmother for what they had done to her.

Since the initial therapeutic work on these ego states and her past trauma, Maria has made slow but significant progress. During one of her last communications with the therapist, Maria indicated that she realized she is not "crazy," just hurt very deeply. She has started a new career and is beginning to make new friends. Finally, Maria stated that her subparts have expressed some of their pain and this is allowing her to begin to heal.

CELESTE—REGAINING HOPE AND FAITH

The second case study concerns a seemingly well-adjusted, respected, and happy woman. Celeste is a 37-year-old single woman from a large Catholic family. An excellent student, she was the one the family admired and pointed to with pride. She entered the convent when she was 18 years old and remained a nun for 12 years. Now she holds an administrative position for a nonprofit organization. While she has been able to make close friends, until recently Celeste had ruled out the possibility of having an intimate relationship. Physically, Celeste has suffered from incontinence, which has been extremely embarrassing, and from chronic strep throat, bronchitis, back pain, and headaches. She has had a complete hysterectomy.

Celeste's therapeutic journey has led to painful confrontations with her family and a discovery of her own ego splitting. This splitting had allowed her to appear normal, even to herself, though she always felt isolated and not quite good enough.

Celeste's disquietude led her into therapy where she seized on her mother's drinking as the source of her internal pain. She joined a group for adult children of alcoholics that helped her in many areas of her life. After several years, though, the isolation, fear of intimacy, and fear of sexuality had not changed. Celeste reentered therapy, this time with one of the authors, and also participated in two forms of group therapy. She uncovered memories of being sexually abused as a child, beginning with her grandparents and filtering into experiences with her father and his friends. She also has memories of her mother participating, as well as some of her brothers and sisters. For Celeste, the therapeutic process has been emotionally and psychologically difficult.

Although some of her ego states have manifested themselves at different times throughout her adult life, Celeste became aware of the splitting process during her therapy. She can readily access these split-off ego states and is now aware that her oftentimes overwhelming feelings of anxiety and depression are produced by accessing younger ego states associated with hurtful memories. Most of Celeste's ego states are very young and correspond to either traumatic abuse memories or to developmental periods that were stunted because of the traumatic experiences.

Some of her poems and letters have been included to illustrate Celeste's defenses, which have protected her against full awareness of being sexually abused. Her writings also illustrate her internal drive to heal. These testaments to the human will are the backdrop that gives Celeste hope even in the midst of the terrifying re-experiencing of her youth. For Celeste, like most survivors of childhood sexual abuse, the internal drive to be healed and whole again results in a profound tension between this need and the need to forget or deny the pain of the abuse.

One of the first ego states Celeste recovered was a 3-year-old girl (see Figures 1 and 2). She was encountered hiding under a couch. Completely petrified, she initially did not trust anyone, including Celeste. This young girl split during a very brutal rape scene when her father took her for a sexual encounter with one of his friends. This experience seems likely to be linked to her incontinence. The following letter from Celeste refers to the recent encountering of this 3-year-old and is an attempt to begin processing the memory of the rape.

Letter #1

> That little girl you talked with last week doesn't know me as an adult . . . Thank you for encouraging me and giving me affirmations last week about "good work, this is hard," etc. and saying it more than once. I needed to hear that. I still do.
>
> I feel like a fish in water that is too shallow. I don't know how to wriggle back to where the water is deeper and I can breathe easily again, and I am petrified that any

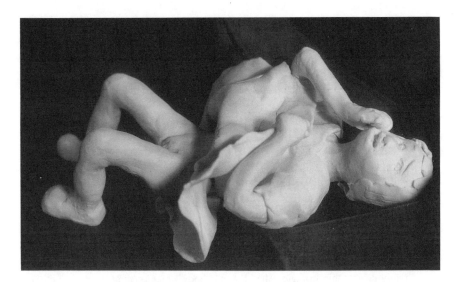

Figure 1   3-year old girl showing terror of rape.

Figure 2   3-year-old girl cowering after rape.

wriggling I do will only get me shallower and put me in mortal danger. It reminds me of when I walk the canals as they are being drained and see all the fish there that have nowhere to go to stay alive. Maybe all my water is draining away too and I should just hurry up and die and get it over with.

I know I told you that this memory is stored on my right side and with it my right side is all scrunched up. It's been so scrunched the last few days that my left leg hurts trying to compensate for the shortness of the right leg. It makes for little sleep . . .

I wish I could cry about this—I need to—but I can't connect with my feelings deeply enough these days, can't make myself slow down enough to let all of this sink in. Maybe it's like that fish who can't overcome the will, the impulse, to stay alive and so cannot surrender to death, but keeps wiggling, no matter how futile the action.

The messages communicated in this letter illustrate a pattern that is consistent with that of most survivors. Once an ego state is encountered and associated with the initial trauma, fear and survival mechanisms surface. The fish metaphor accurately depicts this struggle. Also, how the body stores specific trauma is aptly described by Celeste as the extreme discomfort she feels in her right side and left leg.

The second split occurred when Celeste was 6 years old and in bed with her father and mother. Her father forced her to perform sexual acts with her mother. Since this was too overwhelming for the feminine ego state to handle, Celeste created a 6-year-old boy named Roger to handle the shock of being forced to do what she thought a girl was forbidden to do. It is common for both women and men to have an opposite gender ego state handle sexual abuse. The letter that follows arrived shortly before Celeste abreacted or re-experienced this particular sexual trauma.

Letter #2

I've been wrestling with a 6-year-old all day. Tell me it gets better. I'm surprised at how strong Roger is, how overpowering. Maybe I'm lucky that he has been comatose this long—up till a few weeks ago.. . . . He wants to smash and destroy things.

One day at a time, Celeste. Tonight I will sack out in my safe place. This letter, if I have the courage to send it, is a cry for help. This feels like an emergency, but emergencies happen quickly like a tornado or a crash or an explosion. This is a long drawn out slow motion emergency. I'm preparing for it with my own internal helicopter and some paramedics.

Friday p.m. And it's a good thing. No sooner had I written that and Roger slit his throat. He really wants to be dead. I was immediately on the scene with I.V. and bandages and whisked him off to emergency surgery. He's in stable condition and they have him strapped down so he can't hurt himself anymore. It's interesting how many sore neck things there are with this cough (that kicks up when I am feeling this).

I think the crisis is over for now. We are not finished with the memory yet. I'm still weighing whether to send you this.

The drama depicted in Celeste's letter recapitulates the types of dramas experienced by women who have been sexually abused as children. For years the term hysterical, which has a negative connotation, was used by mental health professionals to describe these types of behaviors. This glimpse into Celeste's experience, however, gives us a chance to understand how overwhelming the internal experience of the sexual trauma can be. The women going through experiences such as these also must endure their trauma externally in order to be healed. These are not things that can be faced without considerable courage. That is why they are so often hidden from awareness for such long periods of time.

Celeste also gave us permission to use two of her poems, "Question" and "Hollow," which capture the anguish of her betrayal and the glimpses of hope needed to recover (see Figure 3).

Question

You have seen me broken
bleeding my
spirit like shadows across the room;
each spurt from my soul's artery
spewing crimson drops of
life into these tiny children.

We plumb my pain,
bind me to it,
fettered with truth.
My screams
echo through your veins
You join me
rather than stop your ears;
couldn't cradle me as
I lay
whimpering and bare upon the floor,
and hold me now.

I writhe against your care
So easily you cherish
the weakness I abhor.
How do I
heal
from this?

Figure 3   Internalized male figure comforting 3-year old girl.

Hollow
Ocean's roar
through convoluted curve
of conch
once home to busy life
now cast
on yellow sand
mottled emptiness
where once were
children
resonance moans.

Framework of dreams
wrapped around empty air
brittle bone
unyielding
encircles silent space.
Tearless faces

watch empty eyed
as hope drains irretrievable
bleeds into soft sand
mingles with salt foam
vanished;
life's loss unclaimed
keened by wind
through empty shell.

Celeste is beginning to heal. She has reintegrated several of her ego states, although the process has been very painful and frightening. She has had to become estranged from her mother and father and some of her siblings in order to begin to recover from the sexual trauma. One positive outcome for Celeste is that she has renewed her faith in God.

ANGELA—CHILDHOOD PATTERNS REENACTED AS AN ADULT

Angela is a 43-year-old woman with two children and a husband with a highly successful career. Although she is currently a full-time homemaker, she is contemplating returning to school to develop her art skills. Her sexual abuse started at age 3 with her father and later included her grandfather, her father's friends, two uncles, and two cousins. Angela's physical problems have included scoliosis, sinus problems, chronic constipation, chronic urinary tract infections, and vaginal yeast infections.

As a result of being sexually abused, Angela split into four ego states, each well developed and having a protective function. Presently, all the ego states have processed their particular traumas, and Angela is now reintegrated. For the first time, she reports that she "feels solid and has boundaries."

Angela is now planning to confront her entire family through the use of a video in which she describes her sexual abuse experiences and the profound damage she has suffered. She will be sending it to her parental family and key extended family members. Angela is hoping that the horrible family secret will be exposed for the first time and that future generations of children in her family might be spared her fate—the abuse and the resulting ego splits.

The four ego splits represent the roles and feelings that Angela was forced to adopt to cope with the betrayal and abandonment generated by the sexual abuse. The first ego state was a protector who took on the persona of a tomboy. This tomboy was tough and did not know about the abuse; her view of girls was that they are weak and can be easily hurt. The second ego state was a fantasy girl who thinks she is special if she looks pretty and behaves seductively with men. She laughs easily and can be described as charming and attractive to men. At parties, she is a whirlwind of jokes, gaiety, dancing, and flirting. Angela feels that this ego state was what her father wanted and her mother encouraged—a charming, smiling girl who does not feel or express any sadness. The third ego state felt ugly and had a stick-like body and buck teeth. Always feeling alone and abandoned, she archived the information about the abuse. It was her responsibility to be the keeper of secrets that were not to be shared. A fourth ego state was actually involved in the sexual acts and was ashamed about this. Since she participated in the sexual activities, she experienced the physical pain and all the emotions related to the abuse. Feeling used and abandoned, she believed that she would not be acceptable to God.

Angela has struggled through many roadblocks in order to heal from the sexual abuse. She has repatterned her whole relationship with her husband and believes that she will be risking losing her family when she sends the video detailing her experiences.

For Angela, when she is in different settings, different ego states dominate. For example, when she is in social settings, the flirtatious, charming girl is her persona. It was this ego state that experienced being raped by a group of men who were friends of a girlfriend when they all were at a party. Since this assault approximated earlier sexual traumas, Angela forgot it by the next day but complained of soreness in her pelvic area and thighs when she came for her therapy session. When she was put into a light trance, she remembered the rape in detail. Her gynecologist substantiated that she had been sexually brutalized when he examined her and found large tears in her vagina.

Angela is nearing the end of therapy. Her ego splits are chronicled in her art work but not experienced directly anymore. Feeling almost healed, Angela finally has hope for a future that will allow her to grow and not constantly protect against or relive the pain and cognitive distortions that were products of her childhood sexual abuse.

SUE—THE TURQUOISE LADY TO THE RESCUE

Our last case is a 45-year-old women who at first glance seems stable and relatively happy. A professional woman and mother of three, she and her husband genuinely care about each other and seem able to share this loving bond with their children. Their eldest son has had difficulties related to a bipolar diagnosis; however, the other two children appear to be well-adjusted. Like many women,

Sue juggles her professional responsibilities, initially in nutrition and more recently in mental health, with the needs of her family.

With such a seemingly normal life, what prompted her to come to therapy? Sue had lapsed into a deep depression about 8 years ago. Not being able to work or to think clearly and lacking energy, Sue sought pastoral counseling. She continued in counseling for 2 years. It was during this time period that she first discovered that her mother was an alcoholic, which helped her to understand that some of her present difficulties might be associated with past family dysfunction. Also, she began to come to grips with feeling that no matter what she did, it was not good enough, nor could she feel good about her accomplishments.

Since the depression had not lifted in spite of insights gained through the pastoral counseling, Sue sought the help of a female psychologist. This $2^{1}/_2$ year therapeutic relationship was seen as very helpful in strengthening her ability to parent more effectively, to form friend relationships, and to establish appropriate boundaries with others. Although this psychologist suspected that Sue had been sexually abused by her father, Sue's panic at dealing with this issue and the psychologist's reticence about directly confronting the possibility served to keep Sue's awareness of being sexually abused from surfacing.

Even with the gains made with this psychologist, Sue decompensated several times during the process of therapy—she became scared, suicidal, depressed, and had flashbacks. Since this psychologist was relocating, Sue was referred to one of the authors. Sue had just decompensated, and her psychologist was concerned that the sexual abuse needed to be addressed.

Sue's experience is an excellent example of the years of therapy that most survivors have gone through with sexual abuse issues never being directly addressed. Even though Sue made gains in stabilizing her present ego functioning, the splitting caused by the abuse still impacted her life in significant ways.

Like other survivors, Sue's physical problems have paralleled her psychological depression. As an adult, Sue has suffered from ulcers, irritable bowel syndrome, symptoms related to mitral valve prolapse, chronic bladder infections, and TMJ. Since she was frequently hospitalized as a little girl, she felt abandoned by her family.

Sue's struggles in therapy have been monumental at times. She has discovered that the abuse started when she was only 2 years old and continued until she was 14. It involved her grandfather, father, mother, and a neighbor. In addition, her mother physically abused her. The toll of living in her dysfunctional family not only affected Sue but also her brother. At age 19, he died from an overdose of drugs, which Sue strongly suspects was suicide. Although Sue had never talked to her brother about being sexually abused, her brother tried to burn down the family house when he was 7 years old. He started the fire in a bedroom closet—the same place where Sue's father had molested her.

Sue split into many ego states in order to cope with the knowledge and emotions surrounding the abuse. The oldest ego state is a young adolescent, and the other ego states decrease in age to about the age of 2. Unique among these ego states is an ego state Sue calls the Turquoise Lady. The Turquoise Lady serves as a guide who has stored the knowledge of the splitting pattern and the damage that has been done to Sue.

For many survivors, the information and help possible from guides such as Sue's Turquoise Lady are invaluable. While not all survivors have an ego state who functions as a guide, when a guide is present, it is a powerful ally for the therapist. Precious therapeutic time can be saved by having this internal helper.

When Sue first came to therapy, she was asked to make an artistic creation depicting her defenses that had prevented her from knowing about the abuse. She first brought in a magnificent cloth dragon that contained many internal layers, much like Russian nesting dolls, and then a cloth box filled with objects (see Figures 4 and 5). Later, she brought in a circular box that contained sculptural representations of all of the ego splits inside of her. The Turquoise Lady offered these creations as a way for Sue to begin to explore her abuse.

The dragon was a test for the therapist. Sue later said, "I knew if you couldn't understand her, then any further work would be futile. I don't know if you ever realized just how important it was for you to get it, and how afraid we were that you just might." The therapist did understand the meaning of the dragon, and Sue began to reveal more of her past. Like Sue, many clients will devise tests for their therapists before really trusting them with such overwhelming, hurtful self-revelations.

The cloth dragon was an amazing soft sculpture. Sue wrote a description to clarify the meanings of the five layers of the dragon.

Layer One: The surface layer was the dragon itself. Sue wrote about this dragon, "She's a dragon Lady. We all know that dragons are magical, mystical creatures that blow fire and smoke and scare the townspeople with their fury. They're showy creatures who never let anyone get close enough to see anything but the anger which we see by the smoke and fire. Things get burned that happen to fall in their path. We can certainly see what the aftermath of their fury does to the innocent who happen to be near. But in addition to the angry facade they put on, dragons are fearful timid creatures." In the beginning of therapy, Sue frequently presented herself as a dragon lady—angry and curt.

Layer Two: Underneath the outer layer was a grey cloak. On the inside of the cloak were threads of many colors. In describing this cloak, she wrote, "The grey cloak is that of obscurity or invisibility. Underneath the anger is the timid crea-

Figure 4   Defenses: The layered dragon.

ture who hides from contact. But by running or hiding in the shadow, one conceals the being they are. The sounds of their colors, their full panorama are hidden from view, not only from others but from themselves as well." Sue thought that she had no talents and shied away from friends. In many ways, Sue's consciousness is the grey cloak; it hides who she is, even from herself.

Layer Three: Inside the grey cloak was a black cape that was blood red on the inside. Sue described this cape with the following words, "But the obscurity conceals more, fear and anxiety. They wrap around like a thick cloak concealing and impeding any movement, binding creativity. Under the fear is the blood . . ." The blackness, like the black inside her closet, was the core of Sue's hurt and depression. The pain she was still feeling from the rape is depicted in her inability to finish the sentence about the blood.

Layer Four: The fourth layer showed a brown knit-and-purl pattern that resembled a knight's chain mail. "The brown mail is her sin—her utter unworthiness. She carries it with her; it defiles everything she does or touches. Everything she creates is tainted with the stain of her uncleanliness." Brown is the color of dirt and human waste. Like most survivors of childhood sexual abuse, she feels dirty, unclean, and therefore unworthy of love and respect.

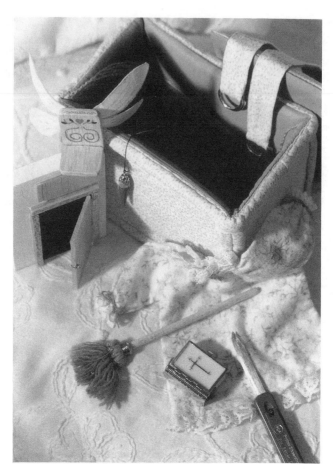

Figure 5   The box: Symbolic representations of childhood sexual abuse.

Layer Five: The last layer was an old woman burdened with rocks at her feet. On her back, she is carrying a little baby, papoose style, who has stars around the bunting holding her in. "The baby is a star child as are all babies born, even if only for an instant. She was born with all the yet unrealized potential and beauty of innocence, knowing simultaneously that the baby is bound in the bunting of unrealistic expectations that can never be achieved. While I was working on the bunting, I developed compassion for the ugly, old woman. She is struggling under the burden on her back carrying this baby, all the unrealistic expectations, and trying to protect the baby. Originally, I intended the old woman to portray everything I found defiled and despicable about myself. The woman is old—old before her time from carrying the burdens. Her long grey and dark hair shows that her face is masked in the frustrations caused by living her burdens and pain.

Her blue dress is the last remaining control that she has. It is significant that there are bands around her breasts, genitalia, and legs, but I don't know why. She has no arms. She is defenseless. She can't fight back. Her black belt is her depression. It is always present no matter how many layers we go down. The rocks weight her down and tie her to the earth. They also serve to stand her up and give her support." The baby is the innocence she should have been, but the old woman is the product of the abuse.

The first cloth box was shunted off with the comment that it was stupid and meant nothing. At the time, Sue did not have a conscious memory of what she had put in the box, which was secured with two straps. The inside of the box was turquoise and red and contained small objects which, through the process of therapy, were identified as symbols of her abuse. The box itself was later discovered to be a replica of her top dresser drawer where she had stuffed her repressed memories.

The first object in the box was a three-dimensional wooden representation of her closet. When the door was opened, she had painted the interior black. This was the closet in which her father had played "sexual games" with her in the dark. The second object was a shoelace that represented the ropes he had used to tie her during one of the closet games. The third object was a miniature doll nightgown that symbolized what she was wearing when her father slipped into her bed after she had fallen asleep. The fourth and fifth objects were related to the sexual abuse by her grandfather. The fourth object was a dowser's pendulum much like the one her grandfather had used to look for water, and the fifth object was a broom. For the 2-year-old, the penetration of her grandfather's penis was like a broom handle being forced inside of her. The sixth article was a wine chalice, emphasizing her mother's alcoholism. The seventh object was a wooden chip that symbolized how scary her grandfather's hands looked to her as a little girl. A Bible was also included. Sue's father was a devout church attender and lectured her on believing everything written in the Bible, and on how she was going to hell for sinning. The final object was a small pocket knife that Sue had kept under her pillow as a child, telling herself that she always had the option of killing herself. As an adult, she still slept with the same small knife under her pillow without knowing why.

The third box, brought to a later therapy session, contained all her split-off ego states (see Figure 6). In it, ego parts were represented that knew about the sex with her mother, the sex with her father, and the various ego states who kept the emotions: a male comforter, one ego part who did not know about the abuse, and a part that was angry at her for being weak and sickly. Because of the presence of these ego states, Sue was able to grow up in spite of an abusive family where there were no models for love and caring.

All three artistic creations were revealed by the Turquoise Lady. She also assisted the process of therapy by showing the therapist how to negotiate therapeutic impasses. The following letter written to the therapist by the Turquoise Lady elucidates this helping process.

> The purpose of the Red Witch [ego state that hates Sue for being weak] is not to kill anybody, but to cause so much despair that any reason to exist is gone. You were given an article on attachment some months ago. That is what is happening here. It's not depression, that is the long term effect. It is about despair, that is where the intense pain is. That is what is going on in here. The despair is from no one being there, from whenever there was attention, it was mixed, wrong and right, good and bad. It seems as though everything was both good and bad in the extreme. Not just shades of gray, but black and white in a confusing pattern . . . Good luck with your session with the Red Witch. I will get her to your office (that has been a battle too). You can contend with her. She is sneaky, she lies, and she burns with rage that is fueled by hate and resentment.

Figure 6   Client's handmade representations of her split-off ego states: (a) figures representing all ego states; (b) close-up of selected figures; (c) male protector figure comforting client after she was sexually abused.

In this short letter, the Turquoise Lady advises the therapist about the origin of Sue's depression and how being abandoned has influenced Sue. She is trying to help the therapist so that Sue can take the small steps necessary in her journey to heal.

SUMMARY

Ego splitting occurs for most sexual abuse victims. This phenomenon initially protects the child from knowledge of the abuse and the physical sensations and emotions surrounding being molested. If the split parts remain separate, however, when the child becomes an adult, a myriad of physical, emotional, and psychological symptoms and dysfunctional behaviors can develop. When the split-off ego states are discovered, processed, and reintegrated, many of these symptoms and behaviors will disappear. In addition, cognitive distortion and repressed feelings can be accessed and changed.

In the four cases cited above, the women knew that something was wrong with their lives, and they started with some conscious memories of their sexual abuse. Each of the splits supplied missing puzzle pieces to help explain each woman's perplexing struggles with life. In essence, by retrieving their ego splits, their lives made sense for the first time and healing could proceed.

Chapter 7

Interventions: How Therapy Works

Once a diagnosis of childhood sexual abuse is confirmed, the client and therapist have to agree to a therapeutic contract. In this contract, the approximate length of therapy is considered, the number of meetings per week decided, a fee arrangement agreed upon, adjunct group therapy is discussed, and a summary of what to expect in therapy is reviewed.

LENGTH OF THERAPY

There is no definitive time line that delineates how long therapy will take. For each client, it will depend on numerous factors as well as on the skill of and relationship with the therapist. Some of the most significant factors might include:

1. *Length and severity of abuse.* The longer the child was the victim of abuse and the more severe the abuse, the longer therapy might be needed to work through all of the ramifications of the abuse. Also, since a child's psychosocial, psychosexual, cognitive, and moral development are impeded by being abused, the therapist will need to facilitate the client's progression through the age-appropriate developmental stages. This can be a slow process. It should also be remembered that the more severe the abuse, the more defense mechanisms are activated and the more resistance will be encountered to remembering and working through the painful effects of the abuse (Bagley & Ramsay, 1985; Russell, 1986; Tsai, Feldman-Summers, & Edgar, 1979).
2. *Age during abuse.* In general, the younger the child was when the abuse occurred, the more difficult the recovery process can be (Courtois, 1979; Meiselman, 1978). Children under 5 years of age who are sexually abused can have significant gaps in their normal developmental processes. Her-

man (1992) has reported that adults with an abuse history have difficulties in cognition, memory, self-care, identity, and the ability to form intimate, stable relationships. Also, since survivors of childhood sexual abuse have had to use numerous psychological defenses to cope with having been abused, they are vulnerable to affective, somatoform, and posttraumatic stress disorder symptoms.

3. *Support systems.* For the child, the availability of a non-perpetrating parent, other relative (such as an aunt, grandparent, or older sibling), or significant adult who spends significant quality time with the child is crucial. The love and caring of this person can serve somewhat as a buffer between the child and the crippling pain of being abused. Sexually abused children who are without the protection and care of another adult are at risk of developing severe pathology as a result of their being sexually abused. Too often sexually abused children have a poor relationship with the nonabusive parent (Cooney, 1988).

4. *Genetic variables.* The extent to which children are vulnerable to experiencing severe symptoms is influenced by their ability to utilize psychological defenses, such as dissociation, repression of memories, and anxiety responses. Van der Kolk (1987) has pointed out that physiological arousal and the ability to handle psychological uncertainty are genetically mediated. Since both physiological and psychological forces come into play during and after sexual abuse, the genetic predisposition of a child can be viewed as one determinant of her chronic stress response, particularly since individuals have idiosyncratic reactions to stressors.

5. *Intimidation factors.* If a child has been physically or emotionally tortured to ensure secrecy, the recovery process will be more difficult. Physical torture might include battering, mutilation, use of hot substances or lamps on the genital areas, or life-threatening gestures such as choking. Women have even related how their abuser tortured or killed a pet or another animal to ensure silence. Emotional torture might include blaming the child for seductive behavior and saying it was the child's fault, threatening to hurt another family member, abandoning or rejecting the child, asserting that it was enjoyable for the child and she wanted to be touched by the abuser, or even blatantly denying that it ever took place. Force has been found to be a major influence on how debilitating the influence of the sexual abuse can be (Finkelhor, 1979; Russell, 1986; Tufts' New England Medical Center, Division of Child Psychiatry, 1984).

6. *Alcohol and drug use.* Many people who sexually abuse their children use alcohol to excess or take drugs. Being under the influence of a chemical substance colors their judgments about appropriate adult-child behaviors;

however, it clearly does not excuse the behaviors or lessen the degree to which they are guilty of violating a child. In the abusive situation, children may also be forced to ingest drugs or alcohol. Not only is the child's physiology not able to adequately cope with being chemically stimulated, drugs cause mental confusion and a profound distortion of the child's reality that can lead to chronic psychosocial symptoms.

7. *Degree of defensive adaptation.* For many adult survivors, defense mechanisms like dissociation, amnesia, and repression have shielded them from either partial or full knowledge of having been abused. The strength of these defenses can be a double-edged sword. Their intactness indicates excellent survival mechanisms; however, the strength and maintenance of these defenses could preclude recovery or make it considerably slow.

8. *Pressure of silence.* Adult survivors of childhood sexual abuse can be stymied in their recovery by secrecy. Since there is a taboo associated with incest, many survivors feel stigmatized and keep silent. They feel self-hate or loathing because they participated in the relationship. A second kind of silence results from the pressure encountered if the survivor has attempted to disclose this information previously but has met with disbelief or outright scorn. Well-meaning teachers, ministers, counselors and other helpers may have dismissed the claim as being fantasy or causing too many waves. Many survivors have reported being condemned by others for breaking their silence. A third kind of silence is fostered by perpetrators and the family. Survivors' claims of being abused upset the homeostasis of the family, and there is tremendous pressure not to reveal any transgressions or to retract ones already made. It is a family secret that no one is supposed to tell to anyone outside the family, and more often than not, it is not to be spoken of within the confines of the family itself (Bergart, 1986). If no one says the words, perhaps it did not really happen.

9. *Ignorance of the effects of abuse.* Sometimes, people who have been sexually abused are not aware of the overwhelming devastation that often accompanies being a victim of abuse. Often the sexual abuse is the norm in their family with more than one child being abused, or they love the perpetrator who may have favored them growing up. Although many times these victims are aware of being sexually abused, they may react like one of my former clients, "I know my father and uncle played with me sexually when I was young, but it was no big deal." Their defense mechanisms are busy protecting them from the implications of the abuse, making recovery much more difficult.

Once these nine major factors are considered, the therapist should be able to estimate the length of therapy. The client needs to understand, however, that while exploring the sexual abuse and its ramifications, new repressed experiences will often surface. For therapy to be successful, it must address much more than memory work. The cognitive and emotional damage have to be addressed and behavioral changes initiated.

SESSION AGREEMENTS AND FEES

The issue of number of sessions per week has become more complex. With the advent of managed health care, the number of sessions being allowed any one client is being automatically limited. In addition, insurance payments have become more closely scrutinized and caps have been placed on what total amount can be paid for treatment.

Since resolving childhood sexual abuse usually involves long-term therapy, the requirements of the therapy itself are increasingly in conflict with emerging health care trends. Many therapists meet with their clients twice a week and encourage 90-minute sessions. In our experience, once-a-week sessions for 60 minutes have sufficed, with an option to hold longer sessions on an as-needed basis. Many times when an abuse experience needs to be abreacted, additional therapeutic time must be allotted to meet the client's pressing needs.

ADJUNCT THERAPIES

Group therapy is often indicated for sexual abuse survivors. The bonding that occurs in these groups can serve as support for the remembering process and for coping with the accompanying pain and isolation created by this type of thera-peutic work (Westerland, 1983). Because they share common experiences, group members provide effective feedback for the many cognitive distortions each member developed as a result of being abused (Bergart, 1986; Courtois & Watts, 1982). In addition, the group monitors one another's current level of functioning so that each member does not sacrifice their present families and jobs while delv-ing into the past abuse. One of the main benefits of belonging to a group is the support and encouragement of members who have also lived through being sexu-ally abused and are on their own journey to health.

Support groups such as Alcoholics Anonymous, Women in Sobriety, and other 12-step programs can provide many of the same benefits as group therapy. Even though these self-help groups are often leaderless, the participants can have a sense of being in a caring family environment, perhaps for the first time.

Couples counseling and family therapy may also be useful to help alleviate many of the problems that the survivor brings into a marriage or family structure. Since healthy adult and parental role models were most likely absent when the victim of the sexual abuse was growing up, the adult survivor is, in effect, attempting to navigate important developmental periods without a map or with one that is seriously flawed. Many victims of sexual abuse ask repeatedly, "Is what I am doing with my spouse (or children) normal?" They lack confidence in the rightness or acceptability of their own behaviors—in their own ability to make sound judgments regarding their behaviors in these close family relationships.

When the psychological therapy has progressed to a point where the survivor is ready for adjunct therapies, massage and selected body work may assist them in the recovery process. First and foremost, these adjunct therapies can introduce healthy, healing touch into their lives. Also, because the effects of childhood trauma can be manifested at the cellular level, appropriate body work can release emotional as well as physical tension.

A strong word of caution needs to be added at this point, however. The timing of these extratherapeutic experiences must be appropriate. For example, a client heard from one of her close friends that a "rebirthing" experience was very helpful for her. Without consulting the therapist, the client enrolled in a day-long workshop that included participants going through rebirthing. The next day, the client started experiencing anxiety attacks, had difficulty breathing, could not concentrate at work, and was disoriented to such an extent that she could not find her way home from work. The symptoms became so intolerable that she needed to take a week off from work to recover the ground that she had lost from prematurely becoming involved in this potentially beneficial experience. She met with her therapist who worked with her on becoming grounded and reassociated to her body.

Other useful therapeutic modalities for survivors of childhood sexual abuse might include art therapy, psychodrama, hypnotherapy, and music and dance therapy. In particular, the breathing exercises and meditation of yoga can be very beneficial as they allow the person to relax and become centered. Further, since sexual abuse can also involve spiritual damage, many survivors need to reconnect with their religion or explore their spiritual beliefs to provide them with internal grounding in order to work through the trauma of being abused.

THE THERAPEUTIC PROCESS

Therapy for adult survivors of childhood sexual abuse occurs in four stages that often overlap, although more psychologically sophisticated clients might skip some of the preliminary stages.

The four stages consist of Safety, Exploration, Loss, and Fulfillment (SELF):

Safety—establishment of the therapeutic bond and insuring safety for the ensuing work.

Exploration—sexual abuse memory work.

Loss—resolving cognitive distortions and emotional trauma of the adult traumatized as a child in order to change old defensive structures and empower the new adult.

Fulfillment—Integrating the new learning into satisfying couple, family, and social relationships, and pursuing vocational endeavors.

The acronym, SELF, is a reminder that the goal is not just coping with abuse but rediscovering oneself as an integrated human being with a full and vibrant future. Table 1 presents an overview of the therapeutic topics to be covered in each stage.

These four stages are not linear progressions that clearly follow each other. The interventions designed for each phase can be utilized throughout the therapeutic process and oftentimes must be repeated in each new stage. Referring to this process as similar to a spiral staircase, one client stated that she realized that each time an intervention was repeated she grasped its implications at an increasingly higher level of awareness. One reason she was able to move through each phase was that underlying all of the therapeutic work was her belief that she would get better. She had hope.

Hope is the foundation upon which all other therapeutic work is built. It gives the client the strength and courage to face what happened to her as a child and to face a future where the bounds of past experience no longer exist. Her aspirations now include the possibility of intimate relationships, a body free of physical illnesses and hurtful memories, and a spiritual connection to the life around her.

To help readers understand each stage, the therapeutic issues most prevalent in each stage along with therapeutic interventions that are most appropriate for that stage will be listed and illustrated.

Safety

Survivors of childhood sexual abuse enter into therapy with numerous impediments to exploring and resolving their past trauma. Before any memory work

Table 1

Components of the SELF model

Safety	Exploration	Loss	Fulfillment

1. Structure therapy
  Parameters of intimacy
  Therapist's attitude
    toward sex abuse
  Cooperative experience
  Confidentiality
  Therapeutic boundaries
	1. Minimization of the abuse
	2. Bonding to perpetrator
	3. Fearing family reactions
	4. Ego splitting
	5. Threatening childhood
	    messages
	6. Fear from flashbacks and
	    nightmares
	7. Cognitive distortions
		1. What was lost?
		2. Grieving the loss
		3. Acknowledging betrayal
		4. Concerns
		    Forgiving
		    Seeking revenge
		    Compensation
		5. Changes in relationships
		    Family of origin
		    Friends
		    Marriage
		    Children
		    Therapist
		6. Mourning the changes
			1. Reconnecting
			    Physical
			      Diet
			      Exercise
			      Play
			      Relaxation
			      Sensuality
			      Safety
			      Nature
			    Emotional
			      Emotions as signals
			      Freshness of experience
			      Joy and hope
			    Psychological
			      Correct cognitive distortions
			      Decision making assertiveness
			      Confrontational skills
			    Spirituality
			      Spiritual identity
			      Life-affirming activities

2. Self-care
  Compulsions/addictions
  Medical issues
  Daily health care
  Sleep patterns
  Stress management
			2. Caring and Love
			    Renogiate relationships
			    Sexual identity
			    Humor and laughter

3. External world functioning
  Home environment
  Play/exercise
  Support system
  Dysfunctional
    relationships
  Normalizing symptoms
			3. Meaningful vocational pursuit
			    Career aspirations
			    Career counseling
			    Financial planning

takes place, most therapists find it imperative to shore up present functioning while establishing the therapeutic bond. This bond is essential because survivors have learned to be mistrustful of others and trusting the therapist is a slow learning process for them. They need a consistent, secure environment to be established early in therapy in order for them to become vulnerable to experiencing the powerful emotional responses and fears that will emerge as a result of the therapeutic work.

A three-pronged approach to therapy is suggested. First, since survivors of sexual abuse have lived with an ambiguity in relationships that has not fostered trust, the therapist needs to provide clients with a clearly understood structure for therapy. This sets the parameters of the relationship with respect to expectations for therapy and boundaries of the client-therapist relationship. In essence, structuring helps to make the therapeutic environment safe.

The second prong focuses on the client's self-care habits. This is particularly important when crises occur. Each therapist needs to assess the client's crisis management skills to be sure that as the therapeutic work becomes more difficult, the client, with the help and support of the therapist, can successfully traverse the issues that surface.

The third prong revolves around an evaluation of the client's functioning in her external world. Is she coping as effectively as possible in her unique work and social world? Does therapy need to focus on this aspect of her life immediately?

Need for Structure. Entering into a therapeutic relationship can be a frightening experience for victims of sexual abuse. In previous therapies that might not have focused on the abuse, these clients' defensive mechanisms were left intact and the clients remained well-defended from having to deal with being sexually abused. In therapy that focuses on the childhood sexual abuse, old fears and negative attitudes are triggered. These negative attitudes might include self statements such as "people will use me," "I'm bad," "I will be abandoned." In order to alleviate some of these anxiety-provoking thoughts, the therapist must discuss ground rules for the therapeutic work.

One essential ground rule sets parameters for physical intimacy during a counseling session. Two areas of particular concern are physical proximity and touching. Many victims of sexual abuse feel the need to have the therapist sit at a distance that does not invade their personal space and does not threaten them. Therefore, it is important for clients to know that at any time they can request that the therapist move in closer or move farther away. Some clients may even request that the therapist sit next to the door or even leave the door open if there is no one else in the waiting area. Touch should be limited to either holding a client's hand when requested or a pat on the back when a session has ended. These recommendations are based upon the fact that sexual feelings that surface as transference and countertransference can be especially powerful during therapy and the welfare of both the client and the therapist is of paramount concern. A good rule of thumb would be for therapists to ask themselves whether they would be comfortable if the therapy session was being viewed by colleagues through a one-way mirror. If the answer is yes, they are probably behaving in a facilitative manner with respect to physical intimacy. If the answer is no, the therapist needs to carefully examine his or her behaviors or consult with a colleague about any doubtful aspects.

Once the physical intimacy has been discussed, the therapist's personal attitudes about sexual abuse must be stated. Most victims of sexual abuse need to have this preliminary feedback that they are not bad because of being sexually abused, since they are used to judging themselves as either bad or dirty and determining that others have these same judgments. The survivor must be reassured that she will be believed and that sexual abuse is a serious issue having far-reaching implications.

It is important to convey to clients that their myriad of symptoms are not indications of mental illness or defectiveness but are a healthy response to an impossible situation. During therapy, these symptoms can be reframed as coping responses that helped them adjust to the numerous double binds that they encountered growing up. For example, an uncle who was abusing his young niece repeatedly told her that he was "making love" to her because he loved her so much and he was just showing her how much he cared about her. She was in the double bind of being hurt while she was being told that she was loved.

In addition, the therapist needs to convey that therapy will be a cooperative experience and that the client's input and responses will not only be respected but actively sought. Therapy revolves around the client's agenda, not the therapist's.

At the very beginning of therapy, the therapist needs to explain to the client the limits of confidentiality. Since many survivors have been betrayed frequently in their past, they must be reassured that, except for rare spelled-out instances, no one can have access to their records. Sometimes there are perceived or real threats from boyfriends, spouses, or family members who might demand information about what the survivor is saying in therapy. Instances when the confidentiality must be broken vary with state law; however, common instances across most, if not all states, are when a minor is being abused, when there is a court battle for child custody, when the client is a serious danger to herself or others, and possibly when therapy records are subpoenaed by a court of law.

Another source of concern about confidentiality could occur when the therapist is also doing therapy with friends of the client. Even though the temptation to discuss the survivor is present, especially when the friend asks seemingly innocent questions, utmost care must be taken to preserve confidentiality. While the therapist may not talk about information disclosed in a therapy session, the same laws and ethical codes do not govern the behaviors of clients. They are free to say whatever they want to whomever they want without worrying about confidentiality.

Parameters of the therapeutic relationship also need to be clearly specified early in therapy and discussed whenever problems arise. It is the therapist's responsibility to set appropriate therapeutic boundaries for the survivor. These boundaries are multifaceted and include issues such as: extended sessions; extra time outside of sessions; frequency of phone calls; the handling of self-mutilation or suicide threats; information provided to community agencies, especially when the client is court-referred or involved with state-funded health care; contact with a spouse or other family members; gifts; threats by the survivor or against the survivor; and so on. Each one of these issues needs to be treated on an individual basis, but both therapist and survivor need to agree on limits in these areas. Survivors of childhood sexual abuse often have boundary difficulties and tend to exhibit polarized behaviors—either they have very permeable boundaries, letting others in too close and too quick, or they have solid walls that keep everyone at arm's length, allowing them to withdraw if intimacy seems possible.

Once ground rules have been established, survivors need to feel safe and protected during their appointments. Sessions need to begin and end on time. If work is done that is emotionally exhausting or if there is any chance that the client will dissociate, then sufficient time at the end of the session has to be allowed for the client to wind down and regroup before leaving the office. Many therapists have group rooms or other offices that might allow additional time for the client to reassociate.

Self-Care. The second prong of Safety is to resolve any life-threatening situations and to focus on the present strengths of the survivor. Focusing attention on life-threatening conditions helps the survivor to marshall her resources for the journey through the abuse to recovery, and emphasizes present strengths that can shore up the ego for dealing with the fears and anxieties that are inevitably met when the memory work commences.

If compulsions or addictions are not dealt with in the beginning of therapy, they can cause the client to be in a constant state of crisis management. Compulsions or self-defeating behaviors that might be particularly resistant to therapy include anorexia, bulimia, and self-mutilation. Commonly recognized addictions such as alcohol and drug abuse, overeating, gambling, sexual acting out, excessive shopping, and so on can result in loss of jobs, loss of family and friends, and loss of self-esteem. Behavioral contracting for the cessation of these compulsive or addictive behaviors can begin to set limits on these dangerous actions and can demonstrate to the client that she does have some control over her life. Many times these behaviors are triggered by flashbacks of abuse experiences that seep into the consciousness. Working directly with these memory triggers can be very effective in therapy. In some cases, medication may be utilized as a short-term solution until the sources of the distress are revealed and worked through. Self-help groups might be recommended as adjuncts to therapy in the beginning and family therapy might be appropriate as the client makes progress in the individual therapy sessions.

Medical problems that can be an outgrowth of abuse may also need to be attended to in the Safety stage of therapy. Many women survivors have a host of physical ailments—headaches, TMJ syndrome, gastrointestinal disorders, pelvic and vaginal pain or disorders, back pain, heart palpitations, chronic infections, rectal pain, dizziness, and breast diseases. Referrals to the proper physician are extremely important. Since many women have had their bodies invaded against their will and trust for people in authority may be low, the therapist may have to take the initiative during a counseling session to arrange the medical appointment. If this occurs, the therapist needs to follow up with the client to find out whether she did go to the medical appointment. If she did not, this should be a topic of therapy as it is another form of resistance and demonstrates poor self-care behavior.

Once the urgent concerns have been addressed, the survivor needs to be oriented toward daily, healthy self-care. Survivors typically have neglected their physical health. Eating a healthy diet and being involved in physical exercise need to be particularly encouraged in this initial phase. Since the body is seen by many survivors as a source of shame or scorn, nutritional needs and body tone have been ignored as if the body needed to be subtly or overtly punished for its involvement in the sexual acts.

In a similar vein, insomnia and nightmares should be dealt with immediately to help reduce the intrusion of flashbacks or invasive information into valuable time needed for recuperating. Night hours are typically an extremely vulnerable time because the abuse often happened when the perpetrator entered the room of the sleeping child.

In addition, approaches to stress management need to be discussed with survivors. Stress management includes not only modifying the external stimuli, that are seen as stressors, but also adjusting the survivors' physiological and psychological reactions to these stimuli. Survivors are apt to suffer from anxiety symptoms and there is evidence to indicate that they lack the ability to modulate physiological arousal (van der Kolk,1987). In essence, survivors will many times respond to insignificant stimuli as if they are in emergency situations. Therefore, stress reduction strategies allow them to soothe themselves and not be in the grasp of uncontrollable neurobiological reactions. These stress reduction or management strategies might include systematic desensitization, self-hypnosis, muscle relaxation, breathing exercises, meditation, yoga, and exercise. Cognitive coping skills have also been shown to be helpful with anxiety responses. In addition, there are effective antidepressant medications that can be prescribed.

When addressed, these last two pegs of the Safety phase, effective self-care and stress management, create a milieu where the defenses that protected the knowledge of being sexually abused can be gradually unraveled. As the client improves self-care habits, she also needs to be aware of what kind of care she is taking regarding her interactions with her external world.

External world functioning. The third major thrust of the Safety phase is to engage the survivor in utilizing her outside environment and social relationships for the advancement of therapy. The home environment has to be made as safe as possible. This can even mean that an area in the home be designated as a retreat from family or friends. When a survivor goes to this part of the home, she is not to be disturbed. It is her personal "time out" place. If possible, a routine also needs to be established that sets a healthy balance between work and leisure activities. Fun activities are noticeably lacking in most survivors' lives. As noted in the discussion of the Safety phase, it is common for survivors of sexual abuse not to be actively involved in a regular exercise program or fun leisure activities. Feelings of depression that often accompany having been sexually abused can be lessened by active exercise. Also, it is common for individuals to feel better after participating in an enjoyable leisure activity that brings a smile to their face or involves them in pleasant company with others. Survivors too often isolate themselves and forget how to enjoy the simple pleasure of sharing fun activities with friends.

To foster better interpersonal intimate relationships, spouses should be engaged as early as possible in the therapeutic process. Not only do spouses frequently need to be taught how to be supportive, often marital strains caused by dysfunctional behavior patterns connected to the abuse need to be addressed. Sometimes it is helpful to include children in family counseling even if it is just to alert them that their mother was hurt as a child and in the future may be having difficulties as she struggles to understand what happened to her. Extended family members, if supportive, might be incorporated into the therapy. In general, however, it is not a good idea to include any perpetrators or family members who are critical of the victim and her allegations of childhood sexual abuse unless the survivor is psychologically strong enough.

Whether the survivor is still in a position of being sexually or emotionally abused needs to be explored. It is not rare that the original perpetrators still may have access either to the survivor or to her children. If possible, the survivor should be encouraged to take protective measures by making sure that visits with the perpetrator are supervised or by not contacting the perpetrator while therapy is in progress. In the present life of the survivor, new perpetrators of sexual or emotional abuse are often encountered. Explaining or confronting this dysfunctional relationship pattern may help to ensure the present safety of the survivor.

Establishing healthy self-care can be accomplished in a variety of ways. Yvonne Dolan (1991) provides a host of wonderful suggestions for orienting clients to their positive functioning in the present and to changes that will occur in the future. Questions such as, "What will be the first sign that things are getting better, that the abuse is having less of an impact on your life?", "What will you be doing differently when sexual abuse trauma is less of a current problem in your life?" and, "What will you be thinking about or doing instead of thinking about the past?" illustrate the emphasis on impending health rather than focusing so much on what is "broken" in a person's life.

Care needs to be taken to work toward normalizing any symptoms caused by sexual or physical abuse. Survivors have been floundering for many years trying to explain their phobias, depressions, and self-mutilating behavior. They have probably been diagnosed with a variety of illnesses ranging from manic-depression to borderline personality. Survivors have either not been involved in therapy or have experienced failed therapies. They have been told to pick themselves up by their bootstraps, to stop feeling sorry for themselves, to get on with their lives. They are ashamed of themselves, or think they are crazy, bad, or defective.

In this arena of survivor low self-esteem and confusion, the therapist has to point out that the symptoms described by the client are normal, protective reactions to intolerable situations like sexual abuse. Since survivors are understandably secretive about many of their symptoms, it is helpful to discuss the various symptoms of sexual abuse and the purposes they might serve. Even self-mutilation, such as cutting near the vagina, can be normalized by explaining that cutting oneself is understandable even though it must be stopped. For many survivors, this type of self-mutilation is one of the few ways of showing themselves that they exist, especially if they grew up in a violent family. It gives them a sense of control over their bodies, even if it is hurting them. The cutting can also be viewed as an attempt to cut out or damage the part of the body, the vagina, that seemed to be the focus of why they were abused in the first place. The tissue damage and the release of the blood cause the brain to release neurotransmitters that dull the perceptions of pain and have a psychologically calming effect on the survivor.

Deciding to establish good self-care behaviors is crucial for survivors. Too often they were raised in families that were too autocratic, and shared decisions were not allowed, or they were raised in families with such loose boundaries that healthy decision making was not modeled. Therefore, from the first session onward, the opinions of the survivor need be elicited. In addition, how the survivor feels about decisions that are being made is a targeted intervention.

Summary. Once survivors feel supported by the therapist, their social system, and their environment, and are able to ameliorate their symptomatic responses to the abuse, the next phase of memory retrieval is ready to begin. As pointed out previously, the stages of Safety, Exploration, Loss, and Fulfillment are not linear, but the elements that ensure the Safety of the client must be a primary consideration. When a therapist attempts to retrieve traumatic memories too early, they may unwittingly prompt returns to drinking or other dysfunctional behaviors, or they may scare clients into prematurely terminating therapy. A solid, relatively safe foundation in the present will reinforce the survivor when she has to begin to remove or restore the rotten beams supporting the past.

Exploration

Within the safety of the therapeutic environment and with resources readied, the survivor begins to encounter her traumatic narrative, her story of the events of her childhood. Initially, the narrative is remembered in a dissociated state. Emotions or affect is many times not available to the conscious mind and is not owned by the survivor. Numerous therapeutic techniques are available, however, to flush out the memories and allow them to be examined in the safety of the therapeutic relationship.

Childhood sexual trauma has been suppressed or repressed for many reasons. Since these reasons help protect the survivor from many hurtful emotional, psychological, and spiritual issues, the decision to enter them can be painful. They might include minimizing the effects of childhood sexual abuse, bonding to the perpetrator, fearing the family's reaction, splitting during the abuse, not revealing sexual abuse because of threatening childhood messages, fear from flashbacks or nightmares, and harmful cognitive messages. Each one of these issues has to be examined as the survivor delves into her own personal "It."

As memories are being explored, some survivors will minimize the effects of childhood sexual abuse. They or other family members will say something like, "it was no big deal because it happened such a long time ago," "I should be able to put this behind me," "I forgive the people who did this," or even "it was my fault it happened so why blame others." As these rationalizations are encountered, the survivor and therapist must discuss why, if these statements are truly believed, there are so many residual symptoms and so much fear, why they are being blocked from accomplishing either vocational or relationship goals, and what the cost to their lives is by having significant gaps in their childhood memory and experience.

Bonding to the perpetrator often presents significant tension and anxiety when trying to construct a narrative of the abuse. Presenting a paper at the 1991 annual meeting of the American Psychological Association, Dee Graham and Edna Rawlings concluded that bonding to one's tormentor may be a universal response to violence that cannot be avoided. They stated that four conditions lead to this bond:

1. The abuser threatens the person's survival;
2. The person cannot escape or thinks they cannot;
3. The person is isolated from others; and
4. The abuser demonstrates some kindness.

The events that followed the kidnapping of Patty Hearst provide an excellent example of the bond that can form between a victim and a perpetrator and how this bond influences the behavior of the victim. A relatively short time after her capture, Patty Hearst participated in her captors' cause. One of the most compelling photographs of the attachment was taken during a bank robbery with a gun toting Patty Hearst dressed like an urban guerilla. She had bonded with her captors. This type of bonding often occurs between individuals in a differential power relationship with the person in less power attaching to the person in power.

Van der Kolk (1987) explains attachments made by infants even though the target of the attachment may be hurtful to the infant. "An infant seeks increased attachment in the face of any external danger, including threats emanating from the attachment object itself. Thus attachments remain strong, even when the imprinted object no longer provides effective protection and nurturance" (p. 34).

The implications of this bonding are vast. As memories are retrieved and processed, the survivor can either deny that the perpetrator did such a thing or claim that they did it out of love. Both the survivor and the therapist must be aware that this bonding can impede therapeutic work or even cause retractions later on.

As memories are uncovered, survivors begin to panic over their families' reactions to their therapy and any revelations that are being shared. It is not uncommon for family members and spouses to inquire about what is being discussed in therapy. If the survivor shares any details with family members, often the claims are met with outright denial by the perpetrator or with threats if "this nonsense continues." Many times family members take sides regarding whom they believe, and it is the survivor who is most often attacked as crazy or bad for disrupting the family balance.

Often parents and siblings of a survivor will attempt to convince the therapist or survivor that it is either hormonal problems, depression, or personal unhappiness that have prompted her memories. Both therapist and survivor may be inundated with articles about false accusations, depression, and family photographs showing how happy the family is. In the meantime, the survivor may be told repeatedly in letters and phone conversations how the family would support her if she pursued a medical route for her "illness" rather than seeing a therapist.

As has been explained earlier, trauma usually occurs in a dissociated state. This process is called splitting. For many traumatized individuals, ego splitting occurs during the sexual or physical abuse. As the survivor reencounters their experience, the memory will seem vague or have an unreal quality. In the process of the splitting many of the body sensations appear to be outside of the body and even the visual and auditory elements are distorted. If the survivor can find these dissociated ego states and integrate them back into her body, the memories become more vivid and kinesthetic elements become more pronounced.

In this memory recovery phase, the threats made by the perpetrator are revivified. Survivors can become convinced that either they or other family members are in danger. Sometimes this is an accurate fear, since the perpetrator might still be violent. There have been instances, however, where this fear is very vivid to the survivor even after the perpetrator has died. There is an ever-present irrational element as childhood experiences and ego states are treated. The fear of the perpetrator has become a deeply ingrained component of their existence. Even though they may realize that it is irrational, particularly if the perpetrator can no longer touch them, it is real to them. As children they were told that the sexual abuse was their fault or no one will believe them if they try to tell. As adults, they still believe that it may have been their fault or that no one will believe they are telling the truth about what happened.

Flashbacks and nightmares increase during this memory recovery phase. These two mechanisms alert the survivor that traumatic material is stored, and it sometimes spills over when conscious control is reduced, such as during sleep or while driving. Both flashbacks and nightmares can be frightening, as the survivor experiences anxiety attack symptoms such as heart palpitations, tightness in the chest, and sweating. Many survivors are unprepared for these intense sensations, and time must be taken to explain them and to reduce their impact.

Cognitive distortions usually are formed as a way of coping with an abusive situation. These misinterpretations can disrupt the retrieval of the memory narrative and must be repeatedly challenged in therapy. Some of the most prevalent core assumptions and the accompanying distortions include:

1. I am responsible for my abuse because . . . I was too pretty. I was bad and needed to be punished. I enjoyed it. I didn't stop it. I was jealous of my father and mother's relationship.
2. Something terrible will happen if I get angry, sad, defiant or critical because . . . When I got angry, the abuse got worse. I was told this was a good experience and I should be happy. Tears make me feel too much of this. It is not right to be disrespectful to your parents.
3. I need to be perfect because . . . If I'm perfect the abuse will stop. If I can act perfect no one will know how bad I am. Someone will recognize or love me if I'm perfect.
4. I can't trust anyone because . . . I am always in abusive relationships. People are out to get something from me. If anyone gets close to me, they will discover how bad I am. Nobody ever believed me before, so why should I trust them. If anyone does get close, they'll leave.
5. I can't handle the memories because . . . I'm not strong enough. They will cause too much disruption in my life. I will make things up, so how can I ever believe my memories?
6. I need to take care of others and act like a saint because . . . If I'm nice to them then they will like me. They won't leave me if I take care of their needs.

These cognitive distortions can exist in polar opposite states. For example, a survivor will believe that all sex is bad and hurtful and withdraw from physical relations, or conversely, she will be promiscuous since all sex is good. Balance between these two attitudes is difficult to achieve.

As the above defenses are processed, the memory work unfolds. Just a few of the therapeutic techniques that can assist this process are hypnosis; visualizations; kinesthetic, visual and auditory cues to the experience; artwork, and journal-keeping. This unfolding can be slow, cyclical, and arduous. Some memories may never be accessible because of the severity of the violence and abuse connected with them, drugs taken, or the early age of the experience. Survivors need to understand that even though the lack of actual memories or slow pace of the therapy can be frustrating, significant progress can still be made on the defenses and symptoms that have bound them for years.

Loss

This third phase of the therapy is perhaps the most difficult since the defenses against the memories have been removed and the horror that had been half or fully hidden is now out in the light. Many survivors contemplate suicide in this phase. This is particularly disconcerting to therapists and survivors who may have envisioned the client making a quick ascent into health. It is the losses and the mourning of these losses that are crucial to the successful resolution of this phase, and this can be a very time-consuming process.

What has the survivor lost? One client summed it up by stating, "Growing up, I was like a fish trying to breathe in the neighborhood pond as they slowly drained it of water. I was always gulping for breath and trying to wiggle into any crevice that might have shielded a deeper pool. Yet, I didn't knowing when it would dry up, too. I was panicked, always anticipating the time when there would be no water left." This heart-tugging description reveals this woman's struggle just to continue existing as a child. It was not until she was "put in a deeper pool of water" as a result of working in therapy that she was able to mourn the loss of her childhood needs for love, safety, and acceptance that had never been met. She had lost her trust in others. She had lost her childhood. Her innocence had been shattered.

Soon after the remembering starts, grieving begins. The survivor usually is confronted with the loss of her defense mechanisms that have sustained her for so many years. Up until this time, she has been able to dissociate from the pain, repress it, or numb it with addictions, such as alcohol or drugs. These protective mechanisms have assisted her in the psychological numbing of the pain. Otherwise, an undirected roller coaster of emotions (hysterical symptoms) accompanies the numerous physical and psychological symptoms. With the reawakening of memories, the survivor is now faced with an overwhelming return of the emotional, psychological, and spiritual pain centered around the abuse. It is not uncommon for the survivor to urgently attempt to recapture the old coping strategies. She may deny once again the validity of her experience or reinstate whatever behaviors that worked previously, allowing her to forget. Such behaviors might have included staying overly busy, drinking, overeating, or seeking constant sexual gratification. As each relapse to past behavior is confronted, the survivor gradually begins to experience the sadness of what happened to her. More often than not, this sadness feels like a bottomless pit. One client described it as a black nothingness that filled her entire chest cavity. There was no bottom, no sides, no boundaries to this hole. It engulfed her.

Within the conceptual framework of this seemingly bottomless pit, sources of the pain and loss have to be faced and dealt with. One of the most difficult is acknowledging that the perpetrator betrayed their trust. Children have an infinite ability to blindly trust the adults they love. When they are abused by those whom they trust, this is a devastating betrayal. Survivors' reactions to this betrayal can range from prematurely saying that the perpetrator is forgiven, before the pain and anger have been worked through, to a desire to hurt the perpetrator as he hurt the survivor, to get revenge. This latter attitude can trap the survivor into a vicious cycle of hate that hinders rather than helps her recover. These two extremes can halt the progress of the therapy and must be carefully negotiated.

Forgiveness is the cornerstone of most religions and if the perpetrator is a family member, then forgiveness often is seen as a way to repair the family disruption caused by any allegations of abuse. Many survivors have been bombarded with comments like, "Why don't you just forgive him and get on with your life?" and "God would want you to forgive him." As explained previously, the survivor may still feel a strong bond to whomever hurt her and want the betrayal to go away in the ritual of forgiveness.

The danger of forgiveness is not that it eventually might happen, but that it comes prematurely. If the act of forgiveness comes before the perpetrator has admitted what he did and offered to make restitution, then it is probably a hollow gesture. One client was sexually abused repeatedly by her father, other family members, and a series of friends in her childhood. When the client alluded to the fact that her father had hurt her deeply, he responded with a letter and videotape. In the letter he asked her forgiveness for not being the best father he could have been and for not being emotionally available. He also apologized for any hurt he might have unintentionally caused her by his actions. The videotape was a religious broadcast preaching that forgiveness is an act of a good Christian. All the client wanted was for her father to admit what happened and to say that he was sorry and to feel that the grandchildren were safe from him. The letter from her father still preserved the secret and did not acknowledge his responsibility for his actions.

The second danger involves the wish to revenge the acts of sexual abuse or to seek compensation from the perpetrator. Some survivors have violent fantasies and dreams of torturing or hurting the perpetrator in ways similiar to those of their own abuse. While brief episodes of imagined violent revenge may help some clients to handle the overwhelming torrent of anger and hate that is released by the memories, prolonged revenge fantasies are non-productive and often hurtful to the survivor. These traumatized individuals run the risk of triggering a variety of symptomatic behaviors by their own violent fantasies. In addition, they need to be reminded that no act of violence can ever bring back their lost childhood innocence or dignify their experience. Only their passage into health can do that.

Survivors, like other types of victims, often want some compensation for their pain. Most perpetrators either do not feel contrition for what they did or never admit it openly. Survivors who demand an apology or money are often frustrated and angry, especially when met with denial or personal attacks. Even though restitution can be an important part of healing, when it is not forthcoming, continuing to demand restitution may be the "stuck" behavior pattern that prevents further healing. Also, the few people who do sue are frequently met with frustration as the court demands proof and rarely if ever is there objective proof of the sexual abuse.

This drive to demand compensation for the pain and lost years can spill over into the survivors' social and work settings. A small percentage of survivors demand from therapists or friends special favors because they have had to experience this type of pain. As the circle widens they may expect social security or welfare to support them for the ordeals of childhood. The therapist has to watch for the tendency of some clients to always remain victims as a result of their never-ending "poor me" attitude. Whenever possible the survivor and therapist have to break this chain and realize that the goal of therapy is to put the damage in the past and let the survivor now be responsible for creating her own intimacy and happiness. At the end of successful therapy, the significance of the perpetrator must be symbolically reduced to a grave headstone that reads, "here lies the effects of the abuse." The survivor is no longer hanging on to these effects and has permanently buried them so she can move on with living.

As the survivor recovers, relationships with friends and lovers may grow more distant. These relationships may have been based on old needs or dysfunctional behavior patterns. As memory work finishes, these connections may need to be severed. Losing part of one's support system is acutely painful, causing many survivors to regret that they ever began this journey because at this point they feel more alone than ever. They have to be constantly reminded that new, more healthy relationships are on the horizon and will come into their lives when they are ready.

Another painful loss is the potential loss of their nuclear family. If the perpetrator is an important family member and the survivor decides to confront him and other family members, the family members typically choose sides or totally reject the survivor. This abandonment can also trigger old defense behaviors. Regardless of the circumstances of the confrontation, most survivors will have to grieve the loss of certain friends and nuclear family members.

Uncovering and working through childhood sexual abuse can also threaten the survivor's marital relationship. For that reason, marriage therapy is vital in recovery since changes in the survivor can shake or weaken marital connections. For example, one client in this phase of therapy experienced overwhelming anger toward her husband. She remembered numerous snubs, insults, and rejecting behaviors from him that formerly had been excused as "no big deal." Her husband was amazed and confused by all the venom his wife was now expressing. In many ways, the survivor and her husband needed to recreate their marriage with new roles and parameters for acceptable behaviors toward each other.

If the survivor is a parent, she may realize how ill-equipped she has been to raise her own children. Some survivors have not protected their own children from potential abuse or have overcompensated by protecting them too much. Survivors have to work to correct their mistakes or forgive themselves for not being perfect. It helps to remind them that they did not have the resources or knowledge of appropriate parenting skills, or the role-modeling of a competent, caring parent.

Finally, the survivor needs to come to grips with the inevitable loss of her therapist. During the Safety and Exploration phases of therapy, the therapist has provided support, safety, parental role modeling (not just nurturing but also the parent who makes mistakes, etc.), stability and consistency in her life, as well as many other needed functions. In the Loss phase, the survivor has to let go of the therapist and to understand that the therapist's ultimate goal is to no longer be a part of her life. As each acquired role of the therapist is relinquished by the survivor, it may feel like a death or rekindle the abandonment issues. Successful passage of each issue further guides the survivor to assume her own support.

The losses of childhood must be mourned in order for the client to let go of them. The type of mourning that must take place was vividly described by one client. In her dreams she saw a frozen rose, beads, and a scapular, a long wide band of cloth with an opening for the head worn front and back over the shoulders as part of a monastic habit. When she drew these objects, she immediately associated them with childhood qualities that had been preserved rather than destroyed during the abuse. The rose represented her innocence, the beads her trust in others, and the scapular her spirituality. As she recovered each, she mourned the damage done to these elements of her being.

Often as a result of the therapeutic process, survivors find that they have to come to terms with their own relationship with God or whatever they identify with spiritually. Many survivors are extremely angry that their concept of God or spirituality would permit such havoc to be wreaked upon an innocent child. Others find that their relationship to God is strengthened as a result of their journey through their personal pain to recovery. A few survivors renounce their spirituality and refuse to believe in the sacredness of a world that would allow such misery and hurt.

In spite of having progressed through Safety, Exploration, and Loss, the seemingly bottomless pit caused by the abuse has not gone totally away. The survivor needs to enter the fourth phase, Fulfillment, which involves her in risk taking, adventure, fun, acceptance of failures, and personal empowerment. These help her move to a future that is a declaration of her individuality, creativity, and value as a person.

Fulfillment

For clients struggling to overcome the traumatic effects of childhood sexual abuse, the resolution is a long, sometimes dramatic battle fought with many minor skirmishes and major confrontations. It is not a battle that is bloodless. Recovery from sexual abuse is a painful process and the trauma of what happened has to be faced and accepted before healing can occur. Each survivor must find her own peace as she approaches the end of her therapeutic journey.

This last phase of therapy, Fulfillment, moves the survivor into a healthier future. As she moves forward, rebuilding her life, she has developed the basic emotional and psychological tools to navigate her life and to protect herself from similar abusive relationships. The survivor can be compared to the eagle on the back of the American dollar bill, which grasps an olive branch in one talon and arrows in the other.

The first aim of this Fulfillment phase is the reconnecting or integrating of the components of the survivor with her life. This occurs both internally and externally. The survivor now has to integrate and utilize her physical, emotional, psychological and spiritual dimensions to foster her own continued growth as an adult. She has to participate in the learning process of experiencing intimacy with others. Finally, she has to determine what her talents are and decide how her vocation will integrate these talents with her own life mission.

Physically, survivors are challenged to nurture the health of their bodies through proper diet, exercise, play, and relaxation. In addition, they must reclaim their own sensuality. For most of their lives, sex has had negative connotations. Since the pleasures of loving sex were not part of their experience, most survivors have neglected important aspects of their sensuality. Sensuality goes beyond the physical acts of sex. It includes aspects of physical appearance such as dress, hairstyle, and makeup—how the woman presents herself to the world. Some survivors may benefit from consulting a clothing specialist, getting their hair styled, or from taking classes that help them with their posture and movements. Examples of movement classes that our clients have taken include ballet, belly dancing, and modern dancing. The goal is for them to be comfortable with their feminine self and not to hide their unique beauty or to be ashamed of their bodies. They need to learn to take loving care of their physical selves.

Since fear of being hurt has predominated their lives, survivors must now learn to ensure their own safety and to confront their apprehensions. To do this, a self-defense course or an outward bound course might be appropriate. Some survivors have taken up sports as active as skydiving, scuba diving, or rollerblading, while others have chosen activities like swimming, bicycling, or tennis. It is important that they learn to approach their fears with a newfound confidence of risk-taking and a belief that they will be all right.

In addition to becoming more physically active and self-assured through these activities, many women benefit from rediscovering their bond with nature. For some this may mean gardening, planting flowers and vegetables, mowing the lawn, or pruning bushes. For others this might mean going for walks in the neighborhood parks, hiking in the woods, sitting outside listening to the wind in the trees or the birds singing, or even visiting zoos. They are re-experiencing their connection to nature and mother earth.

The emotional well-being of the client must bridge the gap between physical health and psychological health. The entire spectrum of human emotions is now available for the client to experience without fear of psychological numbing, or being so overwhelmed by feelings that she will be debilitated. In the Safety phase, happiness and joy seem to be as foreign to the survivor as feelings of anger and hate. Fear is the predominant feeling. As the client progresses through Exploration and Loss, sadness and grief join the repertoire of experienced emotions. In the Fulfillment phase, the survivor learns to access her emotions as signals regarding what she needs to do or not to do. No longer are emotions absent or a confusing overreaction. They are becoming normalized, modulated and directed.

With the sorting out of emotions, most survivors report that they now feel alive for the first time. They seem to see the world with what Abraham Maslow (1971) would call a freshness of experience. They re-experience the beauty around them with new appreciation at each viewing. They really see rather than just look at their world and others in it. People who wear glasses might understand what we are trying to say when they think about the differences in their vision when they get new glasses or even when they clean the daily dust and particles off the ones they are wearing. The new or clear vision might cause them to say, "Ah, there you are world. Aren't you colorful and beautiful!" We help clients in their struggle to develop a new vision of their world and to find beauty and hope in it.

In the psychological realm, thoughts or cognitions serve as guides for healthy decision making. Having experienced components of cognitive therapy throughout the therapeutic journey, the survivor has been prepared for recognizing distortions in her thinking patterns. In this last phase of therapy, special attention is given to correcting these distortions. Other cognitive interventions such as decision making, assertiveness training, and confrontational skill building reinforce the integration of the body messages, emotional signaling, and behavior. Whereas before dividedness and disharmony had ruled the client's existence, wholeness and harmony now take their place.

Spiritually, the survivor also comes to terms with what happened to her as a child. The client has either found her personal answer to her question, "Why me?" or she no longer needs to ask. A spiritual identity reshapes itself, and God or some Supreme Being becomes a spiritual foundation for her growth. It is also likely that the client's world becomes full of life-affirming activities, and spirituality is no longer an issue. In the Fulfillment phase, survivors may reconnect to their old religions, embrace new ones, or just attempt to better themselves and redefine themselves without a spiritual context. The choice is theirs.

Joining with others in caring and love is the second major aim of the Fulfillment phase. Prior relationships were based on old patterns either of defending against abuse or of accommodating the abuse. Now survivors begin to renegotiate old relationships and to develop new ones. Some survivors must circumnavigate the hazards as well as the excitement of starting to date again. For many, marital therapy as an ongoing process during therapy has reshaped this relationship. For others, sexual identities are in flux and alternative lifestyles might be tried. Whatever the path taken by the survivor, they often re-experience the social awkwardness of teenagers during this phase. Any skipped developmental stages are now re-encountered at this later age. A good sense of humor and ability to laugh at what is happening are invaluable as the survivor traverses the full range of emotions available in relationships.

One client who had been married to a physically abusive husband experienced persistent, severe headaches. She had despaired of ever finding a loving relationship and felt she would be a burden to any partner. Once the pain subsided through a new drug regimen, she cautiously started dating. After a couple of casual relationships, she became involved with someone 10 years younger than she was. As a survivor she had to take a risk and determine that this relationship was good for her in spite of any cultural norms against women dating younger men. She took the risk and found a loving, supportive relationship.

The last goal of the Fulfillment phase is for the client to discover what is fulfilling as a career and to develop her own unique talents in the pursuit of her life work. Up until now, survivors have often stunted their career aspirations because of lack of encouragement, opportunities, or feeling like failures. They have stayed in safe niches, have failed to advance, or have careened wildly through many jobs without any emotional attachment to their work. The survivor and therapist must explore career counseling themes and plan for the future. If money is a concern, then financial planning is also very important.

As the therapy draws to a close, both the client and the therapist need to acknowledge that periodic return appointments are acceptable for "tune-ups." Also, the client needs to understand that in future crises she could re-experience some of the same symptoms caused by the sexual abuse. This does not mean that she may be doing something wrong.

It is helpful toward the end of therapy to have a ritual ceremony that celebrates the journey and gives meaning to the words "sexual abuse survivor." There is a Navajo ceremony that one client used when she was ready to end therapy. She took an egg and cracked off one end. After removing the inside of the egg, she filled the shell with many bits of different colored paper which represented all her different talents that had not been used or were still being protected. She used papier-mâché to close the egg. During her last therapy session, she removed the papier-mâché end and recited a Navajo prayer, while the therapist sprinkled the colored bits of paper over her to remind her that she had regained all of her talents and abilities.

Another ceremony used by many clients is to symbolically remarry themselves. In preparation for taking a vow to love and care for themselves, they write marriage vows that elaborate on how they want to be united with their emotions, attitudes and rediscovered talents as they grow as individuals. As they complete the ceremony during therapy, they may choose to present themselves with a ring to symbolize that they are again whole.

Some women want something less complicated and choose to create a collage that pictorially expresses all they wanted to be from birth to adulthood. In the creating of this collage, they recapture every part of themselves. They can also put this collage in a place in their home that will remind them of the gains they have made and how rich their lives can be.

SUMMARY

When the client has worked through the four phases of therapy, Safety, Exploration, Loss, and Fulfillment, she no longer needs the therapist. She is ready to continue growing on her own. She has begun the process of integrating the four basic components of her humanness—physical, emotional, cognitive, and spiritual—into a healthier self. She needs to realize that this is a never-ending process, that she will continue to grow if she stays open to life while appropriately protecting herself from those who would abuse her. She has regained her SELF.

Chapter 8

Techniques for Helping Clients in the Recovery Process

There are many different interventions or techniques that can be used during the four phases of the SELF model. Although individual techniques are listed under each of the four phases of the SELF model, they may be appropriate for use in more than one phase. Some of these techniques need to be implemented during the therapeutic session, and others are suitable as homework for the client.

SAFETY

1. *Gifts for one's self.* At all phases of therapy, the client can plan for and give herself gifts for having survived the sexual trauma and having the courage to heal from it. The gifts can include music albums, small trips, flowers, long distance calls to a treasured friend, a new makeover or hairstyle, attending an interesting seminar or lecture, or going to the movies or the theater. The gifts should be presented to oneself formally with a card. This exercise furthers the learning of self-nurturing behaviors. The survivor is becoming her own best friend.

2. *Self-hypnosis.* Most trauma occurs in "bad" trances or altered states of consciousness where the person dissociates to escape overwhelming physical and emotional pain. Trance experiences do not need to be negative, and survivors can be taught how to control the trance state so that it is relaxing and helpful in countering the earlier negative experience. The following two trance inductions, both known as sensory induction, are easy to master and can be beneficial:

a. Induction 1: The person finds a safe place to sit or lie down. She then repeats to herself three different things that she can see and follows these statements with a fourth statement about relaxing into trance. For example, she might say, "I can see the picture on the wall. I can see the color of the paint. I can see the flowers in the picture. And these allow me to relax just a little bit more." The next step is to make three statements about three different sounds that she hears, such as the sound of traffic outside, music playing, the air conditioner blowing, or the tick-tock of a clock. These three statements about sound are followed by the same fourth statement. Next she makes three statements about things she feels followed by the fourth statement. Things felt might include the weight of her feet resting on the floor, the air in the room touching her skin, the texture of the cloth on her hands, or the pressure of her tongue on her palate. After three or four repetitions of these sets of statements, she can instruct herself to spend 10 minutes quietly relaxing in a mild trance. Gilligan described a similar pacing induction in 1982.

b. Induction 2: Relaxing each body part, the survivor can start at her toes and progress up her body, instructing each body part to relax. Some people find the contrast between tensing and relaxing each body part more helpful in that it helps them recognize the differences between holding tension in a muscle group and having that muscle group be relaxed. Many tapes and books describe this method of deep relaxation. After relaxing her body, the survivor can put herself into trance by counting slowly down from 20 to 1.

3. *Purposeful dreaming.* This technique allows the client to take control over her dreaming by doing it in a controlled, aware state. Clients who are fearful of memories can close their eyes and ask themselves to dream their fearful memories in symbolic form. By so doing, they will be protected from the fearful content resulting from understanding it consciously. This allows the dream to be dealt with in smaller, more manageable doses. In addition, for clients with nightmares, an instruction can be given to dream the nightmare while in the safety of the therapist's office. But, working with therapist, the nightmare is given a controlled ending that allows the client to come to a safe resolution of the traumatic material.

4. *Dialogue journal.* Unlike the typical journal, this is a journal in which the client makes her notes and then leaves space for the therapist to respond. In this dialogue journal, the therapist can influence the daily thoughts and feelings of the client. The client can mail her journal to the therapist daily and the therapist needs to respond in a timely fashion that promotes the

client's growth. Because of the daily mailing, a loose-leaf notebook is recommended so pages can be easily removed and inserted.

5. *Breathing meditation.* The client sits in a comfortable position on the floor or in a chair in an environment that has minimal distractions. Deep, diaphragmatic breathing is recommended. In doing this breathing, the client focuses or rests her hand on the area immediately above her navel. As she inhales, filling her lungs as full of air as possible, her diaphragm (the muscle separating the chest and abdominal cavity) expands and is pushed down causing the abdominal cavity to bulge out. As she exhales, the diaphragm will contract and naturally push the air up and out of the lungs. As this process of deep inhalation and exhalation continue, the client will enter a quiet meditative state.

6. *Signed Stones.* Many survivors need transitional objects during crisis times or during flashbacks. Stones that have been painted bright colors with the therapist's initials on them seem to be helpful. Clients can carry their stone in their pocket or purse and feel connected to the therapist without having to actually contact him or her. The stone is solid and reminds the client of the strength she is getting from therapy. One client even left a signed stone in her car since that was the place that seemed to trigger most of her body memories. Instead of signed stones, some clients prefer to carry a picture taken with their friends or loved ones to have handy in a crisis.

7. *With a little help from your friends.* The client needs to identify a close friend or a loving relative whom she trusts. Taking the point of view of this close friend or relative, the client writes to her inner children (the younger parts of herself) who were hurt or betrayed by the sexual abuse experience. These inner children write back. Perhaps for the first time, the client will be able to feel supported and understood by those who are important to her even though they were not directly involved in this exercise. Writing back while in the role of her inner children, she can share her experience with those whom she believes would have shown concern for her had they been aware that she was being abused. Before, she felt all alone. Dolan (1991) has also presented exercises where writing from the perspective of others has been helpful for survivors.

8. *Spirit guide.* Often a survivor feels safer if she has a sense that someone or something is protecting her as she is doing therapy and may want to visualize a spirit guide who is constantly available to her. This guide, which may be part of the client's unconscious, can help pace therapy by choosing which memories need to be processed. In our experience, this guide has shown up as religious figures like Moses, Jesus, or guardian angels, car-

toon characters such as Gumby or a clown, a Crone (a wise old woman in mythology), a close relative who is deceased, and even as a white devil. For some women, they appear as power animals who symbolically give their wisdom and strength to the person to whom they are connected. In a sense, the guide is the observing part of the ego which does not become emotionally involved in events. If the survivor is open to this type of visualization, therapeutic decisions can be assisted in numerous ways.

9. *Safe havens.* When flashbacks or anxiety threatens to become overwhelming, the survivor needs to have safe places in her home or at work where she can retreat either physically or mentally. In the home, a favorite chair and blanket might be part of this environment. Some women may find that hugging a stuffed animal, particularly during the evening or night hours, is helpful. At work, special pictures and keepsakes can be placed on her desk as a reminder that she will be OK, that she can handle the anxiety. An audiotape from the therapist or a friend with a soothing voice giving instructions on how to calm down can be very helpful in counteracting anxiety.

10. *Tape recorder self-help.* To facilitate the client's increasing sense of self-control, it is often helpful to have her make an audiotape with self-instructions for relaxing during times of high anxiety or panic. These instructions need to be recorded when she is feeling stronger and more in control. On the tape, the client can remind herself that although what she is experiencing is very difficult, she always survives it. Compassionate statements about her own courage for doing this and about the importance of the present pain should be part of the recording. Also, a list of alternative helping mechanisms, such as contacting supportive people, playing music, exercising, making self-statements, doing art projects, or writing to get the feelings out, should be part of the audiotape.

11. *The A-Team.* On television, no one can defeat the A-Team when they all work together to solve a problem. This same analogy can be used with survivors of childhood sexual abuse. Forming their own personal A-Team or support system of friends, children, husbands, or significant others to coach them when they are going through a difficult period can be very helpful. Sometimes these people can be brought together in therapy and be officially designated as the support team. The client's own A-Team has specific support tasks that are initiated when the survivor asks for help or lets them know in some way that she is hurting and needs their support.

12. *Mantra or litany.* To help the client cope with body memories or flashbacks, it may be helpful to have her repeat her name over and over as a way to ground herself. Some women have found it helpful to count num-

bers, to say their rosary, to repeat a mantra such as Om, or to hold onto any solid, stationary object that will help ground them. Even ripping up newspapers or molding clay can be useful. Anything that will ground the person and take them out of a trancelike flashback can be used.

13. *Relaxation.* Many relaxation methods need to be encouraged and taught. These might include progressive muscle relaxation, yoga, visualizations, self-hypnosis, autogenics, and meditation. For trauma victims, the nervous system has been so enervated that new modes of soothing oneself have to be developed.

14. *Time line and life chart.* Many survivors have blank periods in their childhood memories. Recollections, anxiety attacks, and flashbacks are often triggered by certain dates such as birthdays, holidays, or days that they were abused as children. Frequently overwhelmed by ambiguity and fear, survivors do not feel grounded and feel at the mercy of seemingly random events. Therefore, it is helpful to do a time chart on butcher paper with all available significant memories filled in, leaving room for any that might be recovered in the future. A special emphasis might be placed on positive experiences, deaths of people who cared about them, abuse dates, and so on. This time line can be filled in with different colored pencils to signify different types of events and can be ongoing in therapy as more issues are processed. As holidays approach or other significant dates occur, this chart can be invaluable in grounding the survivor in present day reality.

15. *Flashback Containment.* Flashbacks can be scary, particularly since they occur spontaneously. A number of approaches can be used to contain them:

a. Have the client visualize herself having the flashback. This visualization is projected onto a movie screen. The client has the power to change the screen until a soothing scene appears.

b. Have the client visualize the flashback and then use white-out to erase it. The client can also visualize the flashback appearing on a blackboard and use an eraser to get rid of it.

c. Self-control can also be established by having the client count down from 20 to 1 and tell herself to come out of the flashback trance.

EXPLORATION

1. *Inner circle of ego states.* Many survivors of sexual abuse experience different ego states that range in age from very young children through adolescents to adults. A circle of chairs should be imagined either internally in

a safe place or in the room where the client is actually sitting. Each ego state can be placed in one of the imagined chairs and then be allowed to communicate with the other ego states. The youngest ones who are not yet verbally articulate can either use art therapy or have one of the older ones communicate for them. For most survivors of childhood sexual abuse, there is not just one inner child but a subjective experiencing of many inner children and adults. Having them converse with each other prepares the survivor for reintegrating them into her personhood.

2. *Future healed self-helper.* The client imagines herself 2 years in the future, when she is healed. In this future state, she writes a letter to her present self giving herself advice to be used when she feels scared or doubts her healing process.

3. *Eye movement desensitization reprocessing.* Shapiro (1990) has discovered a method called eye movement desensitization reprocessing that utilizes saccadic eye movement (also known as rapid eye movement) to release anxiety and fear associated with a traumatic experience. The treatment proceeds by having the client re-experience one or more of the following: (a) an image of the memory, (b) the negative self-statement that is associated with the experience, or (c) the physical response of anxiety. When this experience is clearly formed for the client, she is led through rapid eye movements as a way to desensitize the trauma associated with the experience. It is strongly recommended by Shapiro that only therapists specifically trained in using this technique employ it.

4. *Shrink the perpetrator.* In most flashbacks and nightmares, the perpetrator is seen from a child's point of view. Craning their necks to look up at the grown-up, children see them as being huge, having huge hands and bodies, or being gigantic monsters. It can be highly effective to help the client visualize these adults as shrinking to a miniature size so that the fear is more manageable. This is much like the shrinking that takes place in *Alice's Adventures in Wonderland.*

5. *Sensory change in traumatic memory.* If the conscious memory of the childhood sexual abuse is too overwhelming, then the survivor can be told, "Make a small change in the events so that it somehow seems different to you, although you know what really happened. The changes can occur in objects in the environment or in the sound of voices, smells, tastes, and so on." For example, one client put the happy sound of a music box in the background of her traumatic experience so it would not seem so scary. Another client changed the color of her dress. A third made the threats uttered by her perpetrator sound like Elmer Fudd's voice. Making these changes transforms the stock, repetitive quality of the trauma experiences.

6. *VCR processing.* This is another exercise for which the survivor's ability to imagine is important. First, she needs to create a mental video recording of the traumatic memory. The video recording allows her to have control over the memory and to play it back to herself from a dissociated point of view. The therapist instructs the survivor to play the VCR memory in reverse in black and white. Other variations are also possible. For example, it can be played in fast forward or fast reverse so that only glimpses of what happened can be seen. The pause button can be pushed at any time if fear starts to overwhelm the client. The VCR can also be turned off. This VCR processing scrambles the original memory, so the fear response associated with this memory is lessened.

7. *Integrating Splits.* During traumatic events people will often dissociate, and part of their essence or experiencing of the trauma becomes disconnected from their body (see Chapter 6 for detailed discussion of this process). For instance, a client who was gang raped in a parking lot dissociated so that the physical pain rested on top of the car hood and the fear went under the cars. If the therapist can track the specific feelings, knowledge, behaviors, or sensations that have been dissociated, these dissociated parts can be retrieved and reintegrated into the body. Once this is accomplished, the client might feel relief for a variety of physical and psychological symptoms.

8. *Magic.* Flashbacks usually are fearful re-enactments of some portion of a traumatic incident. The client can gain a sense of control over these re-enactments by imagining that she is just part of a scary children's story and the villain can be destroyed through the use of magic. The therapist can walk the client through this process because she may initially feel hesitant about her ability to destroy the villain. Also, it may be helpful to act out the flashback with a therapist and have alternatives suggested for the end of the flashback. Both activities give the survivor a sense of control over the flashback.

9. *Containers.* Many traumatic memories are stored in specific areas such as in some type of container, in a drawer, or sometimes even in back of the head. If the location of and container for the memories can be found, with the help of the therapist, the client can exercise control over the memories. She has access to opening the container when she wants and can find a way to keep the memories from leaking out until she is ready to deal with them. In this way, some of the effects of body memories and flashbacks can be controlled and halted.

10. *Sculptured masks or figures.* Concretizing people who are feared, such as physically and sexually abusive perpetrators, can be an effective strategy

for overcoming the fear fostered by these individuals. A client may choose to make a symbolic representation of the perpetrator (a drawing, a clay figure, or a mask), which can be left in the therapist's office or with friends. These representations can be locked up or even buried. By concretizing the perpetrator, the client can have a sense of control over her reaction to the perpetrator and the influence the perpetrator has on her.

11. *Flashback intervention.* List the sequence of events in the flashback with all cognitive, emotional, and sensual components detailed. For example, one client would wake up from sleep feeling little, see a man in her bedroom, get nauseated, tremble, hear a screeching sound in her head, and then scream, "Don't kill me." Once the sequence of events was established, a specific three-step intervention can be used as part of the therapeutic process.

   a. The first step is to intervene at each event that is part of the sequence. For example, the client could be asked to concentrate on just slowing her breathing to control the trembling, saying self-statements for coping with nausea, shrinking the man in the room to a smaller size, or turning the screeching sound into a car putting on brakes.

   b. Next, have her interrupt the sequence by adding new steps. She might pick up a favorite stuffed animal after awakening or have a flashlight under the pillow that she turns on.

   c. After the flashback, explore the message of the flashback. Is it just an old message that unconscious material is leaking into the awakening life or is it a message that something in the present life is unsafe?

12. *Journal writing.* Journal writing, particularly when the client takes the perspective of herself as a younger person, can be especially powerful. For example, clients can keep daily journals from the perspective of an inner 5- or 8-year-old child. This is very healing since their seemingly bizarre reactions to things start to make sense. It is also effective to have survivors write journals from a healed perspective in the future but reacting to present events. A third idea is to have them react to the daily fluctuations in feelings from the perspective of the therapist. In this way reparenting can be done in a nonintrusive manner.

13. *Disconnecting.* This procedure was adapted from an approach discussed by Andreas and Andreas (1989). Most adult survivors of childhood sexual abuse are connected to their perpetrators as children. This connection has been labeled codependent. This bonding to the perpetrator can perpetuate or recreate the cycle of abuse. Since the connection for many survivors is concrete, literally or figuratively cutting this connection can have far-reaching effects. This can be done in many ways. Some examples are:

    a. The client should visualize the perpetrator in the room with her as a child at her most vulnerable age. The perpetrator should be placed right next to the child.

    b. Then the client should imagine herself as she is as an adult walking around the pair, noticing all connections. These connections might be physical, such as the child sitting on the perpetrator's lap. Other connections might be more metaphysical, such as a beam of light from the perpetrator's eyes into the child's heart.

    c. After recognizing all of the possible linkages, the adult needs to ask the child if she has any objections to breaking this bond and re-establishing it with her grown-up self.

    d. If there are no objections, then the adult survivor breaks each of the connections. This can be done gently such as removing the perpetrator's arm from around the child, lifting the child off the perpetrator's lap, or unlinking their fingers if they are holding hands. It can also be done more actively such as slicing through it with a laser or taking a pair of scissors and cutting through all of the connections. Applying this same concept to recovering from a broken relationship, other authors have suggested that this process is like unplugging or cutting all the wires from a switchboard.

    e. After the connections have been severed, the child must be reconnected to herself as an adult in exactly the same way. At this time it is very important that they (the client as a grown-up and as a child) be reassured that they will be taken care of and loved.

14. *Ideomotor signaling.* Many clients can access unconscious material through the use of ideomotor signals. These signals are spontaneous. Even though finger signaling is the most accessible and easiest ideomotor signal to use, other signals such as head nodding, sensations in parts of the body, and auditory commands can be used. To use finger signaling, have the client think of something that is a strong personal value. Tell her that when she is ready, an unconscious part of her will transfer this strong value into a movement. When the client is asked a question, one finger will move if she is in agreement with the question. This movement will signal a "yes" to the therapist. There will also be a "no" finger and a finger that will indicate that there is "too much fear." Check these finger signals with questions that would yield yes or no responses. Sometimes signals are delayed up to a couple of minutes before a response is made, so the therapist must be patient. Other times, the movement is so minimal that only the client can feel it. In these cases, asking them may be necessary, especially if they need to protect themselves initially because of fear of being controlled.

Trauma survivors seem to be especially adept at this signaling as it is a relatively safe way to begin to explore the events surrounding the trauma.

15. *Floor plan.* Drawing the floor plan of the house in which the client grew up has several useful purposes. Sometimes it can revive memories if the rooms are described in detail and can delineate who had access to certain rooms, which demonstrates the power structure of the family. This exercise can be connected to the present time by having the client draw the current floor plan of her own house. Discovering the similarities the survivor has recreated in her adult world can be a very therapeutic experience for her.

16. *Abreaction.* Many times clients need to relive the traumatic event. In order not to retraumatize the client, a process is needed that guarantees client safety, titrates the experience, and includes debriefing. A step-by-step plan might be:

    a. Plan the session a week or two in advance and ask the client to prepare for the abreaction by dreaming the content material in disguised form, or drawing or writing something symbolic about what happened to her. Then, she should allow herself slowly to start to feel some of the body reactions while they are in their safe haven (safe place in their home).

    b. The experience itself can be made safe in two different ways: either by doing the abreaction while the body is numb so that the feelings associated with the abuse are not felt (this is a partial abreaction), or by reliving small portions of the memory and skipping over the most traumatic part. [Hammond (1990) discusses alternative procedures for the abreactive experience.]

    c. Once the experience is abreacted, the client usually needs to take the child out of the abusive experience. This is done by having a trusted friend, the therapist, or the survivor herself pick up the little girl who was hurt and carry her to a safe place that was established specifically for this purpose.

    d. The client needs to imagine confronting the perpetrator. Many clients can do this effectively through the Gestalt empty chair technique.

    e. Finally, the client, with the help of the therapist, develops a plan to take care of herself after the session, and a winding down time is provided. This includes debriefing the experience with the therapist.

17. *Anchoring.* This neurolinguistic programming technique allows the therapist to track body memories or flashbacks back to the abuse that need to be worked through. In this process, the client tries to re-encounter her reactions by re-experiencing what she was seeing and hearing, as well as feeling her body sensations while in the flashback or body memory. The

therapist can anchor this experience by holding the client's wrist or touching the client's elbow when she signals that she has recreated the experience. The pairing of the touching of the anchor with the re-creation allows for the touch alone to trigger the re-experience. While being safely anchored with the therapist, the client can go further back in her memory until a situation presents itself in which she had an experience similar to the flashbacks or body memories.

18. *Move the body memory.* To break the pattern of body memories, it is effective to have the client attempt to relocate the painful feelings to a different part of her body. For example, many clients will feel the pain in their chest, stomach, or vagina. By moving the body memory to a big toe or thumb, the signaling mechanism is still present, but the sensation is less central to the person's function and less disorienting. If ideomotor signals have been accessed, the possibility of accomplishing this is greater because of the cooperation of the unconscious.

19. *Memory Segmenting.* The goal of this technique is to have the survivor gradually experience sensory segments of memories until she is ready to integrate and experience all components of a memory. For example, the process can be started by having the survivor view the memory with only the cognitive component and no other input. The therapist could also choose to have the client experience the memory from only an auditory or visual perspective. If ideomotor signaling has been established, it is helpful to view the memory from only an unconscious perspective with no conscious remembering at all. The client can go through the process many times at this level until the fear is reduced to manageable levels. Gradually adding all the sensual components allows for a stepwise integration of the experience.

20. *Sanctuary.* After each memory is processed, the abused child can be gently gathered up and taken to a safe place. For example, one client had an old Victorian home guarded by a chain link fence and two dogs patrolling the outside. As this client worked through the memories at each age period, her different little girls were transported to this sanctuary. Here they were safe from any further harm and were ready to be re-integrated with the adult woman.

21. *Metaphor construction.* Role-playing or enacting the abuse experience can be a powerful intervention. Metaphor construction involves having adult survivors develop their own story of healing by picking a time period, a childhood age, and cast of characters to represent how they were hurt, who hurt them, and how they reacted. For this activity to be most effective, it needs to be completely removed from the client's present life.

For example, one client picked a 13-year-old girl living in the Middle Ages. She depicted her rape by her brother as a scene from the Crusades during which soldiers were pillaging a village. The client acted out all the scenes and each character's behavior and reactions. She was then asked to act out what would happen to the village girl who was raped if she never recovered from the experience and what would happen to her if she recovered fully. This allows a distancing aspect to an otherwise overwhelming experience.

LOSS

1. *Obituary and funeral.* In southern Mexico there is an Indian tribe that stages a funeral for depressed tribal members so these members can realize the impact their depression has on themselves and other members of their tribe. The same type of intervention can be utilized with a client who is severely depressed or suicidal. By having her write her own obituary, she is jolted into realizing what she has accomplished and what she would still like to accomplish. This may be the first time that the impact of friends and family is actually considered by the client. A role-played funeral would have each person who is close to the client say what they thought about the death and what they wanted to remember about the person. This exercise can be very effective in breaking suicidal threats or thoughts.

2. *Family contacts.* Possible contacts with family members should be encouraged if these members can be supportive. If the family members have been perpetrators, the therapist and client have to carefully assess how the contact can be helpful or hurtful. With the permission of the client, eventually it can be helpful to include them as part of therapy. However, if the perpetrator is still harmful either verbally or physically or if the abuse is still happening, then protection of the client is the main concern.

3. *Body work.* Many times tension is held in the body and this is expressed as muscle soreness and back pain. Identifying the area of the body that holds tension and adjusting the posture can be very helpful. The therapist needs to refer the client to a specialist for this type of posture adjustment. Also, survivors usually breath shallowly, using only the very top of their lungs. Deep breathing can be especially useful in providing the body with more oxygen, which helps the body to function better. If the tension persists, what the soreness represents or what the body is trying to tell her through this pain can be very enlightening for the client. In this type of body work, the ideomotor signaling technique can be employed to help identify

sources of pain by asking the body to ache more as a "no" signal and less if the answer is "yes," or vice versa.

4. *Family mapping.* Charting the family structure can be important, especially when it includes all pertinent family members such as grandparents, parents, and siblings. Many family maps or charts are commercially available. Whether the map is commercial or homemade, it is helpful to have the survivor list on the map who is closest to whom and also indicate the family members she feels closest to and those from whom she feels most distant. An additional aid to help the client understand the family dynamics is for her to color code what the revelation of sexual abuse would do to the family map. How does this information change the family and the relationships among family members?

5. *Good-bad split.* Many survivors put their therapists on pedestals at first. During the process of therapy, however, when the therapist makes mistakes, does not understand exactly what they mean, or is not always accessible, tremendous anger is unleashed. It is helpful for the client to keep a chart with two columns headed "good therapist" and "bad therapist." Examples can be discussed briefly in session and the client is encouraged to add to the discussion about what might make her feel one way or the other about the therapist. During the time she is in therapy, she should record feelings and thoughts on this chart. This activity can avert needless stuck places in the personal relationship between the therapist and the client, because the client has learned that it is expected and all right if she gets angry with the therapist. Being frustrated or angry with the therapist does not change the work that needs to be done in therapy.

6. *Confrontation.* Confronting either the perpetrator or family members who are not supportive can be devastating. Therefore, preparation for doing this is essential. Scripts must be carefully prepared and role-played before attempts are made at confrontation. A number of different situations and potential responses or outcomes need to be practiced. The following scripts can help a client plan for the different scenarios that might be enacted during the confrontation:

a. Have the client write out the best possible scenario for the confrontation, one in which apologies are given to the survivor and family members or have the perpetrator ask what he or she can do to make up for what the survivor went through. The survivor should realize that this is the least likely scenario.

b. Have the client write out the worst possible confrontation scenario in which there is denial and condemnation of the survivor. The survivor should also consider possible rejection and being disowned from the family if it is incestual.

c. Explore with the client how she thinks the perpetrator or family will realistically respond. This allows for all possible alternatives to be discussed, planned for, and role-played.

d. Not only must the client plan for how those being confronted will react, she must be aware of her own reactions as a result of initiating and carrying out the confrontation. Reactions of the client to all possible responses of the perpetrator or family members need to be discussed and ways to cope with her resulting feelings need to be planned. Contingencies for healthy self-care need to be explored.

e. As a result of the confrontation, the family may or may not be a group with whom the client wants to be involved. Therefore, she needs to plan for a range of possible options from reentry into the family after secrets have been revealed to planning for a support group of friends if there is no reconciliation with the perpetrator or family.

7. *Family locator.* Utilizing marbles, rocks, colored paper, and various small objects, the client lays out on the floor her extended family in relation to one another according to who is the closest and farthest away emotionally. If a secret or barrier separates anyone, the client draws it and places it in the scheme. This illustration can be used to have the client explore her feelings toward family members by having her move her representation of herself closer to or farther away from other family members and discuss how this feels to her.

8. *A perpetrator's letter.* Clients typically want the family to be healed and to forgive the perpetrator. This can be accomplished symbolically even if it never occurs in reality. The client can write a letter to herself from the perpetrator and other family members who have had extensive therapy. In this letter, each person admits what they did and says that they are sorry. An alternative is to have the perpetrator or others in the letter respond to the client from a healed spiritual position.

9. *Polarities chart.* Most clients act out polar opposite behaviors in their daily lives. To help them understand this, they can chart where they fall in their daily interactions by putting a check on where they are on the polarity continuum. A typical chart of polar opposite behaviors might include these elements:

Smiling excessively/ingratiating ....Frowning/unpleasant
Trusting/naive ....Distrustful/distant
Inhibited ....Uninhibited

Physically unappealing ....Promiscuous/seductive
Poor hygiene/overweight ....Good hygiene/average
Isolated...Overly social
Victimized/controlled...............................Dominating/controlling
Inferior to others/bad ....Superior/righteous
Hysterical...Numb to feelings
Compulsive/addictive ....Restrictive

FULFILLMENT

1. *Forced Bed Rest.* The client has to stay in bed for a week with no distractions such as reading materials, television, radios, art, or writing. (This
time period can be adjusted for work demands or needs of children.) The
three daily meals are consumed in bed, and the person is allowed to get
out of bed only for personal hygiene reasons. Initially, the survivor experiences increased drowsiness, which is followed by mounting agitation as
many thoughts, emotions, and anxieties surface into awareness. By the
fifth day, there is usually a tremendous sense of boredom. Clients who follow this regimen learn that feelings and thoughts are transitory and that
after the boredom they truly want to accomplish something. They want to
be more actively involved with life.

2. *Crystal Ball Intervention.* This intervention has been described by Erickson (1954) and was further developed by de Shazer (1985). In this intervention, the client sits with her palms up resting comfortably on her knees.
She is told to begin imagining how she would like to live her life in 2
years, after the sexual abuse work is finished. Once an image has emerged,
place it in an imagined crystal ball held in her right palm. Then the therapist helps the client recall any experience, whether positive, negative, or
neutral, which will serve as a springboard to accomplishing her future life
goal that is captured in the crystal ball held in her right palm. Have the
client recall an experience that occurred between her birth and her fifth
birthday—whatever comes to mind first should be utilized. Once it is
seen, have her place it in a crystal ball held in her left palm. Each succeeding image will be in 5-year increments until her present age is reached.
Each succeeding image will be placed in an ascending arc of crystal balls
until the image for her present age is in a ball being imaged in front of her
forehead. Then the arc will descend as the person takes 6-month increments. In each increment she is to imagine a new experience that she
would like to have that would lead to her goal. Once all of the crystal balls

form a rainbow leading from the left palm (distant past) to the right palm (envisioned future), the client can now visually link them and let them vibrate. This exercise has been used effectively by Milton Erickson, the noted hypnotherapist. It allows clients to have a thread of success connecting their past, no matter how traumatic, with their future. It provides them with hope. The vibration adds movement into their experience, which enhances the experience by adding another sensory dimension.

3. *Body chart.* Have the client outline her body on a large piece of paper, such as butcher paper. This outline should be life-size. With magic markers have her put in all the significant people in her life and draw lines connecting these people to the parts of her body that seem appropriate. Next, have her list her strengths and weaknesses and connect these to her body. Last, have her list how she has been hurt in her life and connect these feelings to parts of her body. The finished product should be a visual depiction of the association between her body and the psychosocial elements in her life—her emotions, friends and family, and psychology. This exercise is important because most survivors have dissociated from their bodies and this helps them with reconnection and integration—becoming whole again.

4. *Directed tasks.* This technique is based on ambiguous function assignment (Lankton & Lankton, 1986). A directed task allows the client to bring her resources and strengths into conscious functioning without the therapist needing to control the learning. These tasks are most helpful when the client is stuck. The steps to bringing the tasks into consciousness so they can be utilized are:

a. The therapist tells the client that there is something valuable that she needs to learn about her experience and this needs to be discussed in therapy after she has completed this task.

b. The client then is given an activity to accomplish which has a specific time, place, and physical object involved. Movement is also an important part of the task.

c. The client is directed to write or think about how the completion of the task is related to how she was stuck and the solution she needs to progress in therapy. These three steps are like a Rorschach ink blot test applied to a client's creative solutions for herself. For example, one survivor was asked to go to the desert botanical garden at sunset and to walk around. She was also directed to stop three times at exact 10-minute intervals and to discover what the particular plants in each setting could tell her about her recovery process. She was instructed to write down her immediate thoughts and later to supplement these with more information the next day at exactly the same time. What she wrote involved how each plant had a defense system and how there was appropriate spacing between the plants, which allowed them to grow where water was sparse. For this client, the plants and their environment provided her with messages about proper boundaries needed for growth. Precise directions are like doctor's prescriptions; they provide a concrete framework for the client and help to direct the thought processes about the experience.

5. *Forgiving oneself.* Since survivors often feel that they were somehow responsible for what happened to them, it might be helpful for them to experience self-forgiveness. To do this, they need to find a picture of themselves when they were the approximate age that the abuse began. They are then encouraged to watch children from this age group at a local playground, a softball game, an arcade, or any place where children are playing, and to imagine themselves as one of these children. They should be directed to look for the vulnerability of these children, how the world is simple to them, and how they rely on the adults who are with them. Many times survivors need to see and re-experience vicariously the child that they were in order to let go of the guilt associated with being sexually abused. In this activity, they come to accept that they were innocent children and vulnerable to the behaviors of the adults in their lives. By accepting this, they are able to stop judging themselves for what happened and to start placing the responsibility where it belongs—on the adult perpetrator.

6. *Nature trust.* Clients can be told to plan walks or hikes into nature with the specific goal of learning from animals and plants something important for their recovery. This part of the reconnecting process allows the survivor to identify with the outer world. Some suggestions might include:

   a. Going to a botanical garden and picking out the plant most like them and the one they would like to be.

   b. Carefully watching for any animal that they see on their hike and sensing what they need to learn from that animal about protection.

   c. Stopping three times along their hike to write about the interconnections of the land, plants, and animals. They should include themselves in the writing.

   d. Taking a friend on the walk or hike and allowing the friend to blindfold the client and guide the client as they walk along together. This trust walk allows the survivor to experience letting go of unnecessary control.

7. *Photography flashforward.* As the client becomes healthier, it is often helpful to teach her how to have "flashforwards" by creating how she would like to be in the future. For example, the client can be asked to

describe the way she would like to be in the future. After describing how she wants to be, it is often helpful for the client to create a photographic image of this person. There are several ways to accomplish this. Many amusement parks allow people to dress up in ways that represent different time periods. Or, she can take a friend to various clothing stores and coordinate different outfits with styles that symbolize a "new" person. This exercise is called a flashforward because it builds up images of future possibilities.

8. *Counter clicker.* Since survivors are usually hypersensitive to what is dangerous in their environment and are highly critical of themselves, a number counter can be a useful adjunct to therapy. Have the client count the number of times in a day that she has a positive interaction with friends, colleagues, or themselves. A goal is to have the client recognize the positive component of her day instead of always focusing on the negative.

9. *Celebrating life.* To help the client feel alive and growing, it is often effective to have her plant a tree or flowers in her yard to symbolize the part of her that could never be destroyed and is now beginning to grow. Alternatively, she could purchase a house plant that is sickly or shedding leaves and nurse it back to health. Rescuing a dog from the pound that may be too old to be adopted or not wanted for other reasons can be a powerful message for survivors about nursing the neglected parts of themselves.

10. *Paramedic.* In many ways, the client has to learn to be her own caretaker both literally and figuratively. This can be accomplished symbolically by involving the client in the Paramedic technique. First, the survivor identifies all the psychological and emotional wounds on their body and then applies dressings, splints, or bandages to each one. It is important that the client discuss what she needs to heal each wound and how long it will take. This dramatic role play concretely emphasizes that areas of the body have been wounded and develops the survivor's resources to heal.

11. *Pretending.* The goal is to have the client imagine and act out what she will be like when she has healed from being sexually abused. First, she needs to describe in detail how she will be acting, feeling, looking, and reacting when she is healed. After having a clear image of how she will be, she is to pretend to be healed during the upcoming week so that she can practice what it will be like when she heals. The very act of pretending changes her behavior and others' people's reactions to her. This can be very rewarding and self-sustaining.

12. *Cleansing through rituals.* The use of rituals was discussed by Gilligan in a workshop conducted in 1989. Rituals are a way of formalizing an event

or experience. Rituals borrowed from various religions and cultures can be adapted for use with survivors of childhood sexual abuse. For example, being symbolically baptized can help them feel cleansed of the dirt and badness associated with being abused. Borrowing from the Mormon religion, they can develop their own patriarchal blessing and have this blessing conferred on them by a respected elder member of the community. From the Jewish religion, they can go through a Bat Mitzvah to celebrate their passage into womanhood if they shied away from being a sexual being. There are also various Native American ceremonies that are cleansing and can be adapted to serve as cleansing rituals.

The principal components of a ritual are preparation, enactment of the ritual, and integration of the ritual into the person's emotional, psychological, and spiritual self. The resulting change for being involved in the ritual can be externally recognized by some cultural group (such as with a Bas Mitzvah) or internally by the self (personal evolution). Constructing a ritual for survivors typically follows these steps (in parentheses is a step-by-step illustration of how a ritual was used with one sexual abuse survivor):

a. Initially, the behavior or attitude that needs to be changed is identified. (For example, Susan was ready to give up an identity developed as a result of her mother's constant harangue that she could never get anything right, that she was retarded.)

b. All components of the old self are enumerated and described in detail. (Susan talked and wrote about all of the behaviors that enacted her mother's message. These included clumsy acts, failing courses, forgetting appointments, and misplacing or losing valuable papers and keepsakes.)

c. A symbolic object is chosen to represent the old identity. (Susan chose a troll doll to represent her lifetime of feeling stupid and silly.)

d. The desired new behavior or attitude is described in detail. (Susan described a new self where she accomplished her intellectual pursuits and completed her baccalaureate degree.)

e. A symbol is chosen to represent the new self or new behavior. (For Susan, the traditional graduation cap and gown represented the desired accomplishment and the feeling of being competent and bright.)

f. A ritual act is decided on, which mirrors the changes that need to take place to let go of the old and replace it with the new. (Susan designed a multiple-stage ceremony to rid herself of the troll image and to take on the image of a bright, competent undergraduate.)

g. The survivor prepares for the ritual by some form of cleansing or meditation. (Susan wrote about all the behaviors that carried her mother's messages into her present life and then listed all the things she wanted to believe about herself in the future. She then meditated on this list of future beliefs.)

h. The ritual act itself is acted out with detailed, specific instructions. (Susan wrote and meditated for 6 days and on the evening of the seventh day, she gathered her family together in the living room of her home. She let go of the old messages by burning them in the presence of her family. She then went out into her backyard, buried the troll, and planted an acorn where the troll was buried. For Susan, the acorn symbolized new strength and majesty growing out of the remains of the old messages. Susan then adorned herself in the graduation cap and gown and had a graduation party with her family. Traditional graduation music, Pomp and Circumstance, was played in the background.)

i. The client is given a time span and an activity to integrate the new into her life. (For the next month, Susan was to consider how a person with a B.A. degree would handle questions and decisions that needed to be addressed on a daily basis. In addition, Susan enrolled in a community college to make her new behaviors more concrete and real.)

13. *Community service.* For clients who want to take care of others, it can be a valuable experience to become an anonymous donor to a shelter for abused women, work for a crisis nursery, or volunteer to work on a hotline for abused women.

14. *Montage.* Most survivors of childhood sexual abuse rarely received role-modeling of effective and appropriate parenting. These women might want to clip pictures of good parent-child interactions out of magazines or photograph parents playing with their children. It might also be helpful for them to interview the parents on their parenting style and connection to their child.

15. *Candid camera.* To help clients realize that they control their behavior, it is helpful to have them carry the best/favorite and worst/least flattering pictures of themselves. At the end of the day, they record in their journal what they did that day to ensure that they were like the person in either picture. For survivors who feel helpless, this is a concrete exercise in taking control of behaviors that make them feel good (like the person in their favorite picture) or bad (like the person in their least favorite picture).

SUMMARY

Although some of these techniques seem simple and easy to use, the therapist must be constantly aware of the complexity of the recovery process. The reactions of clients to these interventions can be variable, and the therapist needs to be sensitive to individual differences and to when the client is experiencing distress. Pacing is very important, since some clients have few internal resources for dealing with their pain. These clients may need to proceed more slowly as their resources are being built and fortified.

Beginning therapists need to seek the supervision of experienced therapists when working with clients who have been sexually abused as children. These clients, like all clients, deserve the most skilled care possible and should not be learning experiences for therapists. Not only must therapists be very knowledgeable about childhood sexual abuse, they must watch carefully for transference issues, which will arise more frequently in this work and be more difficult to recognize and manage.

The techniques presented in this chapter are only offered as adjuncts to therapy. The heart of the therapeutic process will always be the relationship of the therapist to the client and the therapist's conceptual framework for moving the client through the healing process.

Chapter 9

The Process of Recovery: The Case of Lori

"I dreamed that I was with a man, and I was very happy with him. Then my father came and said, 'OK, let's go to bed.' And it seemed perfectly natural. I realized . . . that I was dreaming of my father and I was a little girl."

This dream was a catalyst for Lori, a 57-year-old woman, to consider the possibility that she had been sexually abused by her father. Although Lori was aware of having been sexually molested by a baby-sitter, she was shocked by the dream revealing an incestuous relationship with her father. She had had other dreams that might have cued her memory, but she had not been able to recognize their meanings of incest. Only with this dream was Lori able to receive the message consciously.

Lori spent 1½ years in therapy focusing on her childhood sexual abuse. As a result of her own healing, Lori wanted to share her struggle with others who have been sexually abused by someone they trusted to protect and to take care of them. Like so many who struggle with the issue of having been sexually abused, Lori found the process of therapy to be both emotionally painful and spiritually freeing. Perhaps the opening words of Dickens' (1859/1981) *Tale of Two Cities* best describes how survivors feel about their therapeutic journey—"It was the best of times, it was the worst of times . . ." During her therapeutic work, Lori experienced brief moments of joy as she slowly healed from the horrible abuse she suffered. Yet, as is so vividly described in *IT*, in order to heal, she had to enter the darkness of the childhood experience and re-encounter the trauma in order to begin the healing process.

In order to understand Lori's journey, we will provide some background information about her. At the time she entered therapy, she was divorced and had been married twice. She married for the first time when she was 21, and that marriage lasted 3 months. Her second marriage, which lasted 8 years, ended when she was

33 and produced a daughter who is now an adult. Presently Lori is a teacher and an artist pursuing a master's degree in art therapy.

During her preschool years, Lori lived in a home where her mother was seldom present. Lori's mother was frequently ill and had to be hospitalized for a series of ailments; therefore, it seems unlikely that Lori's mother was aware of her young daughter being abused.

Lori's first memory of abuse was of being molested by a baby-sitter giving her a bath when she was only 2 years old. The incest with her father transpired when Lori was between the ages of 3 and 5 years old. Not only did her father sexually abuse Lori, he also allowed his brother and friends to have sexual relations with her. Like most children, to cope with this abuse, Lori was able to dissociate during the abuse and later to repress or "forget" what had been done to her.

As an adult, Lori experienced a myriad of physical problems—cancer of the cervix, chronic fatigue, blood poisoning, severe allergies, and hives. In addition to seeking medical treatment, Lori began to realize that these illnesses might also have an emotional component, particularly since she never felt any real happiness in her life. Lori sought the help of a variety of counselors, psychologists, and psychiatrists, but, after spending 7 years in psychoanalysis, 1 year doing stress relaxation training, 3 months in Gestalt therapy, and 1 year of what she characterized as visualization therapy, Lori still did not feel at peace with herself. She described all of these therapies as "not working." In spite of trying to heal herself by seeking professional psychological help, Lori was still troubled—she still had not discovered "what was wrong." In 9 years of therapy, no therapist had asked her about the possibility of her being sexually abused. Like an undetected infection, it was still eating at her and she couldn't get well. Only the symptoms, not the cause of the problem, had been treated. The underlying infection was still there.

In order to help understand the impact of the sexual abuse on Lori, it will be necessary to share her innermost thoughts and feelings as they arose in therapy and during in-depth interviews following termination of the therapeutic relationship. In these interviews, Lori reflected on her discovery of being sexually abused and how it influenced her life. Quotations from the interviews are presented to illustrate her journey. For Lori, sharing her experience and pain is a way to help others who might have been molested as children.

In the first interview, Lori described how she met the therapist and decided that the exploration and resolution of possible sexual abuse needed to be the goal of her therapy. From this starting point, Lori painted a picture of the startling effects that the sexual abuse had had on her physical functioning, her emotional well-being, her interpersonal relationships, her cognitive functioning, and her spirituality. Within the safety of the therapeutic relationship, Lori plunged into the unknown terrain of her childhood as she attempted to remember and process what had happened to her.

As the sexual abuse was gradually uncovered, Lori recounted the pain of regressing to the time of the abuse and how she had to slowly let go of the defenses that her inner self had created. With the peeling back of these layers of protection, Lori finally was able to begin to function normally without the severe effects of the abuse intruding on her life.

EXPOSING THE TRAUMA

Lori met the therapist during a workshop designed to teach school personnel how to run support groups for high school students having trouble with either drugs or alcohol or living in a family where such problems existed. Lori was a member of a small experiential group led by the therapist. During one of the group exercises dealing with intimacy, Lori had a violent reaction in which she had to struggle to breathe and thought she was going to die.

In the following excerpt from the interviews, Lori discussed what was happening in the group, how she responded, and how the therapist interacted with her while she was in crisis.

As part of the intimacy exercise, group members gave each other feedback on how they were perceiving each other. Lori recounted vividly her response to the positive feedback she was given about her nurturing personality. *I guess I felt enough trust with the group and with you to open up and go underneath. I was able to respond to the group, and I said, "That's very nice that you see that caring, social part of me. But that's not the only part. There's a part of me that you don't know, a part that would isolate myself in the middle of a desert on a rock next to a rattlesnake."*

And you [the therapist] *said, "Do you want to explore that a little bit? When does this feeling hit you?"*

And I said, "When I'm getting close to someone."

And you said, "Imagine that you're close to someone in this group, what would happen?"

And I said, "Well, we could share poetry." As I began to describe to you the things that I could do intimately with George [a member of the group], *I began to get violently ill. I mean, like I had never been ill.*

It was so overwhelming that I blocked a lot of it and I can't remember it. But I didn't really know what I was feeling. It was so intense. There were colors associated with it, and I couldn't breathe. I thought I was going to die. But that thought didn't even come at first. I remember saying over and over and over, "I wish someone would tell me what I am feeling, what this is. What am I feeling? What is this?" And finally, I said, "I think I'm dying." And just saying those words started the feeling in my stomach. My arms and legs went numb. They literally went numb. I've never been so nauseated in my life, and it felt like I was dying. It really . . . it felt like I was. And it felt like I needed to stop. Because if I didn't stop, I would have died. I felt like I would pass out and begin to throw up and it would have gotten worse. So, I started pulling out of it. Because I thought I was going to die.

What Lori described is what is known as a body memory. When a person experiences a traumatic event, the memory of that event is stored both physically and emotionally in the body. Any association to the original trauma can trigger the memory emerging either as a bodily reaction (body memory) or an emotional reaction. For example, if the abuser wore a certain cologne, years later the smell of that cologne could trigger the same fear that was originally felt during the actual abuse. For Lori, the developing intimacy in the group probably activated the body memory of the inappropriate intimacy between her and her father during the incest.

Lori's body memory not only caused a violent reaction during the group session, its effects continued to intrude on her life for the next 3 days. Experiencing the body memory, Lori literally regressed to being a 3-year-old girl. Lori described the profound repercussions of this regression and its effects on her relationships and job functioning.

I wasn't entirely sure what was going on. And someone said, "Well, you might have had a spontaneous regression." We were supposed to eat lunch right after that session. I went out, but I couldn't eat. I was in a great deal of pain that lasted over an hour. Then, for 3 days I was literally in the mind of a 3-year-old. And I knew it. The first thing that happened after the session was when I came home and my boyfriend tried to touch me. I wouldn't let him. He tried to touch me and my immediate insight was he wants something from me. He doesn't want to give me anything, he wants to take something from me. He needs something from me. . . . And, uh, anyway I was literally 3-years-old for 3 days. I was talking like a little girl and I ran away at one point and picked a rose. When I came back, I was supposed to be cooking breakfast for my father and my daughter and they said, "Where have you been?" And I said, "I picked a rose." They said, "Weren't you cooking breakfast?" And I said, "You hurt my feelings."

Well, that lasted for 3 days. When I went to school to teach, here was a 3-year-old teaching 12-year-olds, and it didn't work. They were going to devour me and I had, I had to reach down inside of me and force myself back. It took all day, it took 8 hours to get back into me.

Having experienced these profound reactions, Lori knew that something powerful was beginning to happen to her. Something in her past was being forced into her consciousness. Like a tangled mass of thread, something in her was starting to unravel. She knew she needed help to deal with what was happening and what might happen if memories continued to surface spontaneously. For Lori, the best place to get this type of help was in the safety of a therapeutic counseling environment.

THE THERAPEUTIC ENVIRONMENT

When choosing to enter therapy, the first question clients need to ask themselves is whether they would work best with a male or a female therapist. This decision is crucial to the therapeutic process as gender issues often arise for clients who have been sexually abused. In addition to deciding on the gender of the therapist, clients need to evaluate the therapist's professional qualifications and whether there seems to be a good interpersonal match since the therapy process is often long and arduous. Some of the early therapeutic issues that arise are control and trust, while later therapeutic issues might include fear of abandonment and shame. In any effective therapeutic relationship, both the therapist and client work together collaboratively for the client's growth and healing.

For Lori, gender of the therapist was not a significant issue, although she recognized that for many women, it may be very important. What was most important to Lori, because she had an extensive history of therapy that had not been helpful, was that the therapist have expertise in working successfully with sexually abused clients and experience using techniques that would help her accept what had happened to her.

In discussing gender issues, she stated, *I think it depends on the abuse. For instance, if you were raped, I think you might have some difficulty with a man. You'd have to overcome, first, all of your fear, anger, and a whole lot of issues. In my situation, I don't think it made that much difference. I really don't. I really don't think it mattered whether it was a man or a woman. I think what mattered was what worked.*

You didn't allow any kind of rationalization to go on at all past the first utterances. You cut right through that and probed in a very creative way with images to get at what was underneath it. And you wouldn't let me off the hook. You worked me very hard, and you went for the deepest feeling. I was determined to find out something new and I was determined to work when I came in.

I said, "This is not going to be wasted. This is not going to be an exercise. This is not something I'm going to learn for school. This is something for me."

As the therapeutic contract for working together is established and goals are agreed upon, the client and therapist must understand that when a client is a victim of incest, her trust in others has been severely damaged. When the client does not trust the therapist, she will try to control what happens in therapy. This need to control evolves from fear of the unknown that eventually must be explored in order for healing to occur. Trying to take control can be manifested in the emotional depth of information presented, in what issues are introduced for discussion, and in the degree of therapeutic intimacy or support allowed. Often the client is unaware that her behaviors are designed to take control of the counseling sessions.

The struggle for control may last throughout therapy as issues are worked through and resolved and as new issues are introduced. The therapy process is similar to climbing a spiral staircase with each new step taking the client into unfamiliar territory while still dealing with the sexual abuse.

From the beginning, Lori attempted to inundate the therapist with artwork, poems, dreams, and stories about her dissociation. If she could get the discussion focused on these, then she had control.

In reflecting on this, Lori remembered, *The issue of control came up, and you said, "You come in, and you bring all this stuff, and I have work that I'm trying to do with you. I think that we're having a control issue here." And it wasn't until later that I realized that I needed desperately to be in control because of what happened to me. I think I absolutely needed to be in control but I also think that the dreams and the drawings that I brought in were absolutely crucial to remembering what happened to me, because they were telling the story over and over again. They were also putting distance between us. I do know this, I wasn't trying to be in control, but I needed to be in control. And I think that this is something that therapists should be aware of, that this is a very important issue.*

I enjoyed that battle, but there has been a change. At one point in our therapy relationship, you finally got through to me. You finally said, "You know, you bring in all this stuff, and I need you to just come in." And I was finally able to do that.

In the therapeutic relationship, control must be shared. The therapist directs the session to help the client work, which means, initially, that the client's pain often gets worse. The client determines what depth of information and pain she can handle. When Lori decided to let down her guard, a flooding of vulnerability and hurt threatened to engulf her. The therapist was her safety net, helping her to venture into the darkness of her experience but not letting her be overwhelmed by it. This is a slow, difficult process for many reasons. In the current psychology vernacular, this might be known as empowering the client by having her take shared responsibility for the therapeutic work.

For many women, shame and embarrassment are primary emotional components of having been sexually abused. As Lori confirmed, *I think it's always embarrassing to tell someone exactly what, you know, every single thing, just everything that you really think. It's like you're completely nude. It feels good, though, to be able to admit it. But it feels a little scary too. Still, you're just leaving yourself open for someone to say, well, you were really foolish.*

Another primary emotion is the fear of being abandoned. Once Lori let go of her need to control every session, she experienced a fear that the therapist would abandon her. In the next passage, this fear is manifested in Lori's reaction to a mix-up in her appointment time. Since she couldn't be seen that day, Lori felt the pain of the abandonment that had haunted her throughout her childhood. She vividly described how as a child she comforted herself.

When I arrived for one session, you said, "Didn't I tell you that I cancelled? I had to cancel this time, so you've missed your appointment." You had someone else scheduled in the time that I was here. I forgot that I was supposed to come earlier. That was it. I felt really bad. And you know what I did? I did something that is really strange, but I followed my compulsion. I drove straight to the Japanese garden and bought myself flowers, a bouquet of flowers.

After buying the flowers, I had that same spontaneous regression. I was 3 years old again. When I got home, I was still in the state of mind of a 3-year-old. I got into a fight with my family and went outside. I wandered around the neighborhood until I found some flowers to pick.

Whatever happened to me when I was little, probably right after it [the abuse] happened, the only thing that would comfort me was to find a flower. I think what happens to people is that they continue repeating their traumas over and over and over. When I felt abandonment by you, I guess that's all that I could think about doing—going to pick a flower. So, I followed my compulsion and it did make me feel better. But that was a very strong indication to me that something else was happening. A lot was happening that was causing me to relive old patterns.

As a child, Lori comforted herself by picking a flower. As an adult, when she experienced a spontaneous regression as a result of feeling abandoned by the therapist, she picked a flower. This behavior pattern signaled that there was a connection between what she was experiencing in the present and something in her past. One of the reasons Lori pursued therapy was to find out what this powerful connection was and how to change her tendency to react to difficulties in interpersonal relationships by regressing into feelings of abandonment and betrayal.

In order to develop the trust that is needed to explore these feelings of abandonment and betrayal, a bond must be formed between the client and the therapist. Within the safety of this trusting bond, the client can express her fears,
shame, guilt, and vulnerability. Lori offered a perspective on the bond that is necessary to deal with incest issues by comparing it to the bond she has with her art
students.

It's wonderful [happy laughter]. *This is great. I mean, it's the best thing that
ever happened to me. I mean, what a wonderful thing. It's like I'm a teacher and
they come to me, the kids do, to learn how to draw. I immediately look for their
strengths, and then they begin to recognize them. Then they don't need me anymore. When you're dealing from your strengths, you don't need to be taught. And
that's kind of what you were able to give me. What good therapists are able to
give—they're able to point the person back into themselves. And that's much better than depending on another person.*

*I was real attached to you because the idea that I might find out I was abused
made me feel like I was on the edge of an abyss and just about to fall over. You
were my safety net. Or you were holding the rope to keep me from losing what I
thought was going to be my mind.*

As is evident in these comments, Lori trusted her therapist to "be there" for
her. Regardless of what she might uncover about her past, she knew she would
not be abandoned by him. This trust allowed her to explore her experiences and
symptoms that signaled that she might have been sexually abused as a child.

LORI'S SYMPTOMS OF BEING SEXUALLY ABUSED

For most victims of sexual abuse, their symptomatology is extensive and varies
in intensity. For Lori, most of her symptoms seemed to be concentrated in her
interpersonal relationships and were manifested in dysfunctional relationship patterns and numbness of feeling.

As Lori related, *Well, it had to do with relationships. I had been married to a
man for 8 years* [who] *I didn't love and couldn't feel for. I was afraid. I thought
that it was the man and our relationship so I divorced him. Then I became
involved in a very passionate and happy relationship—I thought. But, it didn't
turn out any better because I could feel so much pain. So, I left this relationship.
Then I went through a series of repetitive relationships, and they all ended very
quickly. They were just many affairs.*

*That was when I first went for help, in 1977. I went to a psychiatrist who was
very intellectual in his approach. He figured that it was the loss of my mother that
was causing my inability to have a relationship. So we spent 7 years discussing*

this. I came away with a better understanding of myself, but it was an intellectual one. I was not able to stop repeating the pattern of being in affairs that ended quickly with a great deal of pain. And that became intolerable.

The numbness of feeling happened when I was in permanent relationships, stable relationships. When I was married, someone once asked me if I was happy. It was like a thunderbolt striking me because I had never thought about it. It never, ever occurred to me to think if I was happy or not. I had no feeling at all. That's what started to work on me. That's when I realized that I wanted to feel. I wanted to be in a relationship where I could hold hands with a man and feel something.

Except for pain, Lori only felt numb in her personal relationships. Lori also believes that she chose partners who short-circuited their excitement for life. As a result, her intimate interactions lacked passion.

I don't think of passion as lust, I don't think of it as enjoying sex in a lusty way, but I think of it as an excitement for life, which is passionate, which is intense, which has real depth of feeling. That was missing from my relationships.

When one does not feel passion or real connection in interpersonal relationships, feelings of loneliness often result. Lori suffered from such loneliness even in the midst of relationships.

You know, there's a thing that happens to people who have been abused. It's really hard to talk about. They start withdrawing from people and isolate themselves. That has been a major thing that I've had to fight in my healing. There is a whole part of me that would just withdraw completely even from my dearest friend. When I withdraw, I think that I am trying to show that I don't need anyone and then I can't be hurt. So I don't feel and this is the death that I think I always feared.

This numbness of feeling and withdrawal from intimate relationships is probably a protective mechanism. The part of Lori that is capable of loving and feeling has been dissociated. On a conscious level, it is not available to her.

In a situation when I'm in a relationship with a man, any man, I don't have any feelings for him at all. I don't care. I don't want to talk to him, I don't want . . . It's like I'm not there really. I'm just not there. I can think back in my life and there are many times when I just wasn't there.

Women who have been sexually abused exhibit a variety of symptoms. Symptoms can unfold in many dimensions of their lives, including the physical, emotional, cognitive, interpersonal, and spiritual. For Lori, the primary symptoms were numbness of feelings and loneliness when she was in interpersonal relationships with men. These were accompanied by physical problems and cognitive distortions.

THE JOURNEY WITHIN, TO DARKNESS

The long arduous road to health for Lori involved recovering her personal history. This process occurred in the safety net of the therapeutic environment and utilized Lori's unique talents. Since Lori is a gifted artist, dreams and visualizations were her most powerful tools. Initially, most of the information about her past emerged in symbolic form in her artwork. Lori likened this process to her conscious self hearing the memories stored in the unconscious when the conscious self was ready to listen.

It [the unconscious] *knows you're not ready to hear it* [memories]. *So it's telling you the only way it can, which is in symbols and imagery. It reveals as much as you're ready to hear—as much as you're ready to know. In my experience, I have learned to just really, really pay attention.*

When Lori started therapy, she had a compulsion to draw narrow canyons. These narrow canyons were drawn from many perspectives, but each had a foreboding component.

I couldn't get a dream out [of] *my mind. It was a dream that I had of this deep, narrow canyon. For 5 years, I searched for the canyon near where I had grown up. I finally found that canyon and hiked it. I wasn't disappointed, because it led me to what happened with my father. When I showed him a picture I had drawn of the canyon, he said, "Oh, I know that canyon." I said, "What canyon is that?" He said, "Well, that's where we were when your mother got pregnant with you."*

This got me thinking about my father's life, and I started listening to his stories. I wrote a book about him as he told me stories about his life. I started listening, wrote that book, and that led me to my art. I started photographing and drawing these narrow canyons . . . I didn't know what that narrow canyon meant to me. I didn't know.

Her therapy could only progress when she realized that she had to symbolically go through those canyons and discover what they held. Her unconscious had left the trail, but she needed help to follow it, to get at the minute details. She did this by drawing.

Lori's renderings of the canyon started to change as she began to focus on the rock faces. *What happened was that I was no longer just drawing a nice little picture of a rock that looked like a rock. When I drew the rock all kinds of other things started to come up in it. Like faces that were ugly or were me with my back to the viewer, hiding in the rock. This was a breakthrough for me. What had been happening in my art before this was that I was drawing light airy scenes that were mainly white. Now I was drawing rocks and canyons—tight spaces and darkness.*

What happened to me is I reached a point in my life where the unconscious started pushing me more and more toward the knowledge that something real bad had happened to me. That I was going to have to go through it and it was dark— darkness and a narrow canyon. I could see that there was a light ahead, but another canyon was right there. And it was winding on, and it went forever. I knew I needed a guide.

That was way back in the 1970s and that was the most important dream in my life. It really was. What I had been going through was a dark passage which was acted out as depression. That was what I painted for 2 or 3 years—that deep canyon. What I'm saying is that there's a clock ticking in everyone. I guess the real pity would be if they didn't turn off the alarm and listen to what the clock had to say.

Lori followed the trail into this canyon and her dreams led her to much of the source of her anguish. Lori discovered that she had dissociated into five parts. Also, her sucking on a Sugar Daddy (a kind of candy) conveyed for the first time the betrayal by incest.

When it emerged, it was just like, oh, this is important. That dream was important because it told me that I had divided into five parts. In the dream, it was raining and five drops of water were dripping off of a tree into a pool of water that rippled out in concentric circles. As the water was washed toward the gutter, I was standing in it, sucking on a Sugar Daddy. I didn't understand what it meant when I had that dream. What I thought was, "Gee, that's interesting. I'm starting therapy and I'm starting to open up the past so I'm going to remember something. Obviously, something I should know."

As Lori thought about her dream, she became more and more curious about what it could mean or what it was trying to tell her. *Something happened or something about my childhood that I should know. I had no clue about what those symbols meant. Now it's very, very obvious that there was another symbol in my dream, too. The sky was full of dark, menacing clouds and then it opened up and parted in the middle. What was happening was that the dream was trying to tell me something, but I didn't know how to interpret it. I just knew that things were starting to open up in my unconscious, things were starting to move around. The Sugar Daddy symbol was just right out front—as close as my unconscious could come to saying, "You had a physical relationship with your daddy." But, I couldn't have handled that—that would have been unthinkable at that point.*

I later realized that the five drops of water and the concentric circles were clues that this was still going on in my life. I had this experience that I was in the gutter, you know, and I knew that my unconscious was trying to tell me something, but it doesn't speak easily. It doesn't flow. Besides, I couldn't have listened. If I were to dream, you know, that you were abused as a child, in plain English

. . . Even as Lori's unconscious symbolically expressed her trauma, her conscious mind had to proceed more slowly. The emotions triggered were overwhelming and painful, as was evident in Lori's inability to complete her sentence and to continue talking in the first person.

Lori cautiously explored these dreams that suggested possible sexual abuse in therapy. Like most clients who are victims of incest, screen memories are dealt with initially. Screen memories are less emotionally painful instances of abuse than incest, and they allow the client to learn to deal with the fear and sense of betrayal engendered from having been abused incestuously. As is often the case, the incest memories are too painful to approach directly; therefore, more peripheral abuse is worked on first.

Lori had a feeling that something had happened to her as a child and related a screen memory. *But, I, I just had a very strong feeling of fear that something else had happened to me, that something had happened to me as a child. This feeling kind of washed through me, that there was something else, that I had been abused as a child. That maybe it was to do with the housekeeper. I had talked to my father on the phone that day, and the feeling that came over me was so frightening that I thought I would have to call you . . . and I did call you and say that I think you're going to have to hospitalize me.*

At this point in Lori's therapy, it was safer for her to remember being abused by the housekeeper, although later memories about her father also surfaced. From her knowledge gained from reading, Lori recognized, in retrospect, that this was a screen memory for her.

Very often in cases of adult victims of child abuse, adult survivors, there's a screen memory that comes up first. Someone touching you, or in my case, it was the housekeeper that probably touched me. She used to spend hours with me in the bathtub. I decided this probably wasn't such a bad thing that happened to me, but I don't know for sure. So this screen memory comes up first, because I guess the memory is structured to protect you in that way. If you get anywhere near finding out anything, this will come forth first. There might be several of them.

These revelations about the housekeeper led Lori to the truth about her father. His hints about his role in the abuse gave her further confirmation that she was on the right path.

Well, I just wouldn't let it go. I just kept bugging my father and he said, "No, no, no. You couldn't have had anything happen to you, no, no, no." And I kept saying, "Well, I did have gonorrhea when I was 2 years old. Now, how did I get that?" Well, he didn't want to deal with it. So I called my two aunts and asked them, "What went on there?" One aunt remembered that I was being cared for by many housekeepers. I had 17 housekeepers. When I was 2, when I got gonor-

rhea, I was being cared for by a housekeeper who was mentally retarded. She was about 18 years old and was a prostitute.

So I went back to my dad with that information, and he admitted that it was true and that they had run her out of town when I came up with gonorrhea. I said to my dad, "How did I get it? When I asked my doctor how gonorrhea is transmitted, he said there's only one way, and that's sexual." My dad seemed to ignore this and only said, "It was transmitted by taking a bath with her and sharing the same washcloth." So, I never did find out the exact situation, but obviously, the housekeeper probably used to play with me in the bathtub or something like that. But I don't have any bad feelings about whatever it was she was doing. I think it was loving, because I hadn't been touched prior to that. Now I think that that was probably the beginning of the abuse with my father because then he had to doctor me everyday, four or five times a day. Shortly after our conversation about the gonorrhea, my dad said things like, "Well, I suppose I may have abused you, you know, when I had to put the medicine in you." That's as close as he could come to admitting it. My mother was in the hospital again, and the situation was set up. He was a weak man, and I was a very loving little girl who needed to be touched. I probably just loved being touched. But . . . maybe not, judging from the pictures I've seen of me. I looked devastated.

After the exploration of her screen memory with the housekeeper, Lori was ready to consciously consider the sexual abuse by her father. The narrow canyons in her former dreams prepared her by presenting images of spillways and dams in the canyons. These led her to remember her father being hard and trying to penetrate her.

Well, I just used that image of dams in my canyons. There was a blockage, but sometimes I'd get in the spillway and I'd go inside of there. There were other images of the canyons like a narrow passageway, a dark and narrow passageway. I had lots of canyon dreams. But I kept wondering, Why a box, why a narrow place, why a dam? They all have something in common—blockage, I guess.

Well, the spillway opening would be feelings. Sometimes I never seemed to be able to control what was going to happen. Sometimes I'd just get on a little spillway and I'd go through the main dam. Later I realized this was an image for the sexual experiences that I had had.

Oh, my God, it's hard. . . . I mean, it's hard to talk about. That he would try to penetrate me and he couldn't. And that was part of my dreams. I remember exactly the shape and the size and the way it bent, and a lot of graphic stuff came through in that dream. It was, um, words too! Direct quotes, "This is what your mother and I do, therefore, it's OK. This is what you and I can do."

It comes through in other dreams, but in one it was explicit. It just told me straight out that it wasn't just the feeling for him. For him it was very matter of fact, business-like, let's get right to it, all right scoot down, do this, do that. And I enjoyed it even in the dream. I enjoyed the fun part. But it would seem like for him, it was taking care of business. For him, it would be so exciting that he would come right away and then it would be over.

As the information about her father unraveled, Lori experienced tremendous fear and confusion. Lori's childhood ego state at the time of the abuse was being re-experienced. When this occurs, the therapist needs to help the client with feelings that they are "going crazy." Lori felt like she was losing mental control when she called and asked to be hospitalized. In therapy, pacing is often essential to help the client release stored emotions and to help the client integrate them consciously into an adult framework.

But the screen memory of the housekeeper didn't get into my fear. The beginning of remembering about my father started this incredible fear that something terrible happened to me. I would hyperventilate when I started to think about it. I couldn't breathe, I started to panic. I called you and said, "You have to hospitalize me. I can't go through this unless you do." I said, "You have to put me in the hospital."

I couldn't function, I mean, I just could not breathe. It was like I went into hyper-alert. It's like, I went into a trauma. I couldn't drive. It was true panic.

When Lori reflected on what threw her into this anxiety attack, she realized that her defense mechanisms were being activated to protect her from what she was beginning to find out about her father. It was as if initial danger signs were being activated to prevent her from exploring her past. Also, her father had threatened her if she ever told anyone about what he had done to her.

Fear comes from what you're being told. As you get closer to unveiling that memory, you think you are going to die. So you start to die. You literally stop breathing and you panic. I guess, because you are getting close, you are being warned that if you tell, you'll die. I had many dreams that said I would—that I would be skinned alive or I would freeze to death out in the snow if I tried to run away.

In the midst of all this fear, Lori began to confront her father indirectly. Lori claimed that she could not directly confront her father since he was 90 years old and she was petrified of causing him to die. Also, in her regressed childhood ego state, she was still scared of him and the threats that were made against her. Unlike most victims of abuse who doubt their memories and feelings, Lori's worst fears—that she was sexually abused by her father—were confirmed. Most perpetrators of child sexual abuse rarely admit it.

Well, I just [clears her throat], *I started telling him that I'd seen a show on TV about a girl who had been molested at age 3 and he said, "Oh, you mean he entered her?" And I said, "Yes." Then he asked me, "You mean he just didn't play around with the finger?" I got the feeling right then that it was a kind of confession for him. But then there would always be a cover-up. That's the way it went. He would wind up telling me, but he's a compulsive liar. His pattern is to sandwich the truth. He first tells a lie, then he tells the truth, and then he tells a lie. So, I've learned from listening to him over the years that at some point, he will always tell you exactly what happened.*

He'll tell a story. He'll tell you what happened. He'll say, like he said to my daughter when she was talking to him about abuse—"I knew a lot of people who fingered their daughter. It's OK, as long as you don't hurt her."

Lori decided at this point to share her secret with her daughter. Any victim of abuse has a difficult task when revealing this type of information to family members. Many times the victim's story is vehemently denied, and often she is attacked by her siblings or her own children. This intrusive information threatens the stability of her family life and sometimes is very dissonant with her own experience of the perpetrator. However, in this case, Lori's daughter received startling confirmation of her mother's claims.

My daughter, who is 27, didn't believe me. This was destroying her family. I tell her what I'm going through, and she doesn't want to hear it. Then she had a terrible dream that her house was being torn apart. The house is her foundation, her family. I mean, she loves her grandfather, and all of a sudden he's this dirty old man. So she turns against me, and she doesn't believe me. There's still a part of her that maybe does, and so she won't let it go. One night after I had told her, she was driving home with him. He can't see very well, so she was in the car with him. He was driving his car and I was following in mine. She started questioning and he started talking about a case that he knew about where the man did have sex with his daughter. As he got into it, he got so agitated that he almost had a head-on collision. Then he got so discombobulated he backed into the other lane of traffic and almost rear-ended them. I was just sitting there in my car watching this and that's when we both knew that he was dangerous. He was not only dangerous to himself, but it was her that he would have hurt in that accident. He knows it's wrong. He knows he could go to jail for it. He knew, he knew it was criminal, that people went to prison for this. That frightened him.

With this confirmation, Lori further explored her memories of being sexually abused. As she realized the betrayal of her father, not only did tremendous fear surface but she experienced body memories of the sexual act. Incest is very confusing because the victim often has a dichotomous experience. Not only does the victim endure the fear and pain associated with the sexuality, but she also experiences tremendous sexual stimulation. It is sometimes forgotten when discussing childhood sexual abuse that children need to be touched and to be special to their parents.

Lori vividly described this dichotomy as she relived body memories. *Well, I started reliving the whole damn thing. It was like I was on a roller coaster every night. It was weird, the way the unconscious would work. At first, I woke up at 2 o'clock, then I woke up at 3 o'clock, then I woke up at 4 o'clock. Then I was horribly, horribly, horribly sexually stimulated. I've read other cases and they were, too, once in a while. I mean, it's both repelling and a turn on. It's like a compulsion, you can't stop until you relive the whole damn thing. I'm OK now, but I had to go through months of this. It was hell. I had to relive it in my body. And it was really, really hell.*

Masturbation got me in touch with the fear and the turn on. That's the split. I mean, there's a part of me that loved it and part of me that was absolutely grossed out by it. I think the body just has it's own way of remembering things and that seems to be very common. Every case I've read where a woman starts to remember, she goes through that same period where, just get out your vibrator, because you're going to go through it again. And I know that's shocking to you, but I can't imagine not going through that stage. I can't imagine what would happen if you didn't.

When asked why she found this so shocking, she replied, *The shocking part would be the enjoyment. Now, at my age, I look back at a poor little 3-year-old girl and a grown man, that's shocking.*

When this response was probed by a question about whether it shocked her that she masturbated and enjoyed it, Lori said, *Yeah, sometimes it is, yes. Parts of it are and parts of it aren't. There is a split. That's when I had to split my personality. I couldn't handle that. I mean, here's my father who loves me and that same man abused me. When I was a little girl, he was the only person I really had in my life other than the housekeepers.*

Lori then started to discuss the splitting of her personality. In most cases of repeated childhood trauma, this splitting occurs in order to protect the child from the hurt of the trauma. To the mental health world, this splitting is known as dissociative disorder. The most dramatic form results in what is known as multiple personality where different parts of the person at times control who the person is and the various parts are typically unaware of each other. More common, however, is for the child simply to disassociate during the trauma. While being abused, parts of the child float away from the body taking with them the fear, pain, sadness, and anxiety, leaving the child in a state that is blank and unresponsive. In fact, many perpetrators of childhood sexual abuse have described their victims as looking like rag dolls; therefore, they claim the victim was not being hurt.

After I remembered that I'd been abused, I began to know it in every level of my body—cellular, sexual, every, every level of my body. I knew that it was true. I started having a lot of body memories and I was waking up all night long. Then the dream that I had a double started. And that . . . I knew I was going to need help. I was so in shock, but I knew I had to work through these feelings in order to get rid of them.

For Lori, as for many victims of sexual abuse, memories started emerging in dream form. *All of the information that I've ever gotten about being abused and even on the split has come through dreams. In an early dream, I was trying to live in a house that someone else was using. There was a war between the two people, one was sort of a male and one sort of a female. It . . . I'm . . . this could be the split. I knew that it could happen so I started looking at some of my old poems I had written after having dreams that seem to present two sides of me.*

In these dreams, the girl was a little girl who was very loving, but she didn't have any other feelings at all. I think she was created to protect me. When I was a little girl, my mother said that I was like two different people. In one day, I'd be like a boy and sometimes I'd be like a girl. When I was a boy, I'd wear cowboy boots and long pants and I was tough and nobody messed with me. When I was the boy side of me, I fought and protected the girl side who would do anything to please her father, especially, or her mother. The little girl would try to be beautiful and sexy. She liked dressing up in costumes. I even wrote differently when I was the boy and when I was the girl.

The weirdest thing was when I went to college. They called me eclectic because I had different ways of working depending on which one I was into—the boy side or the girl side. One draws and sculpts, and the other paints. When I was the boy, I made straight A's. When I was the girl, I [didn't] do as well. The boy does better in the cognitive area.

Every time I do photography, it's the boy. And if, God forbid, I should slip and get into the wrong one—I did that last summer—something always goes wrong. Last summer, I went on this horseback riding trip, and I was the girl on that trip. She's not brave, she's not hardy. It's the boy who's brave and hardy and it's the boy who can take 125 miles on a horse. I nearly killed the girl out there. She got vertigo in the middle of the canyon, and they were going to have to drag her out of there. She was covered in hives.

In reflecting on these two sides of herself, Lori did not think that she was that unusual. *Everybody has a male and female part of themselves that they want to kind of integrate anyway. Right? Maybe mine just got polarized at a really early age. But I think that the central personality was in charge of all this.*

I started meditating in the sixties. That helped me to develop a rather strong sense of self. I think if I wouldn't have developed an ego or self, I couldn't have handled all this. I couldn't have withstood it. When all of this started, I began to re-experience both sides. It was devastating. It was like being in madness. Neither one of the sides was a safe place to live.

In response to questions about how the boy and how the girl reacted to the sexual abuse, Lori said, *Well, she had sex and he fought it. That's just as I can feel it, because I don't have access to a lot of memories. But I think she enjoyed it, . . . and she, . . . and she, when it got frightening for her, she'd leave her body and that is when he'd take over. He would say no. And I think he would think of lots of things to sidetrack what was happening.*

The split between the boy and girl helped Lori to keep certain information repressed. Recovering the knowledge of their functions set the stage for recovery.

JOURNEY INTO RECOVERY

While the abuse is being remembered, the process of recovery can begin. Not only do the memories have to be accessed and processed, recurrent patterns of dysfunction have to be changed. For recovery to be complete, victims of trauma have to find meaning in their experience.

In order to break down the barriers in her life that were created by the abuse (so vividly depicted by her as the narrow, unending canyons), Lori had to be open to the full tragedy of the hurt. Like the children in *IT*, she had to re-experience and accept what had happened in order for healing to take place.

Lori described this in detail. *OK. First of all, I think there are stages of experiencing the knowledge that you were abused. First is awareness, and then anger surfaces. At some point, in order to go past this and not spend your life going to support groups with other angry women who have been abused or always feeling sorry for yourself, you have to reframe the abuse as a plus. You have to not only accept what happened to you but embrace it as the wound that has given you much of your power. I know that the idea of embracing something that is unspeakable is pretty foreign to most people. But you are actually embracing the wounded part of yourself. This is what it takes to turn it around from shame to empowerment.*

How can I do that? How can I embrace something as ugly as that? Because what happened to me became a vehicle in my life, driving me to my strongest talents, my strongest powers to survive. When I embraced my woundedness, I began to heal and the abuse began to lose its power over me. Otherwise, I would have been stuck.

There was a point at which I simply said, "I accept that I was abused and now, because of this awful thing that happened to me, now I'm going to grow and I'm going to overcome it. And I'm going to try my best." I'm actually saying, "I accepted what happened to me totally." I embraced it. And when I did that I no longer saw myself as a victim.

Instead, I saw myself as a wounded healer. In Native American cultures, there's a whole tradition around a wounded healer. That's the person who's been really wounded in childhood in either an emotional or physical way—a harelip, a clubfoot, something that really hurt that person. Such a hurt is the tear in your very center that has to happen before you can be. You have to have that hole in order to be fulfilled with the power that's waiting for you. It's there.

In order to move beyond always defining herself as a victim of childhood sexual abuse, Lori realized that the abuse could serve as a catalyst for her growth as a person. While we would never wish sexual abuse on any child, for those who have been abused, coping with it as an adult can provide an opportunity for growth. Although the recovery process is long and difficult, the victim status must eventually be relinquished. By finding meaning in the experience, one's life can be enriched.

In many ways, this process is similar to that described by Victor Frankl (1959) in his book, *Man's Search for Meaning.* Frankl found meaning in being in a Nazi concentration camp and moved beyond always seeing himself as a victim of this terrible atrocity. He reframed the horribleness so that it allowed him to evolve as a person. It allowed him to change on a deep inner level.

As a result of integrating the abuse into her present existence, Lori realized that her relationships with men had to change. With the processing of the abuse, she was finally ready to establish healthy relationships based on love and mutual trust. She also realized, however, that she had to proceed cautiously and learn the steps involved and that the learning could be painful.

Well, my life is really changing a lot. My boyfriend left, and he never came back. He just vanished. I committed myself to my artwork. I began to understand that all the things I looked for in a man were the same qualities that I found in my father. I seemed to look for a man who was already committed to someone else or who was impossible for one reason or another. Either he was too young or he was too this, too that. I began to put it together. I would be with a man for a certain period of time but it was never, even from the outset, going to be a permanent relationship.

Men found me because, because I was safe—I wasn't looking for a committed relationship. I wasn't looking for a long-term thing. I was repeating a pattern I had learned as a child as a result of my relationship with my father.

To unlearn this pattern, Lori decided to just engage in friendships with men for a while. She realized that intimacy has to proceed from friendship and love, not from repeating old patterns of betrayal experienced in the sexual involvement with her father.

I'm not risking sexual involvement, you know, in a way. I think I'm now able to accept companionship and affection. I was not able to do that before. And it feels real good. You know, just a nice hug and spending time with someone.

Another change for Lori was working on healing the split of the boy and girl. She understood that both were crucial to her development as an integrated person. Using imagery and her artistic talent, Lori began to build a rock arc between the boy and girl so that they could finally merge.

I started drawing this image of the rock arc, because I think in terms of rock a lot—how rock is connected to me. I decided to draw a picture of an arc connecting two sides of a canyon. In the center under the arc was water and a solid piece of rock, like a plug.

I was building this image from a composite of three photographs. Every time I would get to this one place in the drawing, where I was supposed to be able to see the reflection of the rock arc in the water, I would draw this plug instead. Then it would be impossible for there to be a reflection. It occurred to me that I was working with a metaphor. So I finally said, "I don't know what the hell this is, but I'm going to take it out." I took out that rock plug and as soon as I did, the reflection showed up.

When asked if she saw this as a phallic symbol, Lori strongly agreed. The sexual abuse, as represented by this phallic symbol, had kept her boy and her girl separate for most of her life. *I took it out and I could join both sides with this arc. It almost became a Dorian Gray picture. Each week I kept painting it more vividly. I knew that the changes were happening inside of me and that I didn't really need to keep doing the Dorian Gray thing with the art, so I stopped.*

With the integration of the boy and girl, Lori described how she left the victim role. One of the major markers of this change was that she now had access to her feelings and thoughts.

I'm not just a victim anymore. I can now feel and think. It's wonderful. It's like joining the real world. It's like having the same game plan as other people. Maybe I'm not there yet, but at least I'm getting there.

It seemed like there were always 10 thousand hidden agendas that I could never see—in business, in people, in relationships. My own daughter has sat me down and said, "Mom, don't you get it?" I always thought, "Get what?" I couldn't understand the abstract meaning behind things. To me, what was, was.

Other changes began to snowball as her career shifted from art teacher to artist. It seemed to Lori that her expressive potential, which had gotten frozen with the abuse, had now begun to flow freely.

Well, I made a commitment to my art and this is the second year that I've had an exhibition. It's really very, very good progress in 2 years. It's been interesting to be able to carry out images and work through them all year long, instead of just a little while in the summertime when I wasn't teaching.

Lori also has continued to evolve in her ability to establish and maintain intimate relationships. *Relationships? I don't feel vulnerable. I don't feel scared. I'm getting nourished from different people. I have friendships and I can accept affection. What I would like to see in a relationship with a man is I'd like to be with someone I could share my art with.*

I see myself not teaching anymore but doing my art. Because of being sexually abused, I'd like to help other people who have been abused. I'd like to do art therapy. I think that what this has given me is that I can be a guide now to the underworld. I know the underworld—I know the darkness. I know what it is.

I can be a guide. I don't know how I'll do it professionally, but I want to do it. It'll happen. It'll be fine. I'm not sure how. Check with me in 5 years and see if this is just fantasy.

Now firmly pointed toward a healthier future, Lori still has pockets of the past that she is resolving. She has shared her very personal experience with the hope that therapists and the lay public will learn from her experience and not ignore sexual abuse. By telling her story, she hopes that other women will have the courage to go through a similar healing journey.

As she said, *The timing is right for people to remember. The time is right for therapists to begin to say, Let's work on it. You know this business of saying it didn't really happen and ignoring obvious information has to stop. It does happen and there are a lot of women of all ages out there who are just beginning to remember and are just waiting to be helped.*

Chapter 10

Patricia Tells Her Own Story: The Friendly Next-Door Neighbor Betrays Her Trust

It always surprised me that other people had detailed memories of their childhood years. Sitting around with old friends from high school, they would often recount tales of what had happened in junior high school or even elementary school. They would turn to me and say, "You remember. . . ." Although I'd nod my head in agreement, I remembered nothing other than stories that had been told to me by my friends or by my mother as we looked at old family picture albums. On my own, there were no memories, just a blank. But this is not how I wanted to begin my story. Let me start over.

When I came to therapy, it was not for body memories or bad dreams or flashbacks. While I was out of town on business, my husband of 8 years decided to leave our marriage. He had not told me that he was even thinking about leaving. In fact, he had sent a dozen long-stemmed roses to my hotel with a note saying, "Happy Birthday. Hurry home, I miss you." Picking me up at the airport, he quietly told me when he was walking me to our car, "I have some bad news. I had to move out when you were gone." After watching me vomit next to the car, he drove me home in silence and gave me a birthday present. He said that this was hard for him, too, but he never gave me any explanation as to why he "had to move." He just said that he loved me and this was just temporary. I was in total shock and disbelief. This couldn't possibly be happening to me, to my marriage. This just had to be a horrible dream. Soon I'd wake up and everything would be fine again.

In response to my pleading, he agreed to enter marital therapy. The male psychologist supported my husband's leaving to find out what he really wanted. The psychologist soon started meeting with each of us individually and kept telling me that I needed to deal with my "abandonment" issues. My own father had died when I was 12 years old, and the therapist believed that my feeling so devastated by my husband's leaving was due to my feeling abandoned as a child. It seemed as if he thought that I was somehow responsible for the breakup of my marriage. I just couldn't understand this and felt that we needed to be working on the marital issues that had caused my husband to leave. The therapist did not agree and wanted each of us to work on childhood issues. This was fine with my husband, who by now had decided that he loved me but not "as a husband." He wanted to still be my best friend but said he would never move home again. He never used the word "divorce" but said he wanted to be "unmarried," just not right away.

In the 5 months since my husband had moved out I had lost 30 pounds and was wearing size 2 clothes, was taking antidepressant and anti-anxiety medications, had gone through a terrifying time during which my physician thought that I had breast cancer and lupus, was barely managing to perform at work, and was having serious behavioral problems with my teenager. Although I was feeling lost and terribly alone, it made no sense to me that the depth of pain and devastation I was experiencing was the result of unresolved childhood issues over my father's death. Instead, I was experiencing a profound sense of loss and betrayal.

My husband had betrayed the total trust I had given him. He had always told me that he loved me and would be there for me, and I completely believed him. Even when he said that his leaving would be for just a few weeks and then he would move home again, I believed him. In my worst nightmares, I never expected him to break his word to me. I also could not believe that, after he had been gone for 5 months, he could be so uncaring when he told me that it was completely over only 3 days after my daughter had made a serious suicide attempt. My life was literally falling apart, and I knew that I had to do something to save myself. I could not look to him to rescue me. He was not my knight in shining armor, I was not Sleeping Beauty, and we were not going to live happily ever after.

It was at this devastating time that I sought therapy from another psychologist. Although I wanted to understand why my husband had left, he refused to discuss it with me. Having no other explanation for my husband's behavior, I blamed myself for somehow being an inadequate wife, for not being good enough in some way, for failing in this marriage. To me, it just was not rational that he could withdraw his affection so completely for no reason. My husband had to have a reason for leaving, and it must have been some deficiency in me. I must have been flawed in some way. I must not have been thin enough or sexy enough or pretty enough or bright enough. In the back of my mind, I irrationally thought that if I could change the flaw, perhaps he would love me again and come home. On the rational level, however, I knew that this was not true. He was gone and I needed to accept that and try to get on with living my own life.

It was with this deep-rooted self-blame and confusion that I began therapy for me, not to save my marriage. In establishing therapeutic goals in my new counseling relationship, I decided that if I could not understand why my husband had left, then I would just have to learn to accept that our marriage was over and divorce was inevitable. I also wanted to work on my relationship with my daughter, who was having a hard time coping with what I was going through, and I needed to overcome my depression. These became my three goals for therapy.

Since my therapist was skilled in hypnotherapy and I was familiar with being hypnotized, we began our work together using both talk therapy and counseling techniques tapping into the unconscious. Under hypnosis, I felt my father telling me that everything would be all right, that it was OK to be alone. I just had to be strong and continue fighting for myself. I had been very depressed and would probably have tried to kill myself if I had not felt a deep sense of responsibility to my daughter. I, who was an eternal optimist, couldn't believe that I would ever be happy again. I felt trapped in a black bottomless pit with no way out and no light visible.

When the therapist asked me to envision myself as a little girl, I re-experienced an autumn scene where my older brother was pulling me in a wagon and we were laughing and playing together. It felt safe and warm being with him. No other memories about my childhood were accessible either through hypnosis or consciously. While I remembered being embarrassed because my family did not have much money and I often had to wear my brother's clothes to school, I had no vivid memories of actually being this embarrassed little girl. These few childhood memories did not cause me to believe that I had abandonment issues with my father as had been suggested by the first therapist.

To help me begin to feel a sense of closure regarding my marriage, my new therapist led me in conducting a eulogy for my marriage. I detailed the highlights of our marriage, from our first meeting at a Christmas party where we sang carols together, to its illness when he started to withdraw all physical and emotional affection, to its death when he said he would never move home again. As part of the eulogy, I imagined what friends and family would have said at the funeral service. For example, I thought that my husband would have said, "I wanted out. I'm sorry that I hurt her, but she is strong. I was right in what I did. Poor me. I'm the victim here. I lost my home and my dog." I thought his father, who was a staunch Catholic, would have said, "He married the divorcee. The kid was a brat. I understand why he left. He was trying to be kind to her." In contrast, his mother would have said, "He couldn't tolerate the situation because he never realized that you make your own happiness. He will just go out and make the same mistakes again. I'll stand by my son, though." My daughter would have said, "I'm glad it's over. He wasn't a kind person. Mom deserves more. I want to be the most important person in Mom's life." Comments from my friends would have included: "He was insincere and is an imbecile for leaving. He only cared for himself," "I always thought he was too perfect to be real," and, "I never really liked him." Finally, our marriage therapist would have said, "He did the best he could. He has a long way to go. But at least he made a decision. I warned her to get on with her life."

This process helped me start to let go of a marriage that I couldn't make successful by myself. Similar to the deep feelings of loss and pain when saying good-bye to a loved one who has died, saying good-bye to my marriage was very painful and sad. In many ways, it would have been much easier if my husband had died. My sense of total rejection would not have been so full of anguish. The eulogy helped me to accept that he chose to leave, regardless of the reason, and that this was his final decision. I needed to bury the marriage in order to continue really living my own life. Since he left I had been existing, not really living.

While I was still grieving my loss and in considerable emotional pain, my therapist encouraged me to look toward my future. I began conceptualizing how I wanted my life to be and what tools I already had to make my life fulfilling again. My therapist led me through the crystal ball technique and had me link my childhood to my early adult life to my marriage to the divorce and finally to the future. Once again, I had no memories of childhood and could only begin relating my life as it was in high school. This crystal ball technique was helpful in that I was able to identify some of my strengths that had helped me make it through other difficult periods in my life and explore how I could use these strengths in my current life. It also gave me a glimpse of a possible future where I was very much loved by a man on whom I could depend. (What woman wouldn't like the image of two people very much in love sharing a quiet moment in front of a blazing fire?) The key to getting to this future was becoming strong again myself so that I wouldn't be looking for someone else to fill a gap in my life. I realized that only when I was whole again could I meet someone as an equal and with whom I could build a life in which we both could grow. For me, being whole meant that I needed to be emotionally, physically, and spiritually healthy again.

In therapy, we discussed my lack of childhood memories and why I might not be able to remember my childhood years. Based on my own readings, I was aware that people often forget in order to protect themselves from painful events. I had always imagined that my childhood, although difficult financially, was relatively happy. I knew that I was a wanted, loved child. As a family, we did have some struggles. My father suffered from a major illness and could not work, so my mother had to assume the burden of supporting the family. My mother told me how the family used to go to church together, how my father played the guitar and I would sing with him, and that my father loved me very much. I was his "little girl." That I had experienced something so terrible that my mind was protecting me by repressing any memory of it was inconceivable to me. But, if there was even a small chance that something terrible had happened that was getting in my way of being OK again, I wanted to explore that possibility. I wanted to be whole and healthy and if that meant facing some trauma in my past, so be it. I was tired of hurting and knew that I first had to walk through the pain in order to overcome it. It was too strong to be ignored or avoided. I trusted my therapist to be there with me as I faced whatever had to be faced.

In spite of my initial success in therapy (I was no longer so depressed that I was suicidal), the deep emotional pain of my failed marriage was taking its toll on my body, even a year later. I was having daily headaches, searing pains in my chest that caused my whole body to be slouched, and aches in my joints on the right side of my body. I described myself as feeling and looking like a ragged old woman who was defeated by her life and had no energy to fight back.

My therapist tried to change the image of the old, defeated woman to a young, vibrant woman doing aerobics and feeling fine emotionally and physically. When I was asked to "see" my headaches, I envisioned a green slime monster. I was able to gather the slime into a small spot but not get rid of it completely. It was playing an important role in my life in that it was distracting me from feeling the total, overwhelming blackness of my emotional pain by giving me actual physical pain. Since there was a family history of brain cancer, the doctors were taking the severity of my headaches quite seriously and scheduled me for an MRI. Although nothing was found, they told me I was suffering from covert migraine headaches that would probably last the rest of my life. In addition, the doctors ran tests for rheumatoid arthritis and lupus because of the aches in my joints on the right side of my body. Again, the tests were negative, but the pains persisted. To me, it seemed that I was punishing myself with real physical pain for having failed in my marriage.

To address the physical pain, my therapist wanted to break the emotional association between my memories of my marriage and my present circumstances. Since I had idealized my husband and remembered only the best parts of our marriage, he helped me work on changing these memories so that I could let go of them. I visualized scenes from our marriage when I had felt particularly happy and then we would make a slight shift in the visualization so that I wouldn't want to hold on to the positive emotions. The shift required adding to the end of each scene the profound feelings of hurt that he was causing me in the present and had caused me in the past.

This simple exercise helped me to let go of an idealized image of my life with my husband and to accept the fact that he had not been perfect and all-good. He was just a man who had caused me a lot of unnecessary hurt by his actions. He had thought only of himself and had failed to consider how I would react to the unexpectedness and abruptness of his behaviors. I had not been allowed to participate in any of the decisions or been given any explanations for them. He stripped me of all control and left me feeling powerless, inadequate, and vulnerable. Although he continued to say he loved me, his actions were not loving. Finally, I started to believe the messages communicated by his actions, not his empty words.

I had now been in individual therapy for 6 months, and we had not worked on my childhood memories. My therapist was still concerned about the lack of memories, so he hypnotized me and asked about early childhood trauma. My unconscious signaled that there would be no information available until after the divorce was final, that there would be too much pain for me to handle all at one time. I would not be ready to deal with childhood trauma until I had made it through the current crises involving my divorce and my daughter.

During the next therapy session, I was asked to describe the parts of me that were helping me cope with the breakup of my marriage. When I closed my eyes, I was able to see a wise old woman holding a small, frightened, 5-year-old girl. The little girl was hiding under a kitchen table and the old woman had gone under the table to hold her and to make her feel loved and safe. This frightened little girl was named Susy-Q. I also saw another little girl about 7 years old who didn't want the adult me to know about any of the bad or unhappy things that had happened in my life or during my marriage. She was the part of me who wanted to remember only the good, positive things. I called her Karen. Finally, there was an adolescent girl about 13 years old who I called Sherry, sitting primly on the sofa. She wanted to take care of my husband and make everything OK.

In some way, each of these three parts wanted to stay in the marriage and, therefore, assisted in hiding or distorting the memories of the hurtful components of the marriage. For example, my husband became like a cold stone wall every time I did something that failed to meet his unspoken expectations of me or when he felt that I was being too easy on my daughter. In bed, he would turn out the light and roll over, moving far enough away from me as to have no physical contact. His turned back totally shut me out physically and emotionally. Instead of being angry and confronting him when this happened, I would just try to be more understanding and would blame pressures at his job for his behaviors. I always made excuses to myself for his polite coldness rather than connecting it to his judgmentalness, negativity, and suppressed anger. Consciously, all I knew was that I was committed to making the marriage work, no matter what it required of me.

In spite of the revelation of these three little-girl parts of me, I decided to stop therapy for a while in order to deal with the "realities" of life. At this time, I thought that these parts were just figments of my very vivid imagination, and I didn't really see any role for them in my current struggles. I had a daughter who was getting into more and more trouble at school, had run away for a short time, and was becoming violent toward me, and I was experiencing problems at work with coworkers who were losing patience with me for being sad and depressed all the time. It had been a year since my husband moved out, and I was still an emotional mess but trying to "get on with" my life without the help of therapy.

After a 4-month hiatus from therapy, I returned when my husband filed for "dissolution of the marriage." I had gotten a lawyer and instructed her to agree to the terms my husband was proposing since he was being more than fair. The last thing I wanted was a fight over property. In spite of all of my friends and family feeling angry toward my husband, I still felt no anger toward him. I was only hurt that he was ending the marriage.

On the day I received the first draft of the property settlement, I returned my wedding rings to my husband with the message that they had meant too much for me to keep them. I also requested that he not call me or try to see me. It was like I finally realized that in order to even begin to recover, I needed to protect myself from any contact with him. If he needed to talk to me, he would have to write to me. Prior to this time, whenever I answered the phone and heard his voice, I would spend the next several days trying to overcome the fresh pain prompted by the sound of his voice. It was like a scab was being torn off a wound that had not healed, so the bleeding would start anew. For more than a year and a half, whenever I heard his voice I would become short of breath, start to shake visibly, and begin to lose self-control by crying. This had to stop. By setting some boundaries to protect myself, I was no longer panicked by the ring of the telephone. For the first time, I felt a bit of safety and somewhat shielded from him.

When I re-entered therapy, I wanted to explore the possibility that I had experienced some childhood trauma that was so severe that it was getting in the way of my recovering from the divorce. I doubted that anything had really happened, but I was curious, and tired of the constant emotional pain I was suffering.

Over the next several counseling sessions, I gradually started to remember my next-door neighbor sexually assaulting me over a 6- to 7-year period, beginning when I was only 6 or 7 years old. This knowledge helped me understand the drastic shift in feelings I had experienced regarding him. As a child, I had felt very special to him and considered him my second father. When I grew up and left home, I was surprised that I felt only repulsion for him. Whenever I returned home to visit my mother, he would come over to greet me. I didn't like him to hug or touch me, but I felt guilty about shying away from him. I told myself, "He was so good to you as a child, you will hurt his feelings if you don't hug him." But I didn't want him to touch me. It was only when I realized that he had sexually abused me that I understood why I felt such a strong aversion to him.

As I remembered more about the sexual abuse, I realized that I had dissociated during the actual experience. These little girl parts were still separated from me. There was a scared part (Susy-Q), an angry part (given no name), a part that stayed so busy nurturing others that she did not know what happened (Sherry), and a depressed part who wanted to remember only good things (Karen).

As I started remembering, I discovered a bit more about the little girls who had dissociated from me. Susy-Q was hiding under the kitchen table in his home, right where I had seen her 4 months earlier when I visualized the parts of me that could help me recover from the divorce. Karen was huddled in a corner with her hands over her ears. Sherry, who wanted to protect Susy-Q and to hold her so she wouldn't feel the pain of the sex, was standing just outside the back door to his home. Sherry had learned to use her sexuality to get what she wanted and felt that the neighbor really loved her and that she was special. She enjoyed the hugs and affection; however, during the actual abuse, she exited through the wall and wasn't aware that he had sex with her. The angry part was just floating above it all, not allowing herself to be affected by what was happening. Each of these parts was encountered in the kitchen of my neighbor's home. The kitchen was spacious, like an old farm kitchen, and had a daybed at one end. It was on this daybed that he sexually assaulted me.

In spite of these memories, the possibility that I had actually been sexually abused by my next-door neighbor still was not real to me. I had enough hurt to deal with in my current life, so I continued to deny that anything like this had happened. I told myself that I had a very active imagination and I needed to get control of it. In spite of being a well-educated, professional woman, I didn't want to believe what was being uncovered in therapy. How could this man whom I had loved and trusted with such childhood innocence have taken advantage of me like that? It just wasn't possible, therefore, it didn't happen. It couldn't have! Not to me!

I found myself praying for understanding. Numerous questions plagued me constantly. Why was my subconscious telling me that I had been abused by a man I had always respected and loved? Why did my husband leave me? What had I done wrong as a wife? Why was my daughter being so hateful to me? Why were people at work being so nonempathic? What was happening to me? Why was my life falling apart around me?

As if in answer to the almost total hopelessness I was feeling, an angel came to me in the middle of the night. I had moved out of the master bedroom after my husband left and was sleeping in a large old antique bed in the guest room. A diminutive angel, brilliantly glimmering in pink light, appeared for a few seconds on the footboard of the bed. The feeling that I had was to be strong and to trust that all of this would be all right—that I would be OK—that I was loved and that

I was ready to grow beyond the events that were happening in my life. For the first time in almost 2 years, I felt a glimmer of hope and felt that there were spiritual beings watching out for me. I was not alone.

When I returned to therapy 4 months earlier, I visualized parts of me that could assist my recovery. One of these parts was a wise old woman who looked like a Crone. I decided to meditate on her and to use her wisdom to understand whether something had really happened to me as a child and how this could possibly be related to my difficulty in recovering from my husband's leaving.

As I continued in therapy, I recalled more details of the abuse. He would stroke my face and clothes, going up and down my body as I lay on the daybed. He would always tell me, "You can rest here quietly. Everything is OK. You're safe here." Over the years that he molested me, he had intercourse with me more than 50 times. No one else knew, not my mother, father, or siblings, or his wife and children. It was a secret between the two of us.

In order to cope with this violation of my body, I dissociated into little girls who hid in different places in his kitchen or just outside of it. I came to understand more about each of these little girls and how they had helped me cope with the sexual abuse. Karen had her hands over her ears so that she couldn't hear the sounds being made. Feeling scared and terrorized, she twisted herself into a knot. Later I discovered that she was the part causing me physical pain on the right side of my body that the doctors thought was rheumatoid arthritis or lupus. In her terror, she was literally twisting my muscles into knots. During previous physical therapy, a doctor had told me that some of the muscles in my back were twisted so tightly over each other that there was permanent muscle damage. I had never had a serious back injury, so there was no reason for this to have happened to me. Now I began to understand some of the reasons for the muscle pain that had been recurring over the last 20 years. Unexplained components of my life began to make some sense.

During the abuse, another part of me left my body and floated near the ceiling of the room. Although I had no name for her, she took my anger with her. For years she had hated me for not stopping the abuse and was angry at me, not at anyone else. My entire life, I had not been able to be angry with others. When someone hurt me, I somehow justified their actions. Even when my husband left me, I had not been angry with him but had blamed myself for being inadequate. For my entire life I had been re-enacting what this little girl part of me did when my neighbor abused me. I found fault with myself and not with the person who was hurting me. Another puzzle piece fell into place.

The adolescent Sherry removed herself to the outside of the back door where she waited for the abuse to be over. Then she would mother the part of me who had been hurt. The fourth part was 5-year-old Susy-Q who was hiding under the table. She took the physical pain of the abuse with her.

Although each of these little girls helped me cope with the violation of my body by my next-door neighbor, the task now was to reintegrate them into my grown-up being. By slowly taking each little girl through the sexual abuse experience and then placing her in the safety of the Crone's lap, reintegration gradually occurred over several months' time. The Crone was always sitting in an old rocking chair on my mother's front porch.

As an adult, whenever I felt stressed or unhappy, I would imagine being on the front porch of my mother's home in the summertime. I could hear the birds singing and smell the flowers that lined the sidewalk as I looked up at the old, cracked white ceiling. I would always find peace when I mentally went to this safe haven. It was not surprising to me, therefore, that this is where the Crone was and where the little girls needed to go to be healed.

During the next therapy session, while we were working on reintegrating my dissociated parts, I told my therapist that I had decided to tell no one about being sexually abused, that it would just bring pain to others, and that would not help me heal. I loved my next-door neighbor's wife and didn't want to hurt her by accusing him of sexually molesting me. In addition, my mother was now in her early eighties and still lived next door to them. When she needed help, they were there for her. I didn't want to upset the balance in her life by telling her what he had done to me. My therapist still wanted me to write to each of these people— my mother, my next-door neighbor, and his wife—but not to send the letters.

When I returned for the next therapy session, I had totally forgotten about my homework assignment of writing the three letters. My therapist explained to me that this was a form of resistance and my memory repressing what had happened. We wrote verbal letters to each of them and I was able to tell them each how I felt about them and the role they played in my life. This was enough for me. I had no need to confront my neighbor or tell his wife about the sexual abuse.

What was more important to me was the dream I had about my husband. We were still not divorced, even though it had been almost 2 years since he moved out. In the dream, he took me to a strip joint, a club named Llapho, located in the basement of a building in the sleazy part of town. The inside walls of the strip joint were painted a gaudy purple and pink, and the chairs were orange and yellow. A woman dressed in skimpy clothes joined us, but I was only partially there. In the dream, I had dissociated again to protect myself from the pain of his leaving the marriage and then taking me to such a sordid place. The woman and my husband were drinking and laughing. He turned to me and coldly said, "I had sex with her and I enjoyed it!" It was as if he were trying to wound me with these words. (For the last year of our marriage he had not touched me in any loving way.)

Suddenly, I was no longer in the club but in the living room of my mother's home. My husband was in my next-door neighbors' home, looking out their window at me. I wanted to pull down the shade so that he couldn't see me. Just having him look at me was hurtful, but I still couldn't be angry with him or with the next-door neighbor. The little girl with no name still was keeping the anger for me, but at least I realized that I needed to protect myself from him. It shocked me to realize that he had become my next-door neighbor in this dream. Both of them had betrayed my childlike trust and had deeply wounded me.

The self-understanding that resulted from this dream seemed to free me from much of my pain. I also realized that I needed to continue to shield myself from both my neighbor and my husband. To protect myself from the neighbor, I decided to return home for visits only when he and his wife would be out of town. To protect myself further from my husband, I totally shut him out of my life. The only contact I had with him was for business reasons such as putting our home up for sale and closing our joint banking accounts and investments. I stopped writing chatty letters to him and communicated only when necessary.

As I approached termination in therapy, I talked with each of my little girl parts and asked what I needed to do to welcome them back. I promised Susy-Q that I would never let anyone hurt her again, that I was stronger now and would protect her. Sherry just came to me and faded into me. She had always been a powerful part of me. My friends often said that I am one of the most nurturing people they had ever known. Little did they realize that the person who needed the most nurturing was me. Karen had taken her hands away from her ears and faced the fact of being abused. She stopped twisting herself into a little ball to avoid the pain. In the safe, caring, therapeutic environment, she also allowed me to re-experience the pain of being sexually abused. When she reunited with me, she tentatively took hold of my right hand and nestled into the right side of my body—the side which had endured all of the twisted muscles and resulting physical pain. Finally, the little girl who was angry came back to me with the words, "Gee guys, wasn't that interesting!" Besides storing my anger, she also had my curiosity. More than any other part, she helped me realize that by rediscovering my childhood sexual abuse, I had an opportunity for spiritual growth. If I came away bitter, I would have stunted this growth and it would not have added meaning to my life. By facing it, working through it, forgiving myself, and then letting it go, I was becoming a more whole adult.

Perhaps in addition to my therapist, the Crone helped me most through this ordeal. I came to realize that she was my God-part. She was steady, dependable, strong, nonjudgmental, and loving. As the little girls reintegrated with me, I noticed that the Crone was becoming younger. She had lost her stoop, and her clothes seemed less faded and worn. She was "youthening," to borrow a phrase from King Arthur. She was becoming more alive.

As I approached the end of therapy, I felt myself becoming justifiably angry with my husband. True to his pattern, my husband filed the divorce papers and it became final without my knowing it. A week before Christmas, I received notice from the court that I was no longer married. From the beginning to the end, I had no control over his actions, but now at least, I was angry with him and no longer blamed myself for some imagined inadequacy. I was "enough," but he just didn't see it or appreciate it.

It has now been 4 years since that horrible night at the airport. During this time, I have worked on forgiving myself for not being perfect and on loving myself for who I am. As I wrote in my diary, I was using my spiritual beliefs and studies to keep me going, but knowing that this happened for my own growth and embracing what happened are two different things. It took me many years to accept that this pain was a catalyst for becoming a more whole person.

I never thought that I would be in love again, but I have found a wonderful man who truly loves me. I had not dated or even been open to meeting anyone for several years, so you can imagine my surprise when suddenly there he was and I almost immediately felt a oneness with him. He is emotionally mature and tells me honestly what he is feeling and thinking. We share deep personal values and a belief in God. It is like I have found my soul-mate. I don't feel that I have to change myself or hide my feelings in order for him to continue loving me. We both know that open communication, honesty, and mutual respect are the keys to maintaining a healthy, loving relationship and that a good marriage takes commitment and a lot of hard work. We plan to get married this summer and are genuinely committed to working on a marital relationship that will allow both of us to grow because of the love we share with each other. It is scary to love again, but the risk is well worth the joy I have with this man. In some ways, I feel that because I have walked through the depth of the deepest human pain, I now can experience the joy of mature love. Part of me wants to write to my ex-husband and to tell him "thank you" for leaving me. I would never have known this level of happiness and love if I had remained married to him.

I feel like I am beginning my life over and everything is possible again.

Chapter 11

What Happens Next?
A Guide for Clients

While reading this book, many therapists may have recognized some of their clients in these pages. If a client was sexually abused as a child but has not yet "worked through" being abused and explored the impact it has had on her life, maybe the ideas and personal stories presented here will help the therapist and the client in the recovery process. The ideas discussed in this final chapter can be used as a road map for a client's journey toward recovery. Since each client's unique journey has to be balanced with the practical restraints in her life, therapists need to help clients choose a path that will best allow them to recover and evolve as healthy, whole individuals.

This chapter also presents ideas specifically for current or potential clients. We make suggestions designed to help these women select the best therapist for their therapeutic journey, decide which modality of therapy will be most helpful, and move from victim to survivor to recovery. We suggest that therapists have clients read this chapter at the beginning of therapy in order to orient them to the process of therapy and what can be expected as they work through the recovery process.

INDIVIDUAL THERAPY

Since the recovery process is so difficult and many developmental issues need to be processed, we highly recommend that clients carefully select a therapist who is trained in this area. An inappropriate therapist can waste valuable time and resources by his or her lack of essential knowledge about, skills for, and experience with treating victims of childhood sexual abuse. In some cases, well-intentioned but poorly prepared therapists can retraumatize victims. For example, no therapist should tell a client, based on what she has said or not said or not remembered, that she is a survivor of childhood sexual abuse. *Symptoms are not conclusive evidence that a client was abused.* Other experiences could cause clients to have symptoms that are often linked to childhood trauma. The source of a client's pain should be determined *by the client* as a result of what she discovers about herself in the therapeutic process. Our message for clients is that if they are in pain, they should seek competent, skilled help; however, they must assume the ultimate responsibility for their own health and growth.

To help clients help themselves, here are some practical ideas and suggestions for selecting the best therapist:

1. *Finding a therapist.* The first referral source should be any friends or family members who have been treated successfully. The success of treatment can be gauged by their experiences in therapy and by observing their recovery process. Remember that many survivors initially appear worse before improvement occurs. Trained therapists can also be recommended by a local chapter of Incest Survivors Anonymous. In addition, some communities have mental health associations or hospitals that keep lists of therapists who might specialize in treating sexual abuse survivors. Referrals can also be provided by employee assistance organizations, managed health care networks, university counseling or psychology departments, and local community mental health agencies and associations. The most difficult task might be asking for a referral. By having the courage to do this, survivors are taking the first step toward their recovery.

2. *Determining whether to see a male or female therapist.* For some survivors, the gender of the therapist may be a crucial consideration. For some women, the prospect of working with a male therapist may be too intimidating for a variety of reasons. Men are the most frequent perpetrators of abuse of female children; therefore, it is not surprising that some women feel unsafe when the therapist is a man. These clients may fear that they may be victimized again, that the therapist might misuse his power in therapy, or that they cannot explore the explicit details of the abuse experience because they are too ashamed to say certain things to a man (Laidlaw, Malmo, & Associates, 1990).

   For other women, the perpetrator may have been a woman. It is also possible that a significant female, in some cases the mother, was aware that the abuse was happening but did nothing to protect the little girl. This is often the most devastating component of the abuse—a mother not stopping it when she knew about it, or even a mother encouraging it. Women who have lived through this betrayal by another woman often come to therapy with a profound sense of distrust and anger toward other women. A male therapist can provide a safe way to explore these feelings and help the client come to peace with her sexual abuse and the accompanying betrayal.

These issues regarding the gender of the therapist are valid regardless of the sexual orientation of the client. The important consideration is selecting a therapist the client can trust, with whom she will feel safe, and who has the skills to help her become whole again. It should be recognized that it is not unusual for clients to feel comfortable with either a male or female therapist. The key is to form a good therapeutic relationship that facilitates growth. Some survivors start with a therapist of one gender and later switch to a therapist of the other gender in order to better meet their needs for continued growth.

3. *Recognizing appropriate therapeutic boundaries.* For survivors of childhood sexual abuse, having appropriate relationship boundaries or limits established in therapy is essential. Too often, these women have not learned to set healthy boundaries in other aspects of their lives and do not know what constitutes "appropriate limits" in relationships. First, women who have been sexually abused as children need to remember that their relationship with the therapist is a professional relationship, not a personal one. The relationship exists for the purpose of helping the survivor and, therefore, is focused on the needs of the survivor, not the needs of the therapist. Any sexual or physically intimate contact between a client and a therapist is unethical and in many states is illegal. In addition, the therapist should avoid being in an outside relationship (friendship, parties, business relationships) with clients. When therapists allow this to happen, they have a dual role with clients that inhibits their ability to be totally objective and most effective in therapy. Although therapists come to care for their clients as they struggle toward recovery, clients need to remember that they are paying for the therapist's help, but they are not buying a friend. If any part of the relationship with the therapist has to be kept a secret, then it is probably outside acceptable, appropriate boundaries as defined by mental health professional and ethical guidelines.

In addition to interactional issues, therapists help to establish suitable therapeutic boundaries by informing clients at the beginning of therapy about fees and payment procedures, appointment times, how cancellations will be handled, and the limits of confidentiality. Professionally appropriate boundaries should include the therapist being accessible for occasional phone calls, letters, and additional sessions. However, if clients are calling every day or if the therapist is always setting aside time for additional sessions, then the therapist is not adequately modeling good boundaries.

Finally, the therapist should be open to discussing any problems that occur in the course of therapy or in the therapeutic relationship. If the therapist wants the client to do something the client does not want to do, remember that the final choice is the client's. However, the client needs to understand the therapist's rationale for asking the client to do whatever was suggested. This is the client's journey. The therapist is only a guide. The client is responsible for the hard work, for re-experiencing the difficult feelings uncovered during therapy, and for her own growth process.

4. *Being wary.* We have already stressed the importance of being wary of therapists who try to tell a client that they know from her symptoms that she was definitely sexually abused and who did it. This is so important that we want to emphasize it again. A therapist can explore the possibility that a client was abused, but *the client is the only one who can determine if it is true.* The recovery process is a collaborative process, but the client must make the final decisions about what she is willing to explore and willing to do to assist in her own recovery.

Clients need to be wary of a therapist who tells them exactly how long the work will take. Mental health professionals do not have a crystal ball that will tell them how long it will take each client to move through the phases of recovery. It is only possible to estimate length of therapy. For most clients, the recovery process is prolonged and gradual. In general, short-term therapy taking place over a few weeks time will not be sufficient for a client to move through the necessary stages of recovery.

Clients also need to be wary of therapists who spend the therapeutic sessions either lecturing or giving advice. Asking a therapist for a plan of how the work will proceed, about establishing goals for therapy, and for markers to evaluate progress are all appropriate behaviors for a client who is learning to assume responsibility for her own recovery.

GROUP THERAPY

The same cautions outlined above for seeking individual therapy are also true for seeking group therapy. However, clients should also be aware of other issues that are unique to the group therapy process. Some of these issues include:

1. *Therapist-led vs. self-help groups.* Therapist-led groups have two qualities typically not found with self-help groups. First, potential group members are screened prior to the start of the group to determine whether the group is appropriate for them. Sometimes, women are just not ready to

work in a group setting, they may need the attention offered best in individual therapy, or they may have serious psychopathologies that would not be treated in a group for survivors of childhood sexual abuse. Second, therapist-led groups offer members professional guidance during each session. In addition to a plan for each group session and definite starting and ending points, these groups are facilitated by mental health professionals. Having a professional in charge may allow many members to feel safer than if a leader were not available. If a group member has serious difficulties or exhibits inappropriate behaviors in a group, the therapist can take responsibility for referring this member to an alternative form of therapy. The leader is there to facilitate group interaction and to do crisis management.

In contrast to therapist-led groups, self-help groups usually form stronger bonds among the group members. Since there is no leader, the members of these groups take more responsibility for the direction of the group. Another advantage is lower fees or no fees. Also, self-help groups such as Suddenly Alone, Women in Sobriety, or Alcoholics Anonymous are available at flexible times and numerous meeting sites.

2. *Group suitability.* In groups, survivors might be at any of the four stages of the SELF model. If group members are more advanced in their recovery process, the issues they bring to the group often serve as a catalyst for others. Sometimes, however, these issues cause severe reactions in a survivor who may not yet be ready to confront a similar issue in her own recovery process. As a result, the member may feel threatened and unsafe in the group. If a group feels unsafe, the survivor needs to discuss it with other group members and with the group leader if one is available. Group members should not be afraid to switch to other groups. The primary concern must be their own safety and growth. This is particularly important if the composition of the problems presented in the group include extremes, such as ritual abuse, and discussion of this is damaging to the survivor's feeling of safety.

3. *Group pressure.* Groups can offer powerful support in assisting survivors to look at their own defenses and to reveal themselves in front of people who have similar concerns. Groups can support survivors who may feel isolated or who are in pain. In addition, they can gently confront survivors who may not be aware of self-defeating behaviors. For the most part, members can model a healthy family atmosphere for survivors who probably learned many dysfunctional behaviors growing up. Survivors need to be cautious of any group member or leader who seems to be using the power of group therapy to force them into accepting ideas or actions that contra-

dict their values or moral structure. The group process needs to enhance who the client is and not coerce her into acting in ways that violate her own values.

FROM VICTIM TO SURVIVOR TO MEANING

Individual and group therapies help victims of childhood sexual abuse move through the stages of the SELF model. Skillful therapists guide their clients as they progress from viewing themselves as victims to seeing themselves as survivors and finally, to becoming healthy, recovered women.

As a victim, a sexually abused client has a multitude of symptoms and some parts of her memory may be repressed or dissociated. By processing her physical, emotional, psychological, and spiritual pain, a victim can begin to make the transition into being a survivor.

As a survivor, she reclaims her existence and begins to take control of her own life. Although she is no longer governed by her past, her status as a survivor of childhood sexual abuse is an integral part of her identity and influences how she interacts with others. She has labeled herself as a "sexual abuse survivor."

In the recovered stage, a sexually abused woman no longer acts out or expresses the abuses of the past and no longer holds onto the identity of being a survivor. Having a much wider focus on life, she is alive to new experiences and establishing and accomplishing her goals. She has integrated the experiences of her childhood into who she is as an adult and has come to peace with how it affected her development as a person. She accepts and loves the person she has become, with all her strengths and imperfections.

As sexually abused women make the transition from being victims to being survivors to becoming recovered individuals, their orientation to the past, present, and future fundamentally changes. Victims are usually oriented to the past. They act out behavior patterns established in response to the abuse or designed to protect them from it. Their present lives often feel hollow or empty to them because they are not flexible in meeting current challenges. Future goals are difficult to establish and often lack meaning.

As victims of sexual abuse make the transition to being survivors, they stop looking backward to the past and exhibiting reactionary behaviors. Their attention shifts to healing the hurts of the past within the context of the present. In spite of the past being painful and involving betrayal and rejection, they now acknowledge that it is past, it is over. What happened needs to be acknowledged, felt, and re-experienced as they move to separate their abuse from their present functioning.

Changes begin to occur both intrapersonally and interpersonally. Intrapersonally, women change their beliefs and self-talk to reflect a healthier view of themselves. Personal truths begin to reflect their own internal journey toward recovery. Interpersonal relationships with family members and friends also need to be modified to reflect the survivor's inner transformations. For survivors, the present can be viewed as both threatening and inviting as their world view shifts to accommodate a new, healthier reality.

A recovered woman is free to experience the present and future with confidence and flexibility. Each new experience is seen as a challenge that utilizes inner resources and strengths. Each decision a survivor faces presents her with an opportunity to shape her life in a way that is consistent with her true self, a self that is not bound by old hurts and attitudes. A former sexual abuse client once said that the abusive past would never be forgotten but now seemed like a hazy memory. Her present life and future goals were so exciting that they took complete precedence over any past ruminations. Like the adult children in *IT* who were able to go on with their lives as the trauma of Derry became only a vague memory, women who have moved into the recovered phase have a new, bright outlook on life. They look to the future, to what is possible. The abuse is seen as a force that has helped to shape who they are, but it no longer controls their interactions and is no longer a major component of their identities. This does not mean that they lead happy lives all of the time. They still experience sadness and depression, as well as happiness and joy. It just means that all realms of feeling are available to them.

Being recovered also means letting go of past addictions which were used to numb feelings that were too painful. Many groups such as Incest Survivors Anonymous, Alcoholics Anonymous, Women in Sobriety, Narcotics Anonymous, Adult Children of Alcoholics, and Sex and Love Addicts Anonymous assist survivors in the recovery process. Parents Anonymous and Parents United are two excellent resources for the prevention and treatment of child abuse.

Being recovered requires that women assume responsibility for the quality of their lives. They need to nourish their physical bodies and to enjoy the pleasures of being a sexual human being. Their lives can be enriched by engaging in meaningful relationships where playfulness and intimacy are natural components of interactions with family and friends. The recovered woman realizes her talents and finds meaningful outlets for these talents. Finally, she has to reconcile her spiritual beliefs about the existence of God or some Supreme Being so that she develops a loving acceptance of herself. For many recovered women, the sexual abuse comes to be viewed as a life challenge that facilitates their spiritual growth and ability to be fully alive.

Since these various dimensions of healthy living may seem overwhelming to women just beginning to find a healthy existence, each will be addressed separately. We hope that recovering women will have a sense of excitement and adventure as they tackle each area. The arduous, painful journey of memory work and grieving provides the soil for the blossoming of their own wonderful individuality. Whereas their lives as victims may have been two-dimensional and black and white, recovery adds wondrous depth and color.

Body and Sensations

As victims and survivors, women often neglect or abuse their bodies. Weight is often an issue for these women. They either strictly control food intake to the point of developing anorexia and bulimia or overeat and have excessive weight gain. Even if they maintain a normal weight, body image problems frequently surface. It is rare for these women to be comfortable with their physical appearance.

Dietary planning can be an extremely useful intervention. Healthy foods can be added to their eating regimen and balanced meals planned. Often, it is appropriate to consult a nutritionist or physician for medical guidance. If overeating has been a lifelong concern, then groups such as Overeaters Anonymous can be suggested. Other groups like Weight Watchers provide a foundation for change in eating patterns and thoughts about food. The advantages of these groups are the social support, meal planning, and the emphasis on behavioral change. For those women who have tendencies toward anorexia or bulimia, numerous local therapeutic and support groups are available. Many hospitals now have programs for women with these eating disorders. When food is recognized as a loving, nurturing, caring gift to her body, the recovering woman salvages her own body from the effects of sexual abuse.

For many women who have been sexually abused, their physical body has been their enemy. Having experienced pleasurable sensations during sexual abuse, they feel as if they were betrayed by their body. Guilt about enjoying touching or sexual arousal causes survivors to hate their bodies for its natural responses or to blame themselves for being abused. Often women who were sexually abused have the distorted belief that since part of them enjoyed the feelings, they must have somehow caused the abuse. It should be remembered that many of these women were children who were starved for touch and the perpetrator took advantage of this need when hugging and stroking the child. Compounding this self-blame, sexual perpetrators often convince the child that the reason the abuse occurred was because her body was so sexually provocative or she was so beautiful that they could not control themselves.

Since women who were sexually abused as children have received such distorted messages about sex and their own sexuality, they may need to discuss issues revolving around sexuality. Sexual arousal and the anatomy of an orgasm might need to be explained, and masturbation as a response to healthy sexual impulses should be explored. The effects of hormonal changes, stress, alcohol, drugs, and emotional states on sexual desire are significant topics for many of these women. If any sexual dysfunctions exist, referral to a competent physician and possibly to a sex therapist may be appropriate.

Since many women do not understand their bodies or their physiological responses during sex, it is helpful to explain healthy sexual functioning to them or to give them books on the topic. It might also be necessary to explain what is meant by sexual dysfunction. The female sexual dysfunctions are:

1. General sexual dysfunction: Lack of erotic feelings that might be associated with the inability to lubricate or the lack of physiological change in the genital area during sexual arousal.
2. Orgasmic dysfunction: The inability to reach orgasm.
3. Vaginismus: The muscles of the vaginal wall constrict so tightly that any penetration is impossible or is extremely painful.
4. Dyspareunia: The experience of painful intercourse (coitus) frequently due to anxiety.

Good touch, touch that is not eroticized, needs to be experienced by survivors who often have learned that just being touched means that the other person wants some sexual involvement with them. Many times holding a friend's hand or asking for a hug from a friend can be a safe way for these women to experience good touch. Survivors also need to learn to touch themselves in caring ways. For example, by rubbing lotion on their bodies, they can learn that their own stroking behavior can be comforting. Having their partner give them gentle massages may also be helpful. When the client is ready, going to a professional masseuse (a woman is generally safer) can be an adjunct to the therapy. Some masseuses are sensitive to the fact that the body stores trauma in muscles, and the massage oftentimes has a cathartic effect.

For many recovered women, hairstyling, using makeup, and appropriate grooming and dress become possibilities for the first time. Some women who have been sexually abused as children try to hide their bodies and sexuality under baggy clothes and disheveled looks. These women need to be encouraged to recognize the attractive components of their appearance and to be unashamed of being attractive. In sharp contrast to women who try to hide their sexuality are the women who have eroticized many aspects of their appearance. Their seductive dress and makeup might need to be toned down, and these women need to be encouraged to dress less seductively.

When one client finished therapy, she decided to go to an Elizabeth Arden's salon for a makeover. They taught her how to apply makeup so that it enhanced her appearance and was not itself the focus of attention, how to style her hair in a fashion that complemented her face, and what style of dress would best suit her body shape. She was shocked to discover that she looked pretty and actually began to enjoy seeing herself in the mirror. She stated that "For the first time, I didn't need to avert my eyes every time I passed a mirror or entered the ladies' room." Accepting her natural beauty without the burden of old negative judgments, she was free to accept and embrace her feminine self.

New Social Systems—Family and Friends

The recovered person has to develop new strategies for expressing emotions appropriately and for building intimate relationships with friends and significant others. The behavior patterns learned in childhood were primarily protective and do not allow for the degree of flexibility and intimacy demanded for healthy adult functioning.

Women in the victim and survivor stages of recovery still have major impediments to the appropriate expression of emotions. Often, they may be unable to express how they feel, particularly they feel anger, or they may overemote and feel out of control of their emotions.

In healthy, mature individuals, emotions serve as signals to attend to important issues and as guidelines for behavior. When these signals become distorted, the person does not know what behavior will be helpful in a given situation. When emotions are not understood, they cannot provide guidelines for the person's behaviors. Confusion results, and victims and survivors must either withdraw into old negative patterns of behavior or look exclusively to the outside world for direction. While withdrawal deprives them of social input that can act as a reality check, constantly behaving in ways designed to meet others' expectations separates them from their own independence and autonomy. If they refuse to listen to any social input, they risk alienating those around them and remaining isolated.

At the most basic level of emotional functioning, victims of childhood sexual abuse are afraid. While growing up, this fear was associated with being abandoned or rejected and with their trust being betrayed. Added to this fear is the current fear of being physically or sexually attacked or used. The fear is ever present and real as many of these women do become involved in abusive relationships. In order to cope with these fears, many women have learned to misuse protective emotions.

Anger is one of the protective emotions. When expressed inappropriately toward others, it alienates them. When it is turned inward, it alienates the victim from herself and causes guilt and a sense of worthlessness.

Another protective emotion is shame. Many women who have been sexually abused as children not only believe that they are dirty and unworthy, they believe that others judge them just as negatively. As a result, these women experience tremendous shame and self-loathing.

Fear, anger, and shame, the most common emotional consequences of being sexually abused, often cause women to feel out of control. They may attempt to manipulate people and situations to gain a sense of being in control. In the other extreme, women may give up any pretense of being in control or of making decisions for themselves. They yield to others. This yielding results in not having to assume responsibility for anything that happens. Being freed of responsibility means that they no longer need to feel guilty for whatever happens, which is an indirect form of control. In a world that is unsafe and unpredictable, either of these extremes brings some sense of order to their lives.

The recovered person has a much wider range of emotions that can be expressed with a flexibility that is dependent upon the situation. Their underlying fears have evolved into a confidence that they have the skills to cope with new situations. Pleasant and unpleasant feelings are experienced both separately and in combination. Pleasant feelings such as love, happiness, relief, excitement, and joy surface when appropriate. Unpleasant feelings such as fear, anger, disgust, sadness, hurt, and shame also surface freely. Each feeling state helps dictate which actions will be taken or not taken. Each emotional arousal state is available to be consciously analyzed and can be the catalyst for future growth and awareness.

Not only is each of the above basic emotions experienced and available, but all the nuances are experienced, too. Joy can be felt on a continuum ranging from mildly pleasing, comforting, happy, or satisfying, to ecstasy. Anger can range from irritation, annoyance, or indignation to blatant hostility. Each shade of an emotion provides important information that allows a person to navigate safely in the world.

As emotions are fully experienced and acknowledged, the ego defenses become open for examination. Previously, these defenses were predominantly unconscious, but as the woman grows more healthy, they are under more conscious control. Recovered women become aware of the defenses that had once protected them but now impede their growth. Defenses that aided them in withdrawing from human contact might include intellectualizing, generalizing, projecting, and rationalizing. Defenses that allowed these women to avoid intimacy by attacking or fighting others include cynicism, competition, and interrogation.

Intellectualizing is one of the primary ego defenses that allows withdrawal from others to occur. When people intellectualize, they are usually analyzing their own or someone else's behavior rather than responding to it. For example, if you are hurt by someone's criticism of you and you excuse this person's behavior because he or she grew up in a tough home and, therefore, didn't really mean to hurt you, you are intellectualizing. This kind of response allows you to avoid confronting the person who made the hurtful comment. Patricia avoided confronting her husband by using intellectualizing as an ego defense.

Generalizing, a second ego defense, removes responsibility for one's actions by attributing the action to vague groups. For example, a person who is feeling sad because a friend did not call and says that people are sad when they feel alone is generalizing. All personal ownership of the emotion, and its ramifications, are lost.

Projecting allows internal, unacceptable attributes to be ascribed to others. Some of the recent sexual scandals involving born-again ministers who rail against the immorality of others is a good example of projection.

Rationalization is an attempt to cover up hurts caused by lack of inclusion by substituting "good" reasons for noninclusion. A married person whose partner is having an affair might say that his or her partner has been under a lot of stress lately as a way to rationalize the partner's behavior. The betrayal and resulting hurt are being excused and not felt.

The "fight defenses" (cynicism, competition, and interrogation) protect the person by striking first. Cynicism is the frequent challenging, questioning, and attacking of others. It does not matter whether the other's intentions are genuine and loving or hurtful. Spouses often use cynicism as a defense against intimacy with each other. Competition is characteristic of individuals who struggle to control or outdo others. Phrases such as "it's a dog-eat-dog world" and "you better get them before they get you" are two examples of a competition mentality. Interrogation is the use of probing questioning or cross-examination to put people on the defensive. Even though this style might be justified as just trying to understand, it distances social interactions and keeps the interrogator safe from having to interact intimately with others.

Recovered women assemble a new sense of family. Hopefully, they can reenter their family of origin in a new and meaningful fashion. However, if incest is an issue, then the repair work could be more extensive. If the family member who sexually abused them, or others who did not protect them, still are involved in the same hurtful behaviors or in denial, then some recovered women have to distance themselves from their family of origin.

In addition to becoming aware of how ego defenses have been used to control relationships and then changing these behavior patterns, recovered women who were sexually abused by either teachers, baby-sitters, clergy, neighbors, or family friends begin to share this information with their families. The revelation of this information may invoke varied reactions such as anger or a desire for revenge. The recovered woman now has the strength to make it clear that this choice is hers and that, although she may appreciate the heartfelt anger, she is the wronged one. Other family members may hint that she is to blame for any transgressions. A woman who is recovered now has the self-confidence and assertiveness to stand up for herself and make it clear that any sexual abuse done to a child is without the child's consent. In the best possible scenario, the family and close friends support the recovered person and there is a sense of compassion for the time spent hurting and recovering. In the best of worlds, the recovered woman feels love and doesn't feel judged by these friends and family members as she reveals what happened to her as a child and the journey she has been making toward recovery.

If incest has occurred, then the journey usually has been more difficult and extensive. When the perpetrator is a trusted uncle or aunt, grandfather or grandmother, or a father or mother figure to the child, the sense of betrayal is felt more keenly. The impact of a mother or father sexually abusing a daughter typically is the most devastating breach of trust and the most difficult to restore.

A recovered woman has the final responsibility for deciding whether to confront a perpetrator and whether to tell others. While the therapist can present the options and consequences of either confronting or staying silent, the choice is the woman's. Silence can be viewed as both harmful and helpful. Many times it is viewed as perpetuating the system that originally allowed the abuse to take place and as continuing to put future generations at risk. Silence may be the optimal path if violence is a realistic concern, if the perpetrator is deceased or no longer present, or if the recovered woman feels the harm outweighs the benefit of confronting the perpetrator. For example, Patricia made a conscious decision not to confront the perpetrator because small children were no longer in his life and her elderly widowed mother still depended on the perpetrator and his wife for emotional support and neighborly help. The value of her mother's relationship with the neighbor outweighed the value of confrontation.

If the recovered woman does decide to confront the perpetrator and to tell family members, all possible reactions, ranging from disbelief, rejection and condemnation to acceptance, should be role-played. Change within a family is a slow process and to help it occur, family therapy should be seriously considered. In addition to the sexual abuse, issues such as role-confusion, misplaced requirements for nurturance, and social isolation must be addressed. Having the perpetrator say, "I'm sorry," sets the stage for family healing to occur; it is not the end!

Spiritual Dimensions

Most women who are victims of childhood sexual abuse explore and come to terms with issues of good and evil and with their own spirituality in the process of dealing with their sexual abuse. The struggle to recover allows each woman to come to terms with her own beliefs about why she was abused, and her relationship to a world where such atrocities exist and are perpetrated on defenseless children.

From a young age, many abuse victims learn that physical, emotional, psychological, and spiritual abuse is a reality and an expected part of their world. It is not evil, it just is. Others learn to dissociate while they are being hurt and to repress memories of the assaults. Some are convinced that they caused the actions and view themselves, not the perpetrator, as evil or bad. These distorted beliefs often result in some survivors hurting others, be it children or adults, in ways similar to the ways in which they were hurt.

One survivor in therapy had a dream that put evil into context for her. When she was growing up, her mother had emotionally abused her and left her alone for extended periods of time. The mother had also allowed boyfriends to sexually abuse her. She had a memory of her mother attempting to strangle her when she was 10 years old using a string of plastic pearls. When the survivor had her own children, her mother was only minimally involved with the grandchildren and rarely talked to her daughter. The only gift her mother ever gave her was a string of pearls for her birthday; no card was included. This gift sent the survivor into a depression that lasted for weeks, but she had no conscious awareness of the connection between the pearls and the strangling incident.

The revealing dream occurred the night after she received a card from her mother responding to her request for more information about different houses they had lived in when she was a little girl and for clarification of dates and names of neighbors. The mother wrote that her daughter had a happy, safe childhood that was filled with love. She repeatedly called her endearing names such as "sweetie" and "dear." In her note, the mother also told her daughter how badly she was doing physically and financially. The last request in the card was a terse sentence saying that she should stop therapy.

In contrast to the messages conveyed in the card, the dream recounted this story:

I am in therapy and the therapist is telling me that I am done. We're both elated and we share a relatively happy and sad time together. At first I think he means that I don't have to relive any more past experiences, but suddenly he is adamant that I am completely done this very second—and now he's wearing glasses and doesn't sound like the initial therapist [later the therapist is identified as looking and sounding like her mother]. *I question him about being through since we haven't finished the experience we're on and wonder about integration, but it does not change his mind, even though he admits that he had believed that initially. I am confused about the course of therapy and its change of direction in midstream, but instead of discussing it, he wants to be rid of me and he leaves immediately. I begin to feel terribly overwhelmed, confused, and saddened by his unexpected change. He is angry with me and just walks out and leaves me there. I remain in the office overwhelmed for a long time, thinking about how I don't understand what transpired or about what I did that caused him to change so completely. I remember that the therapist I had initially was a good and trustworthy person and that he taught me about evil—that evil can change places, can be disguised.*

Now there are three other people [later identified as split-off child ego states] *with me and we're still in his office. They don't understand what is happening either, why we ever started therapy, and what we did that caused him to abandon us. We really know that we're honestly not done with therapy yet, and feel like it's the therapist who needs termination done at all costs. The other three people and I discuss ways to stop him from hurting other people like he hurt us. Together we know that he is a murderer and he will kill us when he returns and finds us— unless we can stop him. The others have childlike plans that I listen to but realize won't work. I know that evil is too difficult to prove and that the others will have to rely on me for this decision. I pick up the phone and call the police. We need a witness and the others can't be the witness. The others want him stopped because they're terrified and saddened by his betrayal and abandonment. I truly don't understand why he needs to kill us. I only know that it's going to happen no matter what I do, but that I need a witness to my being murdered. I need a police witness more then I need my life. It's OK that I have to die, but if I'm going to be murdered, I want that witnessed and the responsible person caught. This time I wake up crying because I was by the evil therapist and I am going to die.*

The content of this dream foreshadowed a crisis for this woman. On a rational level, she knew that her mother was cruel and uncaring. Emotionally, however, she was still a little girl and was terrified that her mother would abandon her if she proceeded any further with treatment. The evil disguise her mother took was that of someone who was supposed to be helpful and caring, her therapist. Perhaps the most frightening part of the dream was the message that her mother had once tried to kill her by choking her and that if her mother got angry enough over revelations in therapy, the survivor was in danger again. The witness part of the dream expresses every trauma victim's desperate need to have someone else hear it, believe it, experience it with her, and comfort her. A human connection is essential in the face of evil.

Like many authors, Stephen King has explored good versus evil in his horror novels. He recognizes that it is the twisting of logic and fear that allows evil to spread. "It had always fed well on children. Many adults could be used without knowing they had been used, . . . but their fears were mostly too complex. The fears of children were simpler and more powerful. The fears of children could often be summoned up in a single face . . . and if bait were needed, why, what child did not love a clown?" (King, 1987, p. 1016). King knows that children are especially vulnerable to cruelty and evil.

Schindler's List, a movie by Steven Spielberg, poignantly explores the evil of the genocide committed by the Nazi Party during World War II and the childlike status to which the Jewish citizens reverted when faced with such overwhelming evil. For the Jewish people, it was unbelievable that anyone was capable of such evil. Over and over, they denied the steps that led to their extermination. For example, in one scene the women living in a work camp barracks are told about the gas chambers, but they rationalize that it could not be true, that they were too valuable as workers to be killed. Also, the Jews are constantly inundated with fear by random shootings, beatings, and forced separation of families. The terror of random violence is exemplified by a scene in which a Jewish engineer tries to explain that a work camp building is being constructed incorrectly. The base commander shoots her in the forehead and then orders the corrections made.

When children are sexually abused, they too experience the fear of being randomly violated. That someone they should be able to trust and love could hurt them defies their logic. Regardless of what happened, though, children do not label this person as evil or bad, but turn the feelings of hate inward. In their minds, they are the one who is evil.

The spirituality of most survivors of sexual abuse is confused, conflicted, or nonexistent. Many believe that God allowed them to be hurt and did not stop it. As adults they are angry with God or refuse to acknowledge any spiritual being. Some children were told that "God wants you to do this because he knows you're a good girl" or "God wanted me to do this to you because your body is so enticing." Even if nothing was said to a child, she may believe that since she is dirty and bad, even God could never love her. Shame is the most prevalent emotion among sexual abuse victims.

It is possible that a survivor will experience a variety of beliefs and emotional responses to the idea of a God or a Supreme Being. Emotional reactions might include explosive anger, shame, or confusion, or turning to a form of spirituality that does not include traditional religious concepts.

Many studies have confirmed that conceptualizations of God and spirituality usually parallel an individual's feelings about his or her parents or significant caretakers. For children, parents are the original and most powerful authority figures in their lives. Often their understandings and beliefs about God are a reflection of their early relationship with these authority figures, most typically one or both parents. For example, if a father abused his child, it is possible that, as an adult, the survivor would have extreme anger at any authority figure. God is a safer authority figure to be angry with than one's own father. Similarly, if a child's mother did not protect her or actually contributed to the abuse, the adult survivor could view God as having turned his back on her. The survivor may believe that God has abandoned and neglected her, just as her mother did. It is also possible that the survivor feels that God is too distant to care and really has no power to help.

Most survivors of sexual abuse believe that they caused the abuse to happen or that because they enjoyed the sexual sensations or touch, they were guilty of wanting it. A prominent emotion for these survivors is shame and humiliation. In their shame, they feel unworthy to seek the presence of God. The story of Adam and Eve in many ways depicts how many survivors feel. When Adam and Eve ate fruit from the tree of forbidden knowledge, they realized that they were naked and had sinned. In shame, they hid themselves from God. When children have been sexually abused, they too have prematurely "eaten from the tree of forbidden knowledge" and feel as if they have sinned and are dirty. They hide what happened to them by maintaining the secret of the abuse or by repressing memories of it. As adults, many survivors often feel ashamed and unworthy of God's love. They usually take full responsibility for being abused and hate themselves for their part in the abuse, or they unconsciously act out the abuser's messages that they were at fault or disgusting for having participated. Again, they label themselves as evil.

If many sexually abusive situations occurred, it is highly likely that many confusing beliefs will be experienced. These beliefs tend to change as the victim works through the SELF stages of therapy. In the Safety phase of therapy, many victims tend to feel bad and dirty about their abuse. Since they habitually excuse the perpetrator for the abuse or repress it, survivors in the first stage of therapy feel mostly ashamed. The language used may convey that they believe that they are dirty, worthless, useless, despicable, or not deserving to be alive. Many have attempted suicide.

As memory work proceeds in the Exploration stage, survivors eventually get angry with their abusers. At the same time, they often express anger with God. This anger is so deep and explosive that many survivors are scared of the intensity and direction of their anger.

During the Loss phase, survivors struggle with the meaning of their experience. This stage is very emotional and can have significant spiritual qualities. Survivors want their experience to have meaning and at the same time fear that it does not. "Why" questions bombard their existence. Why did they go through this horrid childhood experience? Why have they spent a lifetime affected by it and trying to recover from it? Why has it been so physically, emotionally, psychologically and spiritually taxing? Why do they have to bear the financial burden for overcoming what happened? Why is working to feel better so lonely and painful? Finally, they ask, What was the meaning of all this? The standard responses offered include that God wanted it this way, that God loves you no matter what happened, that this is all part of God's plan. These are unacceptable answers and have little or no meaning to the survivor. The idea that they did something wrong and God is punishing them is cruel and perpetuates their self-hatred. In light of these traditional responses as to why bad things happen in a person's life, what meaning is a sexual abuse survivor supposed to find in the aftermath of the abuse?

There is no pat answer. Each survivor has to find her own meaning for the experience. Finding this meaning typically happens in the last stage, Fulfillment. The meanings are varied and unique for each person. There are some patterns that emerge, however. Some women come to believe that there is no meaning to their experience. The world is neither logical nor fair, and they have to accept it and go on acting and living (This is an existentialist view). Other women come to believe that God gives people free choice. While God may be saddened by the abuse that a child endures, God does not interfere in daily lives. This resolution allows the woman to believe in a loving, compassionate God who lets people make choices to follow good or evil. Some women feel that their experience has helped them transform their lives and allowed them a depth of spirituality not possible if they had not suffered childhood sexual abuse. Even though they would not wish to have it, they accept that the world is a place where pain and suffering occurs. The experience of childhood sexual abuse was the crucible that transformed every aspect of their lives and gave them an opportunity for a deeper spirituality and for greater creativeness. Other women find meaning by embracing alternative spiritual outlets. For example, they might explore Native American religions, feminist spiritual writings, or New Age religions. Others accept agnosticism. The choices are as divergent as the seekers. As women who were sexually abused as children come to spiritual peace with their abuse, serenity replaces doubt, acceptance replaces anger, and love replaces self-loathing.

This process is beautifully described in the words of a woman who has successfully made this journey to recovery. Her unfolding is an expression of rediscovering her unique talents, individuality, and spirituality. Only by reclaiming these, can she be fully alive.

The Pearl

When I came to earth, I thought I saw no light and so I hid in the shadows, thinking it would be safe. In reality I came to earth and I had a physical body but I never took physical form.

From the shadows I saw the insanity of life and was determined that this life would never touch me. A part of me was successful in staying above it all and never letting life in, while a part of me vibrated and agitated whenever the pains and truths of life would move in my direction.

Being in the shadows insulated me from the world. No one could see me, but I could see everyone, which was a good vantage point to be in.

But I couldn't stay in the shadows forever. My own light wanted to shine, and it couldn't shine because it was hidden in the dark.

The light from within became a pearl that was born from a grain of sand representing the struggle of my leaving the shadows to stand in the light.

Being a pearl is not enough. I must value and love this pearl before all else. I must love this pearl enough to allow myself to take physical form. I must trust the pearl within me to stand in the light and to be touched, valued and loved by other pearls. Can I do that? Can I totally love and trust myself?

This is the moment of truth, the final step in my journey through life before I move into myself as a real expression of life.

SUMMARY

Every recovered woman has choices. She no longer has to function primarily out of past fears and hurts. She is free to choose help in the form of individual counseling or group therapy. Her emotions and defenses have the flexibility needed to meet daily challenges. Her spirituality confirms her individuality and nourishes her as she actively encounters life. The recovered woman has just begun to grow and learn. The future is an invitation to grow, not a threat to be hidden from. She has learned how to protect herself and create a world where she feels safe. She now lives her life with anticipation and a sense of excitement as the words inscribed above the door of Israeli Holocaust Museum echo in her ears, "Never Again."

Postscript

"A clay pot sitting in the sun will always be a clay pot. It has to go through the white heat of the furnace to become porcelain." *Mildren Witte Stouven*

"Actually, there's nothing wrong with being a clay pot. It's just that some of us can become porcelain. And it's not just a question of being fired or not. Some of us explode in the kiln, some collapse before we reach the kiln, and some develop cracks that refuse to heal." *Anonymous quote*

"Yet probably the saddest response of all is to successfully survive the firing and refuse to become porcelain. All of us have furnaces in our lives. It's up to us to glean the learning from the firings." *Anonymous quote*

REFERENCES

(1993). *Day One: Female Circumcision.* Washington, DC: American Broadcasting Corporation.

Alexander, P. (1991). A comparison of group treatment of women sexually abused as children. *Journal of Consulting and Clinical Psychology, 57,* 479–483.

Alexander, P., & Friedrich, W. N. (Eds.). (1991). *The role of the extended family in the evaluation and treatment of incest.* New York: W. W. Norton & Co.

Andreas, C., & Andreas, S. (1989). *Heart of the mind.* Moab, UT: Real People Press.

Atler, M. V. D. (1991a). The darkest secret. *People, 6,* 89–92.

Atler, M. V. D. (1991b). Say "Incest" out loud. *McCall's, 9,* 78, 82–83, 148–149, 151.

Bagley, C., & Ramsay, R. (1985, February). *Disrupted childhood and vulnerability to sexual assault: Long-term sequels with implications for counseling.* Paper presented at the Conference on Counselling the Sexually Abused Survivor, Winnipeg, Canada.

Barrie, J. M. (1911). *Peter Pan.* New York: Charles Scribner's Sons.

Bass, E. & Davis, L. (1988). *The courage to heal: A guide for women survivors of child sexual abuse.* New York: Harper & Row.

Baum, L. F. (1900). *The wonderful wizard of oz.* New York: Grosset & Dunlap.

Bergart, A. M. (1986). Isolation to intimacy: Incest survivors in group therapy. *Social Casework, 67,* 266–275.

Blake-White, J., & Kline, C. M. (1985). Treating the dissociative process in adult victims of childhood incest. *Social Casework, 66,* 394–402.

Blume, E. S. (1990). *Secret survivors: Uncovering incest and its aftereffects on women.* New York: John Wiley & Sons.

Braun, B. G. (1988). The BASK (Behavior, Affect, Sensation, Knowledge) model of dissociation. *Dissociation, 1*(1), 4–23.

Breuer, J., & Freud, S. (1893–95/1955). "Studies in hysteria" in *Standard Edition,* Vol 2, translated by J. Strachey (London: Hogarth Press, 1955).

Briere, J., & Runtz, M. (1988). Symptomatology associated with childhood sexual victimization in a non-clinical adult sample. *Child Abuse & Neglect, 12,* 51–59.

Browne, A., & Finkelhor, D. (1986). Impact of child sexual abuse: A review of the research. *Psychological Bulletin, 99,* 66–77.

Bruhn, A. R. (1990). *Earliest childhood memories: Vol. 1. Theory and application to clinical practice.* New York: Praeger.

Buber, M. (1970). *I and thou.* New York: Charles Scribner's Sons.

Calof, D. & Leloo, M. (1993). *Multiple personality and dissociation: Understanding incest, abuse, and MPD.* Chicago: Parkside Publishing.

Campbell, J. (with Moyers, B.). (1988). *The power of myth.* New York: Doubleday.

Carnes, P. (1991). *Don't call it love: Recovery from sexual addiction.* New York: Bantam.

Carroll, L. (1865/1968). *Alice's Adventures in Wonderland & Through the looking-glass.* New York: Magnum.

Chase, N. (1975). *A child is being beaten: Violence against children, an American tragedy.* New York: Holt, Tinehart & Winston.

Clark, M. H. (1992). *All around the town.* New York: Pocket Books.

Cooney, J. (1988). Child abuse: A developmental perspective. *Counseling and Development, 20,* 1–10.

Cooney, J. (1987). *Coping with sexual abuse.* New York: Rosen Press.

189

Courtois, C. A. (1988). *Healing the incest wound: Adult survivors in therapy.* New York: W.W. Norton & Co.

Courtois, C. A. (1979). The incest experience and its aftermath. *Victimology: An International Journal, 4,* 337–347.

Courtois, C. A., & Watts, D. L. (1982). Counseling adult women who experienced incest in childhood or adolescence. *Personnel and Guidance Journal, 60,* 275–279.

Cunningham, J., Pearce, T., & Pearce, P. (1988). Childhood sexual abuse and medical complaints in adult women. *Journal of Interpersonal Violence, 3,* 131–144.

DeMause, L. (Ed.). (1988). *The history of childhood: The untold story of child abuse.* New York: Peter Bedrick Books.

de Shazer, S. (1985). *Keys to solutions in brief therapy.* New York: W. W. Norton & Co.

Dickens, C. (1859/1981). *A tale of two cities.* New York: Bantam Books.

Dolan, Y. A. (1991). *Resolving sexual abuse: Solution-focused therapy and Ericksonian hypnosis for adult survivors.* New York: W. W. Norton & Co.

Ellenson, G. S. (1986). Disturbances of perception in adult female incest survivors. *Social Casework, 3,* 149–159.

Erickson, M. H. (1954). Pseudo-orientation in time as a hypnotherapy procedure. *Journal of Clinical and Experimental Hypnosis, 2,* 261–283.

Erikson, E. H. (1963). *Childhood and society.* (2nd ed.). New York: W. W. Norton & Co.

Erikson, E. H. (1968). *Identity, youth and crisis.* New York: W. W. Norton & Co.

False Memory Syndrome Foundation. (1993, August). Title. *FMS Foundation Newsletter. 2,* 1–19.

False Memory Syndrome Foundation. (1992a, June). *FMS Foundation Newsletter, 1.*

False Memory Syndrome Foundation. (1992b). *Meeting your accused child's therapist; FMSF working paper.* Philadelphia, PA: Author.

False Memory Syndrome Foundation. (1991). *The false memory syndrome phenomenon.* Philadelphia, PA: Author.

Faria, G., & Belohlavek, N. (1984). Treating female adult survivors of childhood incest. *Social Casework, 10,* 465–471.

Farmer, S. (1989). *Adult children of abusive parents.* New York: Ballantine.

Finkelhor, D. (1979). *Sexually victimized children.* New York: Free Press.

Finkelhor, D., Araji, S., Baron, L., Browne, A., Peters, S. D., & Wyatt, G. E. (1986). *Sourcebook of child sexual abuse.* Newbury Park, CA: Sage Publications.

Finkelhor, D., Hotaling, G., Lewis, I. A., & Smith, C. (1990). Sexual abuse in a national survey of adult men and women: Prevalence, characteristics, and risk factors. *Child Abuse & Neglect, 3, 19–28.*

Finkelhor, D., & Williams,L. M. (1992). The characteristics of incestuous fathers. *(ERIC Document,* No. 354451)

Follett, K. (1990). *Pillars of the earth.* New York: Penguin Books.

Frankl, V. (1959). *Man's search for meaning.* New York: Washington Square Press.

Freud, S. (1920). *Beyond the pleasure principle.* London: International Psychoanalytic Press.

Freud, S. (1896/1962). The aetiology of hysteria. In J. Strachey (Ed.), *The standard edition of the complete psychological works of Sigmund Freud* (Vol. 3, pp. 203–243). London: Hogarth Press.

Freud, S. (1905/1953). Three essays on the theory of sexuality. In J. Strachey (Ed.), *The standard edition of the complete psychological works of Sigmund Freud* (Vol. 7, pp. 135–243). London: Hogarth Press.

Gardner, R. A. (1992). *True and false accusations of child sex abuse*. Cresskil, NJ: Creative Therapeutics.

Gelinas, D. J. (1983). The persisting negative effects of incest. *Psychiatry, 46,* 312–331.

Gil, E. M. (1983). *Outgrowing the pain: A book for and about adults abused as children.* New York: Dell Publishing.

Gil, E. M. (1990). *Treatment of adult survivors of childhood abuse* (2nd. ed). Walnut Creet, CA: Launch Press.

Gilligan, S. G. (1989). *A 4-step model for therapeutic rituals.* Unpublished document.

Gilligan, S. G. (1982). Ericksonian approaches to clinical hypnosis. In J. K. Zeig (Ed.), *Ericksonian approaches to hypnosis and psychotherapy* (p. 87–103). New York: Bruner Mazel.

Goleman, D. (1992, July 21). Childhood trauma: Memory or invention? *New York Times,* July 21, p. B5+.

Graham, D. L., & Rawlings, E. (1991, August). Stockholm syndrome: Young women's bonds with abusive dating partners. In L. E. Walker (Chair), *Dating violence: Young women at risk.* Symposium conducted at the meeting of the American Psychological Association, San Francisco.

Hammond, D. C. (Ed.). (1990). *Handbook of hypnotic suggestions and metaphors.* New York: W. W. Norton & Co.

Herman, J. L. (1992). *Trauma and recovery.* New York: Basic Books.

Herman, J. L. & Schatzow, E. (1987). Recovery and verification of memories of childhood sexual trauma. *Psychoanalytic Psychology, 4,* 1–14.

Kempe, R. S., & Kempe, C. H. (1984). *The common secret: Sexual abuse of children and adolescents.* New York: W. A. Freeman.

Kempe, C. H., Silverman, F. N., Steele, B. F., Droegemueller, W., & Silver, H. K. (1962). The battered child syndrome. *Journal of American Medical Association, 181,* 105–112.

Kaufman, J. & Ziegler, E. (1987). Do abused children become abusive parents? *American Journal of Orthopsychiatry, 57,* 186–191.

King, S. (1987). *It.* New York: Signet.

Kirschner, S., Kirschner, D. L., & Rappaport, R. (1993). *Working with adult incest survivors.* New York: Bruner Mazel.

Kohlberg, L. (1976). Moral stages and moralization: The cognitive-developmental approach. In T. Mischel (Ed.), *Moral development and behavior: Theory, research, and social issues.* New York: Holt, Rinehart, and Winston.

Laidlaw, T.A., Malmo, C. & Associates (1990). *Healing voices; Feminist approaches to therapy with women.* San Francisco, CA: Jossey-Bass.

Lang, R. A., Langevin, R., Van Santen, V., Billingsley, D., & Wright, P. (1990). Marital relations of incest offenders. *Journal of Sex and Marital Therapy, 16,* 214–229.

Lankton, S. R., & Lankton, C. H. (1986). *Enchantment and intervention in family therapy—Training in Ericksonian therapy.* New York: Bruner Mazel.

Levin, T. (1980). "Unspeakable atrocities": The psycho-sexual etiology of female genital mutilation. *The Journal of Mind and Body, 1,* 197–210.

Loftus, E. F. (1993). The reality of repressed memories. *American Psychologist, 48,* 518–537.

Loftus, E. F., & Coan, D. (in press). The construction of childhood memories. In D. Peters (Ed.), *The child witness in context: Cognitive, social and legal perspectives.* New York: Kluwer.

Maslow, A. H. (1971). *The farther reaches of human nature.* New York: The Viking Press.

Mason, J. M. (1985). *The assault on truth: Freud's suppression of the seduction theory.* New York: Penguin Books

Meiselman, K. (1978). *Incest: A psychological study of causes and effects with treatment recommendations.* San Francisco, CA: Jossey Bass.

National Center on Child Abuse and Neglect. (1990). National Child Abuse and Neglect Data System: (Working Paper 1, 1990 Summary Data Component). Washington, D.C.: U.S. Department of Health and Human Services.

National Committee for Prevention of Child Abuse (1993). *Current trends in child abuse reporting and fatalities: The results of the 1992 Annual Fifty State Survey.* (Working Paper No. 808). Chicago: Author.

Olio, K. A. (1989). Memory retrieval in the treatment of adult survivors of sexual abuse. *Transactional Analysis Journal, 19,* 93–100.

Ratican, K. (1992). Sexual abuse survivors: Identifying symptoms and special treatment considerations. *Journal of Counseling and Development, 71,* 33–38.

Ritterman, M. (1981). *Hope under siege: Terror and family support in Chile.* Norwood, NJ: Ablex Publishing.

Roland, C. B. (1993). Exploring childhood memories with adult survivors of sexual abuse: Concrete reconstruction and visualization techniques. *Journal of Mental Health, 15,* 363–372.

Russell, D. E. H. (1986). *The secret trauma: Incest in the lives of girls and women.* New York: Basic Books.

Shapiro, F. (1990). Eye movement desensitization: A new treatment for post-traumatic stress disorder. *Journal of Behavior Therapy and Experimental Psychology, 30,* 211–217.

Slack, A. T. (1988). Female circumcision: A critical review. *Human Rights Quarterly, 10,* 437–486.

Stewart, A. C., & Koch, J. B. (1983). *Children: Development through adolescence.* New York: John Wiley & Sons.

Swanson, L. & Biaggio, M. K. (1985). Therapeutic perspectives on father-daughter incest. *The American Journal of Psychiatry, 146,* 667–673.

Terr, L. (1990). *Too scared to cry.* New York: Harper & Row.

Tsai, M., Feldman-Summers, S., & Edgar, M. (1979). Childhood molestation: Variables related to differential impact of psychosexual functioning in adult women. *Journal of Abnormal Psychology, 88,* 407–417.

Tufts' New England Medical Center, Division of Child Psychiatry. (1984). *Sexually exploited children: Service and research projects.* (Final report for the Office of Juvenile Justice and Delinquency). Washington, DC: U. S. Department of Justice.

Vanderbilt, H. (1992). Incest: A four-part chilling report. *Lear's, 4,* 49–79.

van der Kolk, B. A. (Ed.). (1987). *Psychological trauma.* Washington, DC: American Psychiatric Press.

Wadworth, B. J. (1971). *Piaget's theory of cognitive development.* New York: David McKay.

Westerland, E. (1983). Counseling women with histories of incest. *Women & Therapy, 2,* 17–31.

Wheeler, B. R., & Walton, E. (1987). Personality disturbances of adult incest victims. *Social Casework, 12,* 597–602.

Williams, M. (1922/1983). *The velveteen rabbit or how toys become real.* San Diego, CA: Harcourt, Brace, Jovanovich.

Wurtele, S. K., & Miller, P. (1992). *Preventing child sexual abuse.* Lincoln, NE: University of Nebraska Press.

Index

Of similar interest . . .

**Academic journals
in the social sciences
published by
Taylor & Francis:**